RAISING START-UP CAPITAL FOR YOUR COMPANY

RAISING START-UP CAPITAL FOR YOUR COMPANY

GUSTAV BERLE

WILEY

JOHN WILEY & SONS

New York • Chichester • Brisbane • Toronto • Singapore

This publication is designed to provide accurate and
authoritative information in regard to the subject
matter covered. It is sold with the understanding that
the publisher is not engaged in rendering legal, accounting,
or other professional service. If legal advice or other
expert assistance is required, the services of a competent
professional person should be sought. *From a Declaration
of Principles jointly adopted by a Committee of the
American Bar Association and a Committee of Publishers.*

This book contains numerous references with addresses and
phone numbers. These were correct at press time, but the
possibility always exists that they could have changed by
the time this book gets into your hands. Should you find
such a change, please excuse any inconvenience. We would
be grateful if you would notify the publisher of any new
change that should be made in future editions.

Library of Congress Cataloging-in-Publication Data:

ISBN 0-471-51794-1

Printed in the United States of America

10 9 8 7 6 5 4 3 2 1

PREFACE

Money makes the world go 'round, sang The Entertainer in *Cabaret*. He might as well have substituted "business" for "world." Money, the lubricant of entrepreneurial ventures, makes the wheels of business turn more smoothly. Still, many businesses have gone belly up, despite adequate financing, because the importance of capital in the entrepreneurial scheme of things was overblown. If the entrepreneur who drives the venture is inadequate or even incompetent, no amount of lubricant will bring a business safely to its income and profit destination. The ways and means of financing a business cannot ignore the need for management that is ready, willing, and able to serve the public, drive the enterprise on a steady growth path, and, with proper education and skill, prepare for the most thrilling ride of a lifetime.

Most start-up capital (as opposed to expansion capital) comes from the entrepreneur's own resources. This might come as a surprise to those venturing into the business world for the first time. Start-up entrepreneurs rarely find ready sources of OPM (other people's money) or even of more speculative and intrusive venture capital. It does happen occasionally, when a sensational innovation, buoyed by an obvious market need, meets Lady Luck. For most of us, raising start-up capital is a laborious and unsettling task. This book is directed to the majority of entrepreneurs, who face this reality. Utilizing the information and recommendations given in these pages can lead to success spelled with a capital $.

GUSTAV BERLE

Washington, DC
January 1990

ACKNOWLEDGMENTS

If it were not for the Encouragement, Persistence and Research of my own E.P.R., this book might never have been produced. Thank you, Esther Pinto Rosenbloom.

G.B.

Washington, DC
January 1990

CONTENTS

CONTENTS

CONTENTS

CONTENTS

CONTENTS

LIST OF FIGURES

RAISING START-UP CAPITAL FOR YOUR COMPANY

INTRODUCTION

WHERE'S THE MONEY?

Each year an average of nearly $100 billion is being borrowed by small business. During 1988 more than 64,000 would-be entrepreneurs—85 percent of the total requests—called the U.S. Small Business Administration's Answer Desk and asked, "How can I get money to start up a business?"

The idea that Uncle Sam has an open pocketbook that can be tapped by anyone with a dream of business independence is a persistent one. Some years ago the SBA was indeed generous in making direct loans, especially to "socially disadvantaged and minority enterprises." Because many of the borrowers were unqualified, spent their loan money unwisely, and went broke, the losses were quite substantial.

Since the SBA was lending public funds—that is, money collected from taxes—the mentors in Congress quickly put an end to this charitable procedure. Today, no matter what quick-buck artists say to sell their money-making schemes and books, the SBA mainly *backs* loans, and only rarely makes loans directly.

Some writers talk glibly about the "OPM" method of running a business. OPM means "other people's money." It is a grand idea that can work, but is not as easy as it is made to sound. If you are serious about going into business and getting legitimate financing, then you should know the truth.

Of course, you can operate on the OPM principle. The majority of small business start-ups do exactly that—and *must* do so. However, getting other people's money usually means tapping your dear old dad or, better yet, mom, who is generally a softer touch. Other relatives, friends, lovers, all might be prospects for start-up capital. But when you go out into the marketplace to raise capital, you will have to pay a steep price in the form of interest, or give away some of your potential profits to investors and joint-venture capitalists. You could even find yourself out in the cold if you fail to meet the sometimes stiff terms of repayment.

Later on in this book, we will detail the various sources for potential capital—both private and governmental, both informal and professional—and what you must do to open up the treasure chests. Before going into the nitty-gritty of the various approaches, it needs to be stated that a complete, objective, accurate business plan (described in detail in this book's companion volume, *Planning and Forming Your Company*) is a "must." You need it. Why? Because it is your blueprint to building your own business—a road map that can lead you to the land of independence and financial success. Further, there is absolutely no way that a banker or investor will give you a business loan without such a plan.

Even if you have private capital, you probably will have to go to a bank or other professional lending source for some of the money. The process of borrowing money often takes as much psychology—good, commonsense psychology that allows you to look at the bank's loan officer, or any other lender, as a human being—as it does objective proof of your ability to perform and pay the money back. Keep in mind that because lenders expect to make money from your efforts, they *want* to lend you the money you seek—provided that you can offer reliable evidence that you can pay it back with interest.

While there will be more on your qualifications later in the book, be cognizant of the questions that are uppermost in the loan officer's mind:

1. What is the applicant's personal financial status? What assets does the applicant have?

2. What does his or her financial balance sheet indicate?
3. What is the applicant's ability to repay the loan, plus interest, in the promised time period?
4. Will the applicant make reasonable use of the money he or she is seeking to borrow?
5. Has the applicant demonstrated his or her skill in management, especially in the proposed business?

ECONOMIC OUTLOOK

Because each of us is influenced by the general economy, it will be constructive to quote from the last annual Report to the President prepared by the SBA:

> The U.S. economy resumed economic expansion in 1988, overcoming fears caused by the disturbances in the worldwide financial markets. . . . Increased demand in the credit markets caused both short-term and long-term rates to increase. . . . Short-term rates have moved up further as monetary growth slowed down. . . . *Financing remained amply available to small business,* however. Borrowing by small businesses increased at a healthy rate. . . . Equity financing remains relatively inactive in the aftermath of the crisis in the stock market in October 1987. However, offerings by small companies showed smaller declines than total offerings during this period.

If you read between the lines of this bureaucratic pronouncement, you can see that there is optimism afoot. It looks good for small-business borrowing. Let's see how some of this might be obtained by you and you and you. . . .

Section I

Be Prepared

Time spent sharpening ax is saved when you chop wood.

HOW TO BE A BUSINESS BOY SCOUT

1

The Boy Scouts' motto, as all the world knows, is "Be Prepared." This is marvelous advice to follow when you start a business—especially if you want to *stay* in business.

From the moment that the first glimmer of entrepreneurship enters your brain, and all through your business life, being prepared for the present and for all exigencies is as mandatory as keeping track of income and expenses. Being prepared can do more than make your business life easier; it can ensure your continuity and survival.

PREPAREDNESS CHECKLIST

What do you need, or need to do, to "be prepared"? Here are a baker's dozen items:

1. Have a business plan (see Chapter 2).
2. Have a professional, up-to-date financial statement.
3. Have a financial projection of your business activity for the next 12 months.
4. Have a projection of what the money you have or borrow will allow you to accomplish.

5. Have a firm payback plan for any borrowed capital and show proof of how you get this money.
6. Know exactly how much money you need and what interest you realistically can afford.
7. If you have been in business for at least a year, have a professionally prepared P & L statement.
8. Have available a detailed history of your business life or of the existing business.
9. Do some advance inquiry regarding the specific person to see about a loan.
10. Have a current appraisal of all your assets that can serve as collateral.
11. References are always helpful, especially people who have done business with the loan source. These can be trade, financial, and personal references.
12. YOU are the key to your business and to the loan.
13. Have yourself to be proud of. Look in the mirror. Do you like what you see?

BUSINESS FAILURE STATISTICS

The need for sound preparation is underscored by a continuing Dun & Bradstreet study called *Failure Trends Since 1927*. At the peak of America's Great Depression, the failure rate per 10,000 business concerns was 122 (1930), 133 (1931), and 154 (1932). The average liability per failure ranged from $25,000 to $29,000. More recently, in the six years between 1983 and 1988, the failures per 10,000 of listed concerns were 110, 107, 115, 120, 102, and 98, respectively. Average liabilities for these failures ranged from $562,000 to $725,000.

The increase in small-business failures during the first half of the decade can be attributed partially to (1) greater numbers of entrepreneurs, and (2) easier availability of government-backed or direct-government loans. Conversely, the decline in failures during the past two or three years can be attributed to (1) the tightening of "free money" by Uncle Sam, and (2) the realization by entrepreneurs that better preparation is vital to their health.

Causes of Business Failures

What we are concerned with here is the relationship among lack of preparedness, lack of funds, and lack of business success. General economic statistics outrank internal causes in the Dun & Bradstreet studies, but the more important question for our purposes is what else could the entrepreneurs have done to ensure their success.

In the Dun & Bradstreet statistics, a key cause named by respondents for having failed in 1988 was "insufficient profits." This was the principal reason for going out of business given by 22.2 percent of the people surveyed. Apparently they found the investment and effort not to be worthwhile and simply closed up shop.

Inadequate management or insufficient expertise was named in only 12 percent of the cases. This appears to be too low, because management failure is generally cited as the chief cause of business failures. However, the D&B respondents were probably loath to blame themselves for their failures (except in 12 percent of the cases).

Besides insufficient profits, other financial causes were pinpointed in only 26.4 percent of the failures. This reason broke down into the following three subcategories: heavy operating expenses, 11.7 percent; burdensome institutional debt, 8.8 percent; and insufficient capital, 5.9 percent. We can analyze these four financial statistics and try to draw some lessons from them:

Insufficient profits (22.2 percent). This could indicate that initial projections were not done properly. Certainly, the entrepreneur should have known ahead of time what the profit potential of his or her new business would be. Sometimes circumstances arise over which the entrepreneur has no control. It proves that in any financial projections and loan applications, sufficient elasticity has to be built in to account for economic factors such as inflation, and for other factors such as unforeseen expenses, style changes, pilferage, management problems (including health), and even competition.

Heavy operating expenses (11.7 percent). This statistic also indicates a problem with initial projections. Not anticipating true costs created an untenable situation, and it was the third highest reason named. This proves the need to analyze carefully, get estimates in advance, and check and double check your costs of doing business before you put them into your projections. And when you're all finished, add a good cushion for those pesky "unforeseens."

Burdensome institutional debt (8.8 percent). This seems a strange factor to blame for business failure. However, the growth of venture capital support and its high demand on a new company's profits (30–50 percent), could be one reason for the relatively high incidence of this reason. Certainly, normal bank and SBA-guaranteed loans have totally predictable interest charges. Perhaps start-up entrepreneurs, in the flush of their beginning stages, consider the 14, 15, or higher percentage asked for a standard loan as bearable—and later, in a more realistic mood, discover that they cannot afford this cost in their normal operation. Again, caution is the byword. When structuring your sale prices, make sure that the institutional debt, both interest and payments, is accounted for in your expenses.

Insufficient capital (5.9 percent). Running out of money, especially when business growth is slower than expected, or expenses higher than anticipated, or inventory turnover smaller than figured, or combined with any other normal operating reasons, is also a cause for business failure. We would hazard a guess that "insufficient capital" as a reason could be higher than indicated. Ironically, it is sometimes easier to get a $100,000 than a $50,000 loan. The procedure and red tape are just about the same. Make sure you get enough working capital for that first crucial year or beyond. And that should include an allowance for you and your family to live comfortably.

HOW TO PREPARE FOR FUTURE GROWTH

When you are just starting out may not seem like the time to think about future growth, but why not? Entrepreneurs are visionaries. They can see the future better than more pedestrian types. Let's take a positive attitude and assume that your enterprise will be successful and will grow.

You may as well know now that being successful entails needing more operating money. Sometimes, if you are lucky, that extra money will come out of income. In the best of all worlds, sales will keep going up; suppliers will extend credit to you; customers or clients will pay promptly; no great reverses will take place in the economy; inventory turnover will remain high; the popularity of your product or service will rise steadily.

That is, indeed, a wonderful scenario. But don't count on it; everything may not come up roses in your path. The opposite of any of the above hopes and aspirations could occur, or you could get sick.

A more realistic look shows that as your business grows, you need more space, more employees, more merchandise; that all of these expansions require operating capital; and that customers and clients, unless you have a cash-on-delivery business (like a liquor distributorship, a busy gas station, or a successful ice-cream shop), have a habit of paying after 30 or 60 days—or longer. Meanwhile, increased rental, personnel, and merchandise payments must be met—and that requires added cash. Businesses that have grown too fast—that is, beyond the owner's capacity to finance the expansion—have been known to go bankrupt.

What can you do at the very beginning?

- Have your business plan handy and make sure that you account for possible expansions in your cash-flow projections and operations statement (see Chapter 10).
- When you discuss business finances with your banker or other lender, touch on possible future credit-line needs. Cultivate relations with your banker on a continuous basis. Make all loan repayments promptly, and keep your bank contacts apprised of your progress.
- Update your business plan when you notice an increase in your volume, activity, and credit needs, and make sure the lender gets a copy of that revision.
- Pay attention to "soft assets," such as accounts receivable or easily convertible inventory, that can function as collateral for additional loans.
- Explore alternate lending resources, including the SBA guaranteed loan program and its affiliated nationwide economic development corporations that guarantee 30 to 40 percent of long-term loans (see Chapters 8 and 9), and all the other sources discussed in this book.
- If you see low future cash availabilities strapping your progress, think of factoring your accounts receivable for short periods

of time, especially if your business is subject to wide seasonal swings.

As an innovator and entrepreneur, coming up with innovative financing methods can be just as important for your future growth as the development of the product or service that got you started in the first place.

THE IMPORTANCE OF A BUSINESS PLAN

2

If outside investment money is sought from strangers, no amount of charisma, personality, or sex appeal is going to cut any ice. What will crack open the potential investor's checkbook is the oft-touted business plan. Its overall look—including cover, binding, and organization—as well as its grammar, spelling, and completeness, and its apparent sincerity are ingredients that make up the total impression.

In this book's companion volume, *Planning and Forming Your Own Company*, the business plan is discussed in detail, including its overall structure and each individual element, plus pointers given by the renowned MIT Forum on how to create the ideal business plan. Take a look at it again. To review the process, these are the steps in creating a business plan:

1. Do the research.
2. Outline the rough plan.
3. Write it or have it written.
4. Edit and proofread.
5. Be sure all enclosures, forms, and data pages are standard in size and execution.
6. Format it (assemble, bind, etc.)

7. Have a professional check it over for legal and accounting accuracy.
8. Also try to have the plan reviewed by a financing source that will *not* be approached, but whom you know.
9. Individualize the cover letter.
10. Package the presentation, address it properly, and have it delivered by first class mail or messenger.

THREE SITUATIONS

Perhaps you are tired of hearing about the business plan in texts, how-to books, seminars, and workshops. Who can blame you? Writing and publishing a business plan the way it ought to be done is a real effort and a pain in the neck. However, if you are seeking outside investment funds, it is for one of three basic reasons, and all of them require a business plan.

In the first situation, you are a brand new start-up venture. This means the business plan is the only charter you have that states unequivocally, in black and white, what your business is all about. It is necessary for your own mental and physical organization, and it is certainly mandatory for an outside investor. To start without it would be like entering some unmapped wilds; you would become hopelessly lost.

A second possibility is that you are an existing company, and you require additional working capital. Your own company's resources are inadequate, and your personal and family coffers are pretty much depleted. A business plan is necessary to show your performance up to this point and your projection. It is the key tool to attract outside capital.

In the third scenario you are a successful company, but you see an opportunity for adding a new branch, developing a new product, taking on a potentially profitable new line, or acquiring a property that will help you expand and add to corporate profits. The business plan you design will focus specifically on this need. Your partners, board of directors, and any investors who must vote on this expansion will want to know every detail of your strategy.

Thus, the business plan is necessary in any event. It is an exercise in discipline that works like the combination or key to a lock on the treasure chest.

COMPETITION AND OTHER REALITIES

Here is where we must dampen your traditional—and expected—entrepreneurial optimism with a touch of reality. *You* are an optimist because you are an entrepreneur, or vice versa. If you were not, you would seek the safety of no growth or a job. The investor, however, whether he or she is the bank's loan officer, a foundation officer considering a grant application, or a venture capitalist, is by job function, and maybe by nature, a conservative. To compound the difference in approaches, the investor takes a short-range view while you, the inspired entrepreneur, have an unlimited horizon.

Beyond all that, you're in an ocean of competition. Consider an example: You may have heard, through reading, word-of-mouth, or advice from your accountant, that Paine Weber Ventures is a potential source of money. Last year this investment group received several thousand loan applications. In the typical review process, those applications that look promising are read, analyzed, and perhaps brought before a committee for further consideration. About 500—at the most 750—fall into this category. The other thousands are merely returned, like literary manuscripts, each with a brief rejection slip. Of those considered, a mere 1 percent—about six—will actually receive the venture capitalists' financial assistance. You could conclude from this real-life example that you may as well buy several hundred dollars' worth of lottery tickets. But this is the naked truth.

Because the investor has seen hundreds of proposals, yours has to be different, clear, and exciting enough to arouse serious interest. In addition, venture capitalists do not like to commit funds for more than a few years. They want to "cash out" in ten years or less—preferably three or five—so that they can take their profits and return the borrowed capital. Your business plan must take these realities, or philosophies, into consideration. In other words, you have to play to the audience.

What goes into the execution of the business plan beyond bald facts and figures is the psychology of how to phrase your nonstatistical responses, both in the written plan and at a possible personal presentation. An example is to have a businesslike, pragmatic tone: Don't let your personal optimism and enthusiasm run away with reality. Looking at your new product or service through rose-colored glasses without having it backed by factual market research can be the first step into corporate oblivion. The investors know this only too well. Not having your optimism and gung-ho drive, they will look at such unbridled verve with jaundiced eyes.

For a business plan used as a bank-loan application, see Figure 4, in Chapter 4. For a business plan specially geared to seeking venture capital, see Chapter 5.

FORECASTING YOUR FUTURE

As part of a business plan, and as part of running your business and being prepared, you need to do some forecasting. It might be called estimating, projecting, calculating, or just plain "guesstimating"—but it is necessary if you want to have an idea of where your business is going and what kind of financing you need.

A crystal ball will be less useful than your own experience and that of others who have been in your business for some time. Here are some ingredients that will help you form a reasonably realistic picture of what is ahead:

1. Have your own prior sales experience, or have access to others with this experience. If you have been in business for a while, either for yourself or working for someone else, you will have some idea of what creates sales and when these sales accelerate or slow up. If you are just starting, then read, read, read; ask, ask, ask.

2. Market testing is useful, if you can do it. It works with trying out different sales techniques, advertising methods, sample mailings, and sample merchandise.

3. Survey the economic trends in your field and in general to see how they could affect your business. Is yours a needed product or service, or is it a luxury? Is it brand new and "hot," or is it waning in popularity?

Figure 1. Cash Budget Worksheet

Year

	Month:			Quarterly +/−
	Estimate	Actual		
Projected receipts:				
Cash sales				
Charges				
Collections (A/Rs)				
Other income				
Total receipts				
Projected disbursements:				
Merchandise				
Payroll				
Rent				
Utilities				
Interest				
Taxes				
Promotion				
Insurance				
Dues & subscriptions				
Autos & transportation				
Office				
Professional services				
Miscellaneous				
Total disbursements				

17

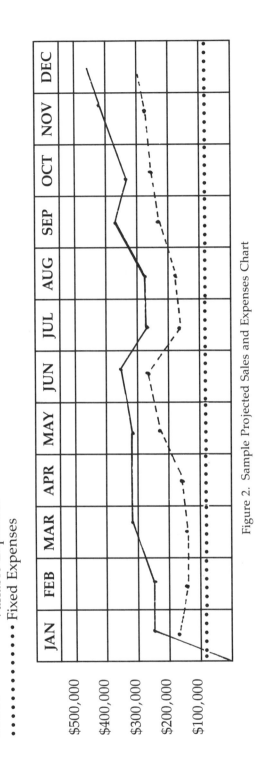

Figure 2. Sample Projected Sales and Expenses Chart

4. Survey your competition to see how they are doing in a commodity or service parallel to yours. What are their employees saying? What do their vendors report?

5. Check the consumer trends in your product or service line. Consumers are fickle; loyalty is a rare commodity, indeed. Is the trend toward your projected or existing business, or do you need to make changes?

6. What are the current technological trends in your specific field? Your trade association and trade publications will give you broad indications. Apply what you learn to your business, making adjustments for local conditions.

Once you gather this information, you will be in a better position to anticipate radical changes. It's a question of being forewarned and forearmed. Forecasting will give you a better than even chance to anticipate adjustments in expenses such as payroll, supplies, and inventory. It will also guide you in making the most of your cash-flow needs and loan requirements. (If you have a good line of credit, there is no need to borrow more than you think you need. Borrowed capital has to be paid back and carries an interest burden to boot.) Another good source of forecasting information is the U.S. Government—the Department of Commerce, the SBA, the IRS, etc.—as well as many state departments of economic development.

In doing your forecasting, you can use the simplified model given in Figure 1, or make up your own cash-flow budget. For instance, you may need to account for fixed overhead such as monthly payments on machinery; you may have a variety of taxes and license fees; and you may want to break "Miscellaneous" down into more specific expenditures, such as travel, entertainment, postage, freelance or temporary help, etc.

Another approach is shown in Figure 2. Some businesspeople like to make graphs to track the trends of various expenditures. Loan officers will be impressed with any evidence of professionalism and clarity. For more detailed accounting information and additional worksheets and forms, see Chapter 10.

Section II

Private Sources of Financing

It's easy to climb the ladder to success if your old man owns the ladder.

INTRODUCTION TO SECTION II

Once the preliminary decisions are made, where will the money come from? Many sources exist. The next section (III) explores government and government-assisted loan possibilities, but this section will cover the private funding avenues, including the following:

- You
- Family and friends
- Local investors
- Banks
- Venture capital investors
- Finance companies
- Credit unions
- Insurance companies
- Mutual funds
- Credit cards
- Savings institutions
- Public stock sales
- ESOPs
- Strategic alliances
- Grants
- Lady Luck

Virtually every one of these money lenders, except possibly your father or your mother-in-law, will want some collateral to ensure the return of their investment in case you and your bright idea go belly-up. Perhaps that's why the most important single source of capital among small operations is owners' own fiscal resources—the category, *You*. About 30 to 40 percent of all small-business capital has come out of the savings of Mr. and Mrs. America.

That leaves 60 to 70 percent that was raised in other ways. Why should an outsider lend you the money to start your new business or help you expand an existing one? No matter how brilliant your proposal or business plan, it is unlikely that a cold call will bring warm results. In the matter of raising capital, this is usually the case: Know who and know how, in that order. Use networking. Get a referral and an introduction from your local banker, your lawyer, or accountant. Anybody who knows anybody should be considered a lead.

A helpful book on this subject is *Start-Up Money: Raise What You Need for Your Small Business* by Jennifer Lindsey (New York: John Wiley & Sons, Inc., 1989). This large-sized paperback, for seekers of $100,000 or less in debt or equity capital, includes unusual financing methods, such as off-shore money raising, and good reference lists.

In the chapters that follow, each of the above-listed funding possibilities will be taken up in turn.

FAMILY, FRIENDS, AND LOCAL INVESTORS

3

FAMILY AND FRIENDS

There are two trends of opinion. One says, don't ever borrow money from friends and relatives; if you do, you can easily lose both. The other trend says, do borrow from family and friends because this is the quickest, easiest, and cheapest form of financing. And in fact, more small-business start-up capital comes from this source than from any other.

Amazingly, not only is the F&F method of small-business financing responsible for an overwhelming percentage of fledgling enterprises, but most of the time the borrower and lender also still talk to each other years later. It proves that the majority of entrepreneurs are basically honest. And it shows that friends and families are loyal and stick together—perhaps even that they share a certain adventuresome attitude toward gain and success.

With all the apparent ease in tapping this convenient source of money, remember two things: (1) Your friends and families are serious about helping you, but, aside from their personal relationship with you, they wish to make money on their investment. You've got to perform. And (2) borrowing money is serious business, no matter from whom. Treat F&F transactions with respect and conduct them legally. Each loan should have your acknowledgment in writing, properly executed and given to the lender, so that there will never be any doubt as to the amount borrowed, the intended payback, and the proposed interest on the loan.

Unrealistic and naive F&F loans *have* ruined many a fine family relationship and friendship. The trauma of such an intimate falling out is not worth it. You need family; you need friends.

LOCAL INVESTORS

Most of the start-up money for small businesses does not come from formal financial organizations. Professional venture capital firms— banks, investors, speculators—provide only 2.5 percent of such financing, according to an SBA study. Forty times as much small-business funding comes from what are called *informal* investors. This means Mr. and Mrs. Jones and others of the one in 115 families in the United States that become backers in a small enterprise. Only one-third of these family backers make in excess of $100,000 a year. Two-thirds of them are moderate-income folks.

Applied Economics Group, a research company in Knoxville, Tennessee, surveyed several hundred investment companies for the SBA and came up with a composite picture of the typical investor backing a start-up enterprise. The description will be revelatory in your search for dollars to supplement your own fiscal resources and those of relatives and friends: "A 47-year-old white male with a college degree in business or engineering, yearly income of $90,000 and net worth of $750,000, who built his own business. This composite angel has invested $131,000 for equity positions in three or four start-up companies and has provided another $75,000 in loans."

If you are going into the financial marketplace to borrow money from such an "average Joe," be mindful of the fact that this person wants to make money on his money—but that this is not the end of his motives. He also wants to be part of the process of building a new business, often because he received similar assistance when he came up the ladder.

EQUITY FINANCING

Besides borrowing money, equity financing is another method (not a source) of obtaining capital for starting or expanding a business.

Equity is what you or your investors or stockholders own in your company. In the past four years you have seen a rash of bank and savings-and-loan ads enticing you to borrow money on the equity in your house. If you do not have enough personal capital, you can also *sell* your equity—in your personal property, commercial property, land, an existing business, a car, or major equipment—for cash.

If you have a partnership or corporation, you can sell the equity in this business enterprise. The investor who buys this equity, or shares in the business, receives a proportionate share in your business profits.

Equity is not a debt. Debt must be repaid with interest, and the lender has no ownership control. In buying equity, the purchaser or lender also buys a measure of control, but is not an actual partner in the operation of the enterprise. Equity has an advantage in that it is fully collateralized, and it will not drain off money in interest charges and loan repayment at the beginning, when your business is most vulnerable. But you do give away a piece of your business. It's the old story: You can't have your cake and eat it too.

Personal Example

This writer set up a small, closely-held business 25 years ago. He figured that he needed at most $50,000 and had about one-third himself ($18,000). An accountant and an attorney who were consulted in the start-up process suggested that he incorporate and issue stock. The stock was divided into 85 percent preferred, nonvoting stock and 15 percent common, voting stock. The preferred stock was offered on the basis that it would pay 12 percent interest and be paid back (that is, retired) within four years or less. In offering the stock, this writer was careful to retain 51 percent of the common, or voting, stock so that he would always remain in control of the company.

This writer, the attorney, and the accountant invited all the friends they had, and nearly 50 people attended a briefing session held at a local hotel. All three sponsors addressed the guests and passed out written business plans for further study. When the smoke had cleared, nine of the attendees signed up for investment participation "packages." One major investor contacted the start-up promoters the following day. Within the week 10 local investors had put up all the needed seed money, and the business was able to start.

Dealing with friends put a special moral burden on this writer, of course. The business *had* to succeed. And it did. The end of the story is that all preferred stock was repaid within, and usually prior to, the four-year deadline. Eight of the ten common stock lots were repurchased at par within seven years. The majority outside investor (22 percent of the 49 percent offered) turned his stock over to a charitable foundation, which agreed to a 10-year payout at a higher value. This is being done punctually. Twenty-three years later, the business is still running and is nominally privately owned.

The F&F method, in this personal case history, was successful—but it was professionally organized and conducted with scrupulous honesty. Further, the former investors and this writer are still talking to each other.

BANKS

4

WHY YOUR "FRIENDLY" BANKER OFTEN SAYS NO

Commercial banks are by far the most visible lenders and make the greatest number and variety of loans to young businesses. Banks, however, are traditionally conservative. About 65 percent of start-up business loans are under $50,000. But then, most entrepreneurs don't realistically need that much. Of all the millions of little businesses scrounging for start-up capital, more than 80 percent need $10,000 or less. Only 20 percent require more than $10,000 to get going. In fact, the SBA has figured that the average small-business start-up requires only $1500 and that most of this start-up capital comes from the entrepreneur's own resources or his or her family and friends.

The banker who smiles and shakes your hand, even invites you out to lunch, is the banker who sees in you a prospect for profits. Maybe this banker can sell you a CD for $10,000, or maybe you will bring in a big new depositor. Also, the business relationship between a bank and a well-run, profitable enterprise can last for 30 years, during which it will earn the bank an average of $150,000. Certainly your banker will smile at you—if you are this kind of prospect.

It's a big "if." Bankers are in business to make money for their banks and not to take risks, and that is why they often say "No." You can read about the few exceptions in the bankruptcy reports, but then failure usually was caused by some high-flying fiscal adventure, not by lending $50,000 or $100,000 to Joe Doaks to set up a neighborhood hardware store.

In all fairness, you must remember that from the banker's standpoint, a loan is not a life jacket to help you keep your head above water, paying your overdue bills, or financing your daughter's wedding. Banks want to lend you money if it is a step toward increasing your business, so that you can make *more* money and, in the process, help to enrich the bank.

Now there is one factor that banks take more seriously than the rest—and that is your ability to pay back that loan plus a profit to the bank (interest). To make sure they won't lose out, banks demand collateral that is as solid as the rock of Gibraltar. Putting up security or collateral for a bank loan does not mean signing over your $100,000 equity in your home for a $100,000 cash loan. What this equity in your personal property will get you is, perhaps, a $40,000 loan. Then, if you default and the bank "collects," it will have no trouble selling your house for more than the $40,000 you owe. Risks? They are for entrepreneurs, not for banks.

Personal Example

This writer's own experience when starting a new business may be typical. The new business showed such good prospects that in six months this entrepreneur needed $14,000 to meet current, recurring bills that would allow him to continue. The bank with which he did business turned down his loan request because it was insufficiently collateralized. So he turned to a private investor, who took an equity position for the $14,000 loan. In other words, the investor took $14,000 worth of stock in the fledgling business, and the project was saved.

More than a decade later, when the new business had proved reasonably successful, the same bank manager *offered* additional financing unsolicited. But by that time the company had built up equity, and a loan was no longer needed. The struggling years were over. The early investor, meanwhile, has collected dividends double the amount of his investment and, 23 years later, is still collecting on his original "faith deposit." So much for bank loans when you don't have collateral.

Many a loan seeker has intoned the old adage that "a banker is always happy to lend you money when you don't need it." Still, loans are needed, and loans are being made. That's what keeps banks in business. So how do you go about getting one? Despite the above example, don't discount the importance of developing a personal relationship with your banker. While banks have rules and parameters by which they judge loan applications, the personal opinion of the loan officer is equally as important.

One bit of advice given by a banker was: "Get your banker involved in your business plans right from the start. Don't get all your ducks in a row, and then look for a banker to come running with the feed."

WHAT KIND OF LOAN?

In borrowing money, you need to understand the nature of the loan you seek. You need to know the difference between operating money and long-term money. You need to know how much you need, so that you ask neither for too much, nor too little.

Operating money pays for your day-to-day expenses. You will need some before you even start in business, and you will need enough to pay your bills promptly once you get rolling. At stake is your reputation and your relations with your suppliers and public. And, believe it or not, you'll need more money even than your projections say. It's easy to forget some little item required in your day-to-day operation. Or it could take longer to open up than you had planned. It certainly will take longer to collect money from your customers or clients. And all of this delay *takes* money. Be sure to give yourself some breathing room and have just a little more money available than you expect to need.

Long-term money (or *capital money*) is what you will use to buy equipment, such as machinery or a truck—expenditures that might never be repeated, or at least not for a long time. This long-term money usually can be paid off over many years, because the equipment itself often counts as collateral.

Working with a commercial bank to obtain financing need not be limited to a straight loan. Banks lend money for all kinds of needs and purposes. Here are just a few types of loans that you can discuss with your commercial loan officer or bank manager:

31

- Straight commercial loan
- Personal loan against personal collateral, such as a home, jewelry, art
- Revolving line of credit that assures you a minimum amount of ready cash in your account at all times
- Loans against your accounts receivable
- Loans against your inventory
- Long-term equipment leasing
- Letter of credit (used especially in foreign transactions)
- Short-term seasonal loans, such as a retailer might need toward Christmastime

And then, of course, there is the loan guaranteed by the Small Business Administration, which is discussed in Chapter 8.

THE SIX Cs OF CREDIT AND OTHER SIGNALS

Despite their conservatism, banks do lend money. That's their business. If you have a good idea and a sound business plan, you might be able to get a bank loan with or without the guarantee available from the Small Business Administration. But it is good to know all the roadblocks in loan applications. Look at them and get them out of the way *before* you make that loan application.

Lenders have a set of preliminary criteria known as "the six Cs of credit." This is what they look for:

1. **Character:** What kind of a reputation do you have? Are you the proverbial boy scout—trustworthy, honest, reliable? Or are you known to live high—above your means? Are you reputed to be a good manager in your personal life as well as in your business dealings?

2. **Capacity:** Does the business you propose indicate that you have the capacity to pay back the loan as promised? Does your cash-flow projection confirm this?

3. **Capital:** How much personal money do you have invested in this business? Do you have enough commitment of your own to work hard, make a profit, and pay back what you owe the bank?

4. **Collateral:** Do you own any real estate, equipment, good accounts receivable, vehicles, stocks and bonds? What is their appraised value, and is this enough to cover the loan and a little more?

5. **Circumstances:** Are the economic circumstances of the times in general, and of your business field in particular, conducive to future growth—and your ability to pay back the loan?

6. **Coverage:** What happens if some catastrophe prevents you from paying back the loan? Are you covered for any eventuality?

Danger Signals

There are other tell-tale signs that a banker watches for. It is good to know about these, too, because they can be useful to you. By being aware of them, you may be able to make assets out of the following loan-seeking liabilities:

1. *Not enough available revenue:* Every business goes through crunches, especially during the start-up years. Do you have sufficient personal reserves to come up with the loan installment on time, in case collections are a little slow during one month?

2. *Overextended account:* Deficit financing may be okay for the U.S. Treasury. When it runs short, it can always sell more bonds or print more money. However, if your bank account shows consistent monthly overdrafts, the loan officer will take this as an indication of bad fiscal management.

3. *Too many unpaid bills:* If the latter have piled up beyond your capacity to meet them, the loan officer will not be likely to bail you out. If you have the collateral to cover the loan, the banker will still ask, "Why didn't you use that to pay your trade bills on time?"

4. *High inventory:* If you carry too much inventory in relation to sales, you may look like a bad buyer and planner.

5. *Too many fixed assets:* If you have more machinery than you can profitably use in your business, as with the preceding, it indicates bad management and planning—a reason for turning you down.

6. *Long-term debt:* If you have bought lots of equipment or property and are getting behind on your payments, the banker will probably be unwilling to add to your long-term debt.

7. *Unexplained loans:* If your books show loans to owners, officers, and others for seeming nonbusiness purposes, the red light goes on at the bank loan office.

8. *High personal income:* If your records show that you have paid yourself or your family members unusually high salaries or other benefits, you'll have some explaining to do.

9. *Too little, too late:* Sometimes even a loan won't save your business. You have waited too long and the bank will realize this very quickly.

10. *Too small a loan:* Ironically, if you apply for a business loan that is too small for the bank to process, you could be turned down. It costs the bank the same to process a $1000 loan as a $100,000 loan. If your needs are deemed too small, look for another lender or get a personal loan.

11. *One-person risk:* Lending to a one-person proprietorship is considered a high-risk loan by the bank. The loan needs to be covered by sufficient insurance to guarantee a payback in case of illness, injury, or death.

12. *Lack of a track record:* The time when you need money the most—when you first start up a new business—is precisely when it is the most difficult to obtain. The bank is looking for a "track record," not for a speculative adventure. You may need to tap friends, a partner, a private investment company (at higher interest), or the family to get you started.

In considering these caveats, two major conclusions jump out: Your *personal integrity* is vital, and so is the need for *collateral*. You are in more control of the first than the second. Still, both are as important in making a successful loan application as your two legs are in walking and running.

THE LOAN PROPOSAL TO YOUR BANK(S)

After getting acquainted with the bank's loan officer—either by doing business at the bank or by someone's introduction or referral—ask for one of their loan application forms. You will find a sample of a brief two-sided form here (Figure 3). However, a more thorough and attention-getting approach would be to create your own appli-

PERSONAL FINANCIAL STATEMENT

IMPORTANT: Read these directions before completing this Statement.

☐ If you are applying for individual credit in your own name and are relying on your own income or assets and not the income or assets of another person as the basis for repayment of the credit requested, complete only Sections 1 and 3.

☐ If you are applying for joint credit with another person, complete all Sections providing information in Section 2 about the joint applicant.

☐ If you are applying for individual credit, but are relying on income from alimony, child support, or separate maintenance or on the income or assets of another person as a basis for repayment of the credit requested, complete all Sections, providing information in Section 2 about the person whose alimony, support or maintenance payments or income or assets you are relying.

☐ If this statement relates to your guaranty of the indebteness of other person(s), firm(s) or corporation(s), complete Sections 1 and 3.

TO:

SECTION 1 - INDIVIDUAL INFORMATION (Type or Print)	SECTION 2 - OTHER PARTY INFORMATION (Type or Print)
Name	Name
Residence Address	Residence Address
City, State & Zip	City, State & Zip
Position or Occupation	Position or Occupation
Business Name	Business Name
Business Address	Business Address
City, State & Zip	City, State & Zip
Res. Phone / Bus. Phone	Res. Phone / Bus. Phone

SECTION 3 - STATEMENT OF FINANCIAL CONDITION AS OF _____ 19____

ASSETS (Do not include Assets of doubtful value)	In Dollars (Omit cents)		LIABILITIES	In Dollars (Omit cents)	
Cash on hand and in banks			Notes payable to banks - secured		
U.S. Gov't. & Marketable Securities - see Schedule A			Notes payable to banks - unsecured		
Non-Marketable Securities - See Schedule B			Due to brokers		
Securities held by broker in margin accounts			Amounts payable to others - secured		
Restricted or control stocks			Amounts payable to others- unsecured		
Partial interest in Real Estate Equities			Accounts and bills due		
see Schedule C			Unpaid income tax		
Real Estate Owned - see Schedule D			Other unpaid taxes and interest		
Loans Receivable			Real estate mortgages payable		
Automobiles and other personal property			see Schedule D		
Cash value-life insurance - see Schedule E			Other debts - itemize		
Other assets - itemize					
			TOTAL LIABILITIES		
			NET WORTH		
TOTAL ASSETS			TOTAL LIAB. AND NET WORTH		

SOURCES OF INCOME FOR YEAR ENDED_____, 19___		PERSONAL INFORMATION
Salary, bonuses & commissions	$	Do you have a will?_____ If so, name of executor.
Dividends		
Real estate income		Are you a partner or officer in any other venture? If so, describe.
Other income (Alimony, child support, or separate maintenance		
income need not be revealed if you do not wish to have it		Are you obligated to pay alimony, child support or separate
considered as a basis for repaying this obligation)		maintenance payments? If so, describe.
		Are any assets pledged other than as described on schedules? If
TOTAL	$	so, describe.

CONTINGENT LIABILITIES		
Do you have any contingent liabilities? If so, describe.		Income tax settled through (date) _____
		Are you a defendant in any suits or legal actions?
As indorser, co-maker or guarantor?	$	Personal bank accounts carried at:
On leases or contracts?	$	
Legal claims	$	
Other special debt	$	Have you ever been declared bankrupt? If so, describe.
Amount of contested income tax liens	$	

PFS (Rev. 3/86)

(COMPLETE SCHEDULES AND SIGN ON REVERSE SIDE)

6713

Figure 3. Sample Bank Loan Form

SCHEDULE A — U.S. GOVERNMENTS & MARKETABLE SECURITIES

Number of shares or Face Value (Bonds)	Description	In Name Of	Are These Pledged?	Market Value

SCHEDULE B — NON-MARKETABLE SECURITIES

Number of Shares	Description	In Name Of	Are These Pledged?	Source of Value	Value

SCHEDULE C - PARTIAL INTEREST IN REAL ESTATE EQUITIES

Address & Type Of Property	Title In Name Of	% Of Ownership	Date Acquired	Cost	Market Value	Mortgage Maturity	Mortgage Amount

SCHEDULE D — REAL ESTATE OWNED

Address & Type Of Property	Title In Name Of	Date Acquired	Cost	Market Value	Mortgage Maturity	Mortgage Amount

SCHEDULE E — LIFE INSURANCE CARRIED, INCLUDING N.S.L.I. AND GROUP INSURANCE

Name Of Insurance Company	Owner Of Policy	Beneficiary	Face Amount	Policy Loans	Cash Surrender Value

SCHEDULE F — BANKS OR FINANCE COMPANIES WHERE CREDIT HAS BEEN OBTAINED

Name & Address Of Lender	Credit In The Name Of	Secured Or Unsecured?	Original Date	High Credit	Current Balance

The information contained in this statement is provided for the purpose of obtaining, or maintaining credit with you on behalf of the under-signed, or persons, firms or corporations in whose behalf the undersigned may either severally or jointly with others, execute a guaranty in your favor. Each undersigned understands that you are relying on the information provided herein (including the designation made as to ownership of property) in deciding to grant or continue credit. Each undersigned represents and warrants that *the information provided is true and complete* and that you may consider this statement as continuing to be true and correct until a written notice of a change is given to you by the undersigned. You are authorized to make all inquiries you deem necessary to verify the accuracy of the statements made herein, and to determine my/our credit-worthiness. You are authorized to answer questions about your credit experience with me/us.

Signature (individual) _____

S.S. No. _____ Date of Birth _____

Signature (Other Party) _____

S.S. No. _____ Date of Birth _____

Date Signed _____ 19_____

(USE ADDITIONAL SCHEDULES IF NECESSARY)

Figure 3. (*Continued*)

cation (a specifically tailored business plan). Such a proposal appears on the following pages as Figure 4. It includes these sections:

a. Cover letter
b. Executive summary
c. Company description
d. Market research, analysis, and sales
e. Research and development
f. Operations plan/cost of sales
g. Management details
h. Internal organization
i. Financial information/operating ratios
j. Appendices

a. *The Cover Letter*

Mr. John A. Doe, V.P.
Name Commercial Bank
000 Main Street
Anytown, State 00000

Dear Mr. Doe:

This is an application for a business loan in the amount of
$ _____.

The purpose of this loan is for _____ ,
as detailed in the attached explanation.

The loan is required for a period of _____ and is expected to
be repaid, with interest, within ____ months.

According to our attached Cash Flow Projection, we should be in
an excellent position to adhere to the above schedule.

Collateral is provided to cover the loan by _____ (Name of
Bank) _____ , as detailed on the attached schedule.

We do not at this time have any debt service, other than for minor
current payments, described in attached documents.

Should additional information be needed, I can be reached at 000-
0000 during business hours and at 000-0000 at other times.

Thank you for your consideration.

Cordially,

Your Name
Title and/or company

encl.

Figure 4. Sample Loan Application to a Bank

b. *Executive Summary*

These are the financial highlights in the attached Business Plan, in support of our loan application:

Cash flow:

_____

_____

_____

Assets:

_____

_____

Brief description of the company:

_____

_____

Our product (service)(process):

_____

Our marketplace:

_____

Competition and our position relative to them:

_____

A history of our earnings (if established), or a personal history of achievements (if a new business):

_____

Figure 4. (*Continued*)

(*Figure continues on p. 40.*)

Forecast of future earnings:

_____

Profile of company management:

_____

_____

_____

[*Note*: The loan officer is most of all interested in your company's financial and management data (the last three items). These sections will probably be reviewed first, so be sure they are carefully executed and accurate.]

c. *Company Description*

Management:

_____

_____

_____

Track record within the industry:

_____

_____

_____

Goal of company (if established, how this has been reached; if new company, how this will be reached):

_____

_____

Figure 4. (*Continued*)

Financial condition at present:

_____

_____

Forecast of future earnings:

_____

_____

Provisions for (1) substantial increases beyond projections, and (2) emergency measures in the event of major decline:

_____

_____

_____

How management will assure the company's growth projections:

_____

_____

_____

_____

_____

[_Note_: A lender is vitally concerned with your strategy to ensure that your plans can actually be carried out. How can you demonstrate that you can, indeed, make the company successful? How will you make your product or service grow in the marketplace? Your ability to repay the loan will depend on your ability to put your performance where your promise is!]

Figure 4. (_Continued_)

d. *Market Research, Analysis, and Sales*

The following market research (is being done) (has been done) to corroborate our projections:

_____

_____

_____

_____

_____

Documentation attached:

_____

_____

Our analysis of available research data leads us to the following conclusion:

_____

_____

_____

_____

_____

Factors being considered in our analysis (where applicable):

    1. Domestic competition

_____

    2. Foreign competition

_____

Figure 4. (*Continued*)

3. Regulatory requirements

4. General economic conditions

5. Industry or consumer trends

e. *Research and Development*

Registered or pending patents held:

Continuing research being done or projected:

[*Note*: Lenders look at technology as unsecured collateral. They rarely finance research and development, because it is subjective and not concrete. An actual patent or provable technology transfer can have a demonstrable asset value, but the details of this section are for information value only.]

Figure 4. (*Continued*)

(*Figure continues on p. 44.*)

f. *Operations Plan/Cost of Sales*

Here is how we determine and control our production costs:

Sources:

_____

_____

Delivery:

_____

_____

Price assurance:

_____

_____

Payment arrangements:

_____

_____

Employees (salaries, fringe benefits, commissions):

_____

_____

Expense accounts:

_____

_____

Discounts:

_____

Figure 4. (*Continued*)

Markdowns:

_____

_____

Industry averages or ratios:

_____

_____

_____

g. *Management Details*

Past experience of owner/manager:
          (attach detailed résumé, if lengthy)

Others on management team:

_____

_____

_____

Personal references:

_____

_____

_____

Business references:

_____

_____

_____

Figure 4. (*Continued*)

(*Figure continues on p. 46.*)

Previous lenders:

_____

_____

_____

[*Note*: Your prospective lender will also have a standard loan application form that will contain much of the above information.]

h. *Internal Organization*

Employee stock option plan:

_____

_____

_____

_____

Profit-sharing program:

_____

_____

_____

_____

[*Note*: The reason the bank's loan officer wants to know about existing stock option plans and profit-sharing plans is that such arrangements give your employees or associates preference over the bank. In other words, these plans subordinate the bank's position as primary creditor.]

Figure 4. (*Continued*)

i. *Financial Information/Operating Ratios*

Profit and loss statement tied to your forecast
                    [attach]
Cash flow statement
                    [attach]
Balance sheet
                    [attach]
Breakeven analysis
                    [attach—possible graph]
Repayment schedule
                    [attach]

[*Note*: If this is a new business, your forecasts need to take into account seasonal fluctuations traditional in your trade or profession. Since CASH is the only realistic source of earned money that you can tap to repay the loan, the banker will pay particular attention to this segment. Just as a Realtor emphasizes the importance of location *location* LOCATION, so a loan officer concentrates on cash *cash* CASH.]

Operating Ratios:

$$\text{Current ratio} = \frac{\text{current assets}}{\text{current liabilities}}$$

$$\text{Debt-equity ratio} = \frac{\text{total liabilities}}{\text{stockholders' equity (net worth)}}$$

$$\text{Receivable turnover ratio} = \frac{\text{net sales}}{\text{average receivable balance}}$$

[*Note*: These figures might be a job for your CPA or business adviser. Current ratio is affected by your inventory and tight credit policy; easier credit and higher inventory will elevate your ratio and make you more vulnerable. The second ratio tells the banker what is owed and what is owned. A higher ratio increases the risk if sales decline. In the third ratio, a higher turnover indicates a shorter collection period and better A/R collectibility.]

Figure 4. (*Continued*)

j. *Appendices*

Board of directors

Lease

Contracts
  Management
  Leased equipment
  Purchasing
  Sales

Patents

Figure 4. (*Continued*)

VENTURE CAPITAL: THE BOOM OR BUST METHOD

5

Unlike family and friends, and even your bank's loan officer, venture capitalists might make you associate the "V" in venture with the "V" in a notorious bird of prey—the vulture.

What sharply distinguishes private venture capital investors (VCI) from banks and the Small Business Administration, or even regular stock corporations, is the VCI's willingness to accept risk in exchange for equity in the business. A bank loan, if you can get it, especially if it is a partially guaranteed loan backed by the SBA, might be obtained at 12 percent to 20 percent—depending on your reputation with the bank and your collateral. Venture capital investors are likely to bypass such traditional financing means. But the projected return they are looking for is 35 percent or higher over a three- to five-year period. They usually invest for only a few years, during which the young entrepreneur must prove his or her mettle or face a takeover or bankruptcy.

For most entrepreneurs, venture capital is a new and glamorous world of big-time operators. One reason for its aura is its uncertainty, its speculativeness. Another is that venture capitalists deal primarily with start-up companies on the leading edge of technology. Many of them have gone on to spectacular success.

Venture capital is *not* penny-ante business. Each "deal" invariably runs into several hundred thousand dollars or higher. The money comes from wealthy family trusts, groups of private investors, and pension funds. The risk is high, but so are the hoped-for returns. Venture investors are most interested in companies that can mature into the $20 million range or close to it. Moreover, they will be interested in the possibility of a public stock offering, a sale at a considerably higher figure, and their own exit options. Don't forget, they are speculators and investors, not managers.

WHAT DOES THE VENTURE CAPITAL INVESTOR WANT IN A PROPOSAL?

To catch the serious attention of these hard-nosed, experienced, "outside" investors you will have to display the proper empathy toward their needs and bear in mind the four principles that investors consider important:

1. What proof can you offer that a need exists for your product or service?
2. How can you satisfy the investors' needs for high returns during a limited payback period?
3. What is the exclusivity of your product or process, if any? Such uniqueness can be like money in the bank.
4. What is your concentration of marketing and energy? Your management and fiscal resources need to be focused in order to have optimum chance for success.

Your business plan needs to take these concerns into consideration. Venture capitalists are looking for very much ,the same proof as bankers—only more so. Remember, only one percent of all venture loan applicants get the nod. We have assembled a package of guidelines you can follow—*if* you feel deeply and sincerely that you have the enthusiasm, nerve, product strength, growth potential, market research, and all the ingredients that can spell success. Your task is to convince a group of very sharp businesspeople that *you* are the one they should bet on, knowing that they bet only to *win*, not to place or show.

Two general points to keep in mind before you read the venture capital business plan are the following:

1. Pragmatic projections of sales and profits are a must. This may deflate your enthusiasm, but it is better to be realistic than to appear foolish before a board of skeptics. One thing that investors will do with your figures is compare them with industry norms. If they deviate too much from such norms, you'll earn yourself a place on the rejection pile.

2. Mass production has a better chance for growth and profits than customized work. The latter requires specialized personnel, a factor that, in turn, requires higher prices and more guesswork. This is especially troublesome when bids have to be entered with general contractors and government bureaus.

VENTURE CAPITAL BUSINESS PLAN

As with preparing an application for a bank loan, a request to a venture capital group is a pragmatic analysis of your present or proposed business, but with some special nuances. It has to be even better than a bank application for two reasons: (1) It usually involves more money, and (2) only about 1 percent of venture capital applicants are successful. Here is what such an application package should contain:

- Cover letter
- Executive summary
- Table of contents
- Company description and history
- General strategy
- Description of marketplace
- Research and development
- Manufacturing and operations
- Sales strategy
- Management team

- Financial data
- Appendices

Cover letter. Find out the name and title of the person who should receive your application; address the cover letter to an individual. State in one page the purpose of the enclosed application, why your business is a great venture capital opportunity, what you plan to do as a follow-up to your application, where the reader will find your income projection, and the investors' bailout or exit timetable. (If you are filing more than one application, this can be a standard letter to all companies, but each must be individually addressed, of course.)

Executive summary. This might be the only portion of your application that the busy venture capital investor reads—so make it shine. Experts estimate that only one out of ten proposals gets read past the executive summary, and of those that do pass this first acid test, barely half get to the VC committee meeting or conference table. This is where you emphasize the key points, giving an incisive description of your company, product(s), services, and technology, and the market in which you expect to strike it rich. If you have any past history of earnings on which to forecast a rosy future, the VC exec should see them previewed here. Finally, blow your own horn and that of your associates to show why your management is the one to take your enterprise to its zenith.

Table of contents. This shows and briefly outlines all the elements in your proposal, so that the VC executive can pinpoint areas to scrutinize in greater detail.

Company description and history. This is probably the toughest section to write. It should be concise and focus on exactly what your company is about. Tooting your own horn melodiously is not easy.

General strategy. Detail the need your new product or service will fill in the global marketplace. What is your pitch? Do you have a new and superior product, a better method of delivery, a lower price? Are you on the cutting edge of a perceived new trend?

Description of the marketplace. Since venture capitalists are creatures of the marketplace, show here that you understand the complexities of market research. What is the background of your industry? What are its size and chief characteristics? What are the trends? Who are the major buyers? How will the trends affect your own future successes?What are your marketing capabilities? How do you stand, point for point, in the competitive marketplace?

Research and development. Is your proposed product copyrighted or patented? Can this effectively protect your ownership? You will have to be careful not to reveal too much of the technology or secret ingredients of your patent, while still detailing your technological superiority over competitive products, as well as your future R&D development beyond the first-generation product.

Manufacturing and operations. Describe your plans for producing your product, stating how much of the operation will be internal and how much will be subcontracted. What kind of quality control measures will there be? What are your physical facilities like? Or what will they be like if new construction or expansion is intended? What about your working staff and its training? How will your product be priced at varying quantity levels? Show how you can increase profits through financial expansion. What are your capital requirements at the various steps?

Sales strategy. Show how you will move the products or services you produce, including distribution methods, geographical coverage, market penetration, sales force acumen, promotional supports. Who are your actual customers? What sales or seasonal cycles exist in the industry? What are your sales projections and how can you support them?

Management team. Venture capital investors know that after all the theory is expounded, it's the people who run the company and manage their investment that really count. Who will be running your company? What are their track records, backgrounds, expertise, education? What compensation will keep everyone perking optimally? How will you fill in other management requirements during your proposed expansion? How will your management and key-employee picture look two or three years down the road?

Financial data. This is a two-part section presenting both a financial plan and a financial statement. The first part must include your capital requirements and timing for each stage and projections of how this expansion will affect your company's valuation and growth. In the second part, if you have been in business for a while, they will want to see financial statements for the past three to five years, P&L, cash-flow projections, breakeven point. Make sure to include your balance sheet and estimated performance projections in a variety of economic circumstances, R&D costs, tax deductions, interest on obligations, material costs, and payroll expenses.

Appendices. Exhibits should include such general (not proprietary) information as your board of directors, management résumés, any available market studies, product pictures, professional references, and any articles on you or your company that have appeared in the trade or consumer press.

Follow up at a decent interval. Make sure your contact has received the proposal. Try to find out when you can expect a response. Invite further inquiries.

HOW TO FIND THE INVESTORS

As a category, venture capital firms (there must be more than a thousand) have literally billions of dollars to invest. The ways to find a venture capital group are to peruse business magazines such as *Venture, INC., Business Age, Entrepreneur, Nation's Business,* and others and to attend venture capital conferences or expos where the more notable VCI groups come together. Or contact one of the networking organizations that can team you with a venture group. (There usually is a membership charge of about $200 a year before you can participate.) Among these financial "dating services" are the following:

Northwest Capital Network
One Lincoln Center, Suite 430
10300 Southwest Greenburg Road
Portland, OR 97223
(503) 245-5936

Venture Capital Network of Texas
P.O. Box 690870
San Antonio, TX 78269-0870
(512) 229-2124

Venture Capital Network of Atlanta
230 Peachtree Street, NE, Suite 1810
Atlanta, GA 30303
(404) 658-7000

Venture Capital Network Inc.
P.O. Box 882
Durham, NH 03824
(write)

Midwest Venture Capital Network
3338 Olive Street, Suite 204
St. Louis, MO 63103
(314) 533-1393

Venture Capital Network of New York
P.O. Box 248
Lake Placid, NY 12946
(518) 564-3227

There are also venture capital clubs you might want to know about. Three selected ones are the following:

Central Florida Venture Group
2828 Kansas Street
Orlando, FL 32785
(407) 338-6843

Connecticut Venture Group
71 East Avenue
Norwalk, CT 06951
(203) 852-7168

Colorado Venture Group
7153 South Alton Way
Englewood, CO 80112
(303) 850-7611

To summarize, investors look for exceptional cash flow, quick growth, and high profits. If your proposed business is so hot and your confidence in it so solid that you think you could grow 30 to 40 percent a year, the venture capital route might be for you. In a way it's a crap shoot, but these investors have money to spare and are willing to take "flyers" to make a lot more money. If you are up to it, it's a great way to ride a comet into the stratosphere.

It might not be for you, however. If these prospects intimidate you or turn you off, then go the more traditional fund-raising routes.

OTHER PRIVATE SOURCES OF FINANCING

6

The sources covered so far are one's own resources and those of family, friends, and local investors; banks; and venture capital investors. The group of less frequently used sources covered in this chapter includes finance companies, credit unions, insurance companies, credit cards, and savings institutions. Mutual Funds are considered but not found to be a viable direct source.

FINANCE COMPANIES

Commercial finance companies are generally regarded as the places to go when you are unable to secure financing from a bank. Like banks, commercial finance companies are concerned with your ability to repay the loan. CFCs, however, are more willing to rely on the quality of the collateral than on your track record or profit projections. The advantage of this policy to a start-up business is obvious. The disadvantage is that loans from a commercial finance company are usually several points higher than loans from a bank.

Commercial finance companies are sometimes called asset-based lenders or ABLs for short. One of their specialty services is *factoring*. This means the purchase of accounts receivable for a sum somewhat below their face value—usually around 75 to 80 percent of their worth. However, this form of financing is only applicable to operating companies and not to start-ups. ABLs also specialize in equipment leasing, which is useful for beginning enterprises.

Each situation is unique. You should "shop around" for money as you do for groceries. The difference in prices here, however, can run into the thousands of dollars. In any event, you will still need substantial personal assets or collateral. Figure 5 shows a typical CFC loan application form.

CREDIT UNIONS

Government agencies and employees of large companies sometimes set up credit unions that function like savings and loan associations or savings banks. Some of them even grow to equal private commercial institutions in size and services.

Employees often can get loans on very favorable terms—generally only as long as they are employed by the nominal sponsor. In addition to financing employees' automobile and home acquisitions, vacations, and bill consolidations, some credit unions have expanded to take in outside depositors and investors and have expanded their loan capabilities to include commercial ventures.

If you have access to a credit union, look into this handy source of start-up financing, especially if you start up your new enterprise as a sideline, or if your spouse is the one running it.

INSURANCE COMPANIES

Insurance companies may sound like an unlikely source for most small business start-ups. They usually go in for big deals, like financing shopping malls when opportunities exist to get into a joint venture or equity position.

However, many entrepreneurs have long-standing insurance policies that have accumulated a cash value. You can borrow on that cash value, paying interest annually or having the interest deducted from the remaining principal. If you should die before the loan is repaid, the company will simply deduct the loan from the remaining proceeds, and your estate will get that much less.

SIGNAL

DATE **May 8** 19 **89**

022940

PAY TO THE ORDER OF:

☐ **YES** I need extra cash today. Here is my application for credit. I understand that a disclosure statement setting out the terms and conditions of the credit you approve will be sent to me when my application is approved, if none was sent to me with this application form.

THE AMOUNT OF: $

Be sure this address shows through the window of return envelope ▶

MC-NRHP89050017   MSC-1361
Signal Finance of Maryland, Inc.
747 Baltimore Blvd.
P.O. Box 426
Westminster, MD 21157-9946

WRITE IN ANY AMOUNT YOU'D LIKE TO HAVE UP TO—

$15,000 ◀

NOTE: THIS DOCUMENT IS NON-NEGOTIABLE AND IS NOT A CHECK.

INFORMATION ABOUT YOURSELF

(Please make corrections below if necessary)

Name of Second Mortgage Holder
$ $
Second Mortgage Payment Amount   Balance
(   )   (   )
Home Phone   Daytime Phone
(   )
Employer   Employer's Phone

Social Security No.   Date of Birth
☐ Own ☐ Rent
Years & Months at Current Address

Employer's Address

Position   Years & Months There
$ $ per
Annual Employment Income   *Other Income

Name of First Mortgage Holder or Landlord
$ $
First Mortgage Monthly Payment or Rent Amount   Balance
$ $
Purchase Amount   Current Market Value

Number of Dependents (Do Not Include Yourself)
(   )
Name of Nearest Living Relative   Relative Phone

Have You Ever Filed for Bankruptcy? ☐ Yes ☐ No

INFORMATION ABOUT CO-APPLICANT (IF ANY)

Name   Date of Birth

Address (If Different from Applicant)

City   State   Zip

Social Security No.
☐ Own ☐ Rent $
Years & Months at Current Address   Monthly Payment

Mortgage Company or Landlord

Your Relationship to Applicant
(   )   (   )
Home Phone   Daytime Phone
(   )
Employer   Employer's Phone

Employer's Address

Position   Years & Months There
$ $ per
Annual Employment Income   *Other Income

Have You Ever Filed for Bankruptcy? ☐ Yes ☐ No

CREDIT INFORMATION

A. Please list all credit cards you now hold. (MasterCard, Visa, Diners Club, American Express, etc. Include department stores and gasoline cards.)

1.   6.
2.   7.
3.   8.
4.   9.
5.   10.

B. Please list all installment loans and other debts or obligations you now have. (If you need more space write on the back.)

Name of Lender
$
Amount Still Owed

Name of Lender
$
Amount Still Owed

* You don't have to include income from alimony, separate maintenance or child support if you don't want us to consider that income

---

SIGNATURE(S) I authorize you to investigate my credit record, to check statements I've made, to report your credit experience with me and to keep this application. I have completed this application fully and truthfully and I have listed all my debts and obligations.

X _____
APPLICANT   DATE   CO-APPLICANT   DATE

SG BC-6

Figure 5. Sample Finance Company Loan Form

Insurance companies sometimes engage in mortgage loans, usually facilitated through local branch offices or loan brokers. They also make unsecured term loans, but only to businesses with long-term profit-making histories. In the latter case, the risks are minimized, but they are still higher than fully collateralized loans. Consequently, the interest rates will be higher than normal ones.

If you do have cash equity in your personal or business insurance policy and want to borrow, you can expect a loan within a couple of weeks after filing an application. Many veterans also have equity in their VA policies and can borrow on them at below-market rates.

MUTUAL FUNDS

We have found little evidence that mutual funds are significant sources of start-up capital. Some funds, of course, have been set up specifically for speculative investments in venture explorations, but they are hardly mutual funds in the true sense. Some funds specialize in the stocks of new companies, but they are not direct funding mechanisms. The direct route is through venture capital groups.

CREDIT CARDS

People who have credit cards will have credit limits of $1000 to $10,000 to unlimited. You can get cash advances from most of them as well as charge major business start-up needs with them.

When no other options are open to you, credit-card advances are a way of getting the kind of quick, small loan that banks don't want to bother with. Of course you pay up to 18 percent for your "loan" (though in Arkansas a local bank advertises an 11½ percent credit card), but sometimes the credit card is the only game in town.

You might have read the story about an independent filmmaker who borrowed $8000 on his credit cards in order to complete a film. Or the chain-store credit manager who planned for many years to use his credit cards to start a business that the normal loan connections had turned down. He finally accumulated 37 credit cards, with which he raised $150,000. Two years later, he is still paying on the 37 cards, but at least he is in the business he wanted.

SAVINGS INSTITUTIONS

Savings and loan associations have had a rough time of late. Over-extensions by S&Ls in Maryland, Texas, California, and elsewhere have resulted in bankruptcies, takeovers, government hearings, and threats to the federal and state insurance systems. However, real estate financing is their specialty and if you are looking to buy a property for your business, the savings and loan association or savings bank is the logical place to look. Both S&Ls and banks might have distress properties that you can acquire by taking over payments.

The commercial and industrial mortgage is a fairly standard type of loan. The institution makes a loan of up to 75 percent of the property's appraised value, spreading the loan amortization over 15 to 25 years. Interest rates vary with the mortgage market and are quite competitive—sometimes falling slightly below those of other financial institutions.

Savings institutions make their own appraisals, so it is difficult to get a high appraisal and try to mortgage out at 100 percent (your actual cost). The prime criteria they look for are a good location, a marketable property that is not specialized but general and salable, and a business's profitability that will ensure repayment of the mortgage loan. Figure two to eight weeks for such a mortgage loan to be processed.

ATYPICAL METHODS OF RAISING CAPITAL

7

GOING PUBLIC

It seems so utterly simple. Draw up an operations plan for your new corporation and get yourself an underwriter who will sell that stock for millions of dollars. Voila! You've got your financing.

But it isn't simple. On the way to such instant riches, don't forget the Securities and Exchange Commission, the thousands of dollars you'll need in seed money, and the obligations and responsibilities that go with a public stock offering. It's not a common route for a start-up company. Moreover, most entrepreneurs are creative types and not financial wizards. Many of them don't last through those tough growth years, and others take over to enjoy and build on the creative fruits of the founder.

When should you go public? Investment counselors say that a company should reach a $5 million volume and show a 10 percent, or $500,000, net profit before entertaining the offering of public stock. The exception might be that you are a known quantity starting a new company. If the prospects of the start-up business are big enough, making a public offering is a very attractive way of raising start-up capital. Using equity capital from public stock offerings allows the entrepreneur to operate without generating a profit and even opens the door to new stock offerings. The more that comes in, the easier it is to camouflage those profitless growing pains.

Before you leap, remember that this is truly hanging your corporate linens out in public. You will have to file very specific and complete information with the Securities and Exchange Commission and with state authorities. From then on, you come under their stringent regulations, and all of your formerly private financial information will be in the public domain.

The choice of an underwriter, the firm that goes into the public and sells your stock, is a very vital one. Your own attorney or accountant might be helpful. Scrutinize the expenses of such an offering carefully—professional fees, commissions, printing—and be sure that they are accounted for in the price offering.

Two factors will influence the price of your offered stock: the strength of your company and the general condition of the stock market. The first factor is not relevant if you are just starting a company. In this case your own reputation in the industry stands in good stead. The second factor, the general stock-market condition, is beyond your own control. It becomes a matter of timing.

Example

Let's say you have reached the minimum operating level recommended by Wall Streeters, or have sufficient advance business or contracts to generate a $5 million volume. Your actual or projected statements indicate that you can produce a 10 percent return ($500,000) on your first year of operation. Here are the steps in deciding on the price and amount of stock to be offered:

1. You and your underwriter, perhaps with the help of your attorney and CPA, agree on a 20-times earning price for your stock. (This is the industry average.)

2. You want to raise $2 million to ensure future operations and expansion. Expenses will take 10 percent of this, leaving you with $1.8 million if all of the offered stock is sold.

3. If your net is, or is projected to be, $500,000, and your earnings ratio is 20:1, then your company is assigned a net worth of $10

million (20 × $500,000). When you sell $2 million in stock, you will give up 20 percent of your ownership.

4. The authorized number of shares that your company owns under the terms of your corporate charter is 100,000. If you plan to offer 20 percent of your net worth, then 20,000 shares will be offered for sale, and each offered share will be priced at $100 ($2,000,000 ÷ 20,000 = $100).

But don't count your chickens until they're hatched; you might wind up with egg on your face.

USING ESOP

An "ESOP" is an employee stock option plan. Many a young company has increased its liquidity by borrowing low-cost funds from its key employees.

It sounds like a natural. "Share the wealth" has a nice ring to it, and theoretically it ensures the loyalty of employees, increases their efficiency, lengthens their service to the company, and can even be used in place of a pension plan. There is also the possibility of some tax and commercial loan benefits.

And yet, ESOPs are tricky. Don't start one until you have discussed all of its ramifications with your attorney and CPA. Not only are the federal regulations pertaining to employee stock option plans complicated, they also tend to change with each new wave of legislators. Further, an ESOP falls into the category of a public stock offering and is, therefore, regulated by the Securities Act of 1933. Besides your lawyer, you will want to work with a compatible underwriter.

One disadvantage is that you need to provide for a liquidation plan if the participating employee leaves the company. Another is that you actually dilute the earning power of your stock by sharing its proceeds—and that makes it less attractive to outside investors, such as a bank.

An additional caveat is that, if you do plan to establish an ESOP in your business as a means of raising on-going operating capital, you should keep it on a business-like basis. Have all transactions between you (the company) and the ESOP participant (employee) handled by a professional. This eliminates any possible conflict of interest or tendency to give the employee offhand, personal, or confidential advice on shares, which might, at some future date, be embarrassing or even legally compromising.

Conflict can also arise if the ESOP's accumulated money finances another enterprise. Will this one be your future competitor? It has happened, especially in such fast-growth areas as California's Silicon Valley.

Still, the pluses outweigh the minuses, and establishing a participating role for key employees is generally recommended. ESOPs are growing in American industry and are being recommended by many small business advisers.

STRATEGIC ALLIANCES

Strategic alliances are mutually supportive relations between entrepreneurs and suppliers or customers.

Sometimes a major supplier of goods used in your selling or manufacturing process wants to help build what will be a valued customer for years to come. It has the means to support the fledgling enterprise—not with cash, but with courtesies that can translate into cash for you. For example, the supply house will accept "dated" billing; that is, instead of the normal 30 days to pay your bill, it will allow you 60, 90, or more days. The supplier is, in effect, lending you the money for what you have bought for this extended period of time—without interest. Meanwhile, this supply company is building good will with you and assuring itself of a new outlet for its products or services.

Coming from the opposite perspective, a large, commercial customer of the new enterprise might look at the start-up as a new supplier, which provides a needed ingredient in its own operation. Now the customer is building a "feeder industry." To encourage this symbiotic arrangement, the customer might pay more promptly or even in advance, so that the new enterprise has the capital to buy raw material and labor. It might go further and bankroll some of the start-up expenses, securing its money by placing the new supplier under contract but guaranteeing to purchase a certain amount, if not all, of the new company's production.

Some danger to the entrepreneur exists in this close a relationship. There is the chance that the "Big Brother" customer would want to dictate the final price or dominate the entire production of the new enterprise, which would limit the entrepreneur's ability to obtain higher prices from smaller customers and resist making price concessions to the large one. This has happened.

One season, a gigantic retail/mail-order corporation bought the entire output of one of its suppliers. When the next buying season came around, the giant outfit dictated the price, which was lower than previously, to the small supplier. The latter could not exist with such a circumscribed profit and had to liquidate its business—which was promptly taken over by the triumphant customer. Beware of agreements that could have Faustian implications.

Another strategic alliance that might be arranged would be between a service supplier and customer and would allow partial or step-by-step payments to be made as the work progressed. A builder, carpenter, or painter, for example, could have such an arrangement with a client.

GRANTS

A qualified small-business start-up might be boosted by obtaining a grant from a private or public foundation. Such a foundation could range from the giant Ford Foundation to a small local one. Some foundations give money for specific fields; others because you are located in a specific geographic area and can benefit the residents. Numerous federal and state foundations offer grants to stimulate agricultural production, low-income housing, training, or export.

From start-up capital to research grants, here is an opportunity worth looking into. Start by checking out a valuable book: *Free Money for Small Businesses and Entrepreneurs* by Laurie Blum (New York: John Wiley & Sons, Inc., 1988). The author has compiled a comprehensive listing of 300 foundations, private funds, and some government agencies that give out money in the form of grants.

LADY LUCK

Perhaps this gal has no place in a serious book of business advice. But human nature being what it is, she should be given a moment's consideration.

Who is she? She is the trip to Las Vegas or Atlantic City to check out the gaming tables. She is the weekly "Oh, well, we might as well blow a buck on a lottery ticket," prompting you to stop at a grocery, newsstand, or liquor store in Maryland, Virginia, New York, Pennsylvania, Florida, or any place where state lotteries have turned ordinary folks into millionaires overnight.

The chances of having Lady Luck finance your start-up enterprise are probably comparable to the discovery of an old aunt Agatha who passed away and willed you the million dollars she kept hidden under her mattress. But hope springs eternal in the human breast.

Got a buck to blow? You could stop by at the friendly neighborhood tavern for a short draw, get half a shoe shine, buy a cheap magazine—or take a chance with a lottery ticket. If you were to put that dollar into a savings account each week, you might wind up with a $400 nest egg. If you bought a lottery ticket each week, you just might. . . .

Section III

Government-Assisted Financing

Going into business is lifting yourself up by your bootstraps. You've got to supply the boots. Uncle Sam only lends you the straps.

INTRODUCTION TO SECTION III

There is financial assistance available from federal, state, county, and municipal governments. You have to remember that governments do not create financial resources except through taxation, permits, bond issues, and punitive measures. The money thus raised all comes from you and you and you. When we ask one of the government units to give or lend us money, we are borrowing money from our fellow citizens—and from ourselves.

It seems more impersonal that way. Some entrepreneurs feel that they have such money coming to them by some magic transformation of their tax dollars into personal handouts. In past years, much government money was indeed passed on to individual entrepreneurs. Often the latter were poorly prepared and only vaguely investigated, and they turned out to be far from qualified or even honest. Billions of dollars were squandered, and bankruptcies rose proportionately. So things changed.

Governments do have money. They sometimes even make free grants, or they lend seed capital and help start-up entrepreneurs get off the ground with training, personal counseling, and leads to sales. Most often, government agencies back or guarantee loans made by local banks or economic development organizations. In all cases where money is lent or guaranteed, the borrowers must go through a process of close scrutiny, in which they come up with collateral to ensure paybacks and, in that and other ways, convince the examiners that they are good risks.

While many states have small-business loan programs, as well as programs to allow new businesses specific tax relief for a period of time, it is the U.S. Government's chief entrepreneurial division that facilitates loans most of the time. This is the U.S. Small Business Administration.

Entire books have been written on how Uncle Sam lends, or, more accurately, guarantees money lent through commercial banks and investment companies. It's a vast subject. Two that will be useful to you are the following:

Free Help from Uncle Sam to Start Your Own Business by William Alarid and Gustav Berle (Puma Publishing Co., 1989), available by writing to 1670 Coral Dr., Santa Maria, CA 93454. This is a useful reference that describes more than 100 federal programs, some of them little known. Includes actual success stories, helpful indexes and telephone numbers, as well as some nongovernmental resources.

SBA Loans: A Step-By-Step Guide by Patrick D. O'Hara (New York: John Wiley & Sons, Inc., 1989). This is a large-sized paperback by a California PhD that tends to concentrate on that state. It is, however, the latest and most complete treatment on the SBA. Includes all necessary forms, which should still be checked through local banks for possible current changes.

Obtaining money from the government or getting an SBA-guaranteed loan is by no means a uniform or cut-and-dried process. The rules often change in midstream depending on supply and demand, whims of Congress, who's in and who's out, and how much money is left in the budget at the time you apply for the loan.

Then, too, there are special circumstances. If you are handicapped, a veteran, or a member of a minority or socially disadvantaged group, you will have a better chance of approval. There even might be, at the time of your application, seed money available to support such a special case *directly*. It's worth a try.

THE SMALL BUSINESS ADMINISTRATION

8

GENERAL DESCRIPTION

While considerable misinformation is broadcast, telecast, and published about the SBA, the facts are published by this government agency itself and updated frequently. Here they are: The U.S. Small Business Administration (SBA) was created by Congress in 1953 during the Eisenhower administration. Its purpose is to assist, counsel, and champion America's small businesses.

The SBA's mission is to help people get into business, stay in business, and win federal procurement contracts. It is an independent agency in the executive branch, whose administrator is appointed by the President and confirmed by the Senate. The agency has nearly 4000 employees and appointees who work out of 110 offices. SBA offices are in every state, in Puerto Rico, the Virgin Islands, and Guam. A list of these offices appears in this chapter (see Figure 7).

Definition of a Small Business

According to SBA Bulletin No. 39: "SBA generally defines a small business as one that is independently owned and operated and is not dominant in its field. To be eligible for SBA loans and other assistance, a business must meet the size standards set by the Agency. There are 18 million small (non-farm) businesses in the U.S. by SBA standards.

"SBA makes special efforts to help those who face unusual difficulties in raising capital and finding sales markets, including women, minorities, the handicapped and veterans."

FINANCE AND INVESTMENT ASSISTANCE

The SBA offers a variety of loans and financial assistance to eligible small businesses, to privately owned small business investment companies (see Appendix), and to area development companies (page 214ff). It should be noted once more that the vast bulk of SBA loans are made *indirectly*, with partial guarantees to the commercial lending institution.

Example: In Fiscal Year 1987, the SBA approved 17,110 business loans in the amount of $2.7 billion. This was only slightly more than in the previous year. Of these loans, ninety-eight percent were guaranteed; only 2 percent were direct loans, which gives you an idea of your chances of getting direct government money (50:1!)—unless you are disabled, a socially disadvantaged member of a minority, or a victim of a natural disaster.

Percentage of All Loans

Even so, the number of start-up and other small businesses that get either direct or guaranteed loans through the SBA is proportionately small. If more than 600,000 small enterprises get started this year, and about 17,000 get SBA loan assistance, that number translates into approximately 3 percent. Most businesses get traditional loan money. Still, an SBA-backed loan is a valuable option to know about, particularly in marginal cases when your own resources are too meager to satisfy a bank loan officer. One indication of this is the current loan-loss ratio—banks report a 2 percent default by small business lenders; the SBA, a 3.17 percent loss.

Value

Another advantage to getting an SBA-backed loan is that the bank might go for a smaller amount than the loan amount that many banks consider worthwhile for a commercial loan. As a small entrepreneur you might not need more—nor can you qualify for more—than $10,000 or $20,000. But there is as much paper work with a $10,000 loan as with one for $50,000 to $100,000, and a commercial bank might turn you down on your request—unless you go to a smaller or rural bank or request an SBA-guaranteed loan.

The value of SBA action can be appreciated from the following report made by the U.S. General Accounting Office (GAO) in a survey of 739 commercial banks across the country:

> About 82 percent of lenders said that the small businesses to which they made loans would not have been financed without the SBA guarantee or would have had different financing terms and conditions. Although it is difficult to project what would have happened without the SBA Loan Guarantee Program, banks are often reluctant to make unguaranteed loans to small businesses under terms or conditions suited to their needs. Entrepreneurs contemplating the start of new businesses often find that financing is difficult to obtain. Many commercial lending institutions consider new business ventures as poor risks. Such ventures usually are supported by weak collateral and lack an established track record.

It should be noted that despite the small percentage of entrepreneurs actually aided by the SBA-guaranteed loan program, without it those that have been helped might never have gone into business.

Expansion

Further, SBA-assisted businesses have contributed to the national welfare, and the SBA can demonstrate a 10 percent return on its investment. With the promise of considerable additional funding from Congress, the SBA will have more money with which to underwrite commercial loan applications—and to publicize this fact to banks and the small business community. Already, under the leadership of the new administrator, Susan Engeleiter, a Bush appointee from Wisconsin, 60,000 brochures have been mailed to banks all over the nation announcing expanded SBA financial services.

HOW DOES THE LOAN PROCESS WORK?

The following information on how to work with and through the SBA is excerpted from SBA Publication OPC-6, revised, on "Business Loans from the SBA." *Note*: A variety of sample loan forms and guidelines for applying for an SBA-guaranteed or direct loan appear in the Appendix.

Two Basic Types of Business Loans

1. GUARANTEE LOANS are made by private lenders, usually banks, and guaranteed up to 90% by SBA. Most SBA loans are made under the guaranty program. The maximum guaranty percentage of loans exceeding $155,000 is 85%. SBA can guarantee up to $750,000 of a private sector loan.

There are three principal parties to an SBA guarantee loan: SBA, the small business applicant, and the private lender. The lender plays the central role in the loan delivery system. The small business submits the loan application to the lender, who makes the initial review, and, if approved for submission to the SBA, forwards the application and analysis to the local SBA office. If approved by SBA, the lender closes the loan and disburses the funds.

2. DIRECT LOANS have an administrative maximum of $150,000 and are available only to applicants unable to secure an SBA-guaranteed loan. Before applying for an SBA direct loan, an applicant must first seek financing from his/her bank of account, and, in cities over 200,000, from at least one other lender. Direct loan funds are very limited and, at times, available only to certain types of borrowers (i.e., businesses located in high-unemployment areas, or owned by low-income individuals, handicapped individuals, Vietnam-era veterans, or disabled veterans).

How to Apply for an SBA Loan

1. Prepare a current business balance sheet listing all assets, liabilities, and net worth. New business applicants should prepare an estimated

balance sheet as of the day the business starts. The amount that you and/or others have to invest in the business must be stated.

2. Income (profit and loss) statements should be submitted for the current period and for the most recent three fiscal years, if available. New business applicants should prepare a detailed projection of earnings and expenses at least for the first year of operation (a monthly cash flow is recommended).

3. Prepare a current, personal financial statement of the proprietor, or each partner or stockholder owning 20% or more of the corporate stock in the business.

4. List collateral to be offered as security for the loan along with an estimate of the present market value of each item as well as the balance of any existing liens.

5. State the amount of the loan requested and purposes for which it is to be used.

6. Take this material to your lender. If the lender is unable or unwilling to provide the financing directly, the possibility of using the SBA guaranty program should be explored. The lender should be encouraged to contact the nearest SBA field office if additional program information is needed. An SBA direct loan may be possible for credit-worthy applicants who are unable to obtain a guaranty loan, depending on availability of funds. Contact the nearest SBA field office for advice on the possibilities of a direct loan.

Terms of SBA Loan

Working capital loans generally have maturities of five to seven years. The maximum maturity is 25 years; however, the longer maturities are used to finance fixed assets such as the purchase of major renovation of business premises. Interest rates in the guaranty program are negotiated between the borrower and the lender subject to SBA maximums. Generally, interest rates for loans with maturities of seven years or more cannot exceed 2¾% over New York prime, and loans with maturities of less than seven years cannot exceed 2¼% over New York prime. Interest rates on direct loans are based on the cost of money to the Federal Government and are calculated quarterly.

Collateral

SBA requires that sufficient assets are pledged to adequately secure the loan to the extent that they are available. Personal guaranties are required from all the principal owners and from the chief executive officer of the business, irrespective of his/her ownership interest. Liens on personal assets of the principals also may be required where business assets are considered insufficient to secure the loan.

Eligibility Requirement

To be eligible for SBA loan assistance, the business must be operated for profit and qualify as small under SBA size standard criteria (except for sheltered workshops under the Handicapped Assistance loan program). Loans cannot be made to businesses involved in the creation or distribution of ideas or opinions. These would include such businesses as newspapers, magazines, and academic schools. Other types of ineligible borrowers include businesses engaged in speculation or investment in (rental) real estate.

General Size Standards

For business loans, size standard eligibility is based on the average number of employees for the preceeding 12 months or on sales volume averaged over a three-year period.
Manufacturing: Maximum number of employees may range from 500 to 1,500, depending on the type of product manufactured.
Wholesaling: Maximum number of employees may not exceed 100.
Services: Annual receipts may not exceed $3.5 to $14.5 million, depending on the industry.
Retailing: Annual receipts may not exceed $3.5 to $13.5 million, depending on the industry.
Construction: General construction annual receipts may not exceed $9.5 to $17 million, depending on the industry.
Special trade construction: Annual receipts may not exceed $7 million.
Agriculture: Annual receipts may not exceed $0.5 to $3.5 million, depending on the industry.

Credit Requirements

A loan applicant must

- Be of good character.
- Demonstrate sufficient management expertise and commitment for a good, successful operation.
- Have enough capital so that, with an SBA loan, the business can operate on a sound financial basis. For new businesses, this includes sufficient resources to withstand start-up expenses and the initial operating phase during which losses are likely to occur. SBA generally requires that owners inject one-third to one-half of the total assets needed to launch a new business.

• Show that the past earning record and/or probable future earnings will be sufficient to repay the loan in a timely manner.

SPECIALIZED SBA LOANS

The SBA, as well as private-sector lenders, might have special considerations for specific trades. One of them that deals in large sums and short-term loans is the building business.

General Contractors

Because most residential, as well as commercial, structures are mortgaged once they are completed, the working capital needed by a construction firm is for a relatively short duration—six months to two years, perhaps. Such loans are generally well collateralized, because the property (ground) can serve as security, as well as the title to the property under construction. Further, it is customary that the client or customer for whom the contractor is erecting the building will make some upfront payments.

Fact Sheet No. 17 (Figure 6), entitled "Loans to Small General Contractors," is typical of such "specialized" loans.

Socially and Economically Disadvantaged Entrepreneurs

Small start-up or operating companies run by "socially and economically disadvantaged persons" can obtain federal contracts and monetary assistance under the Section 8(a) Program. This program was started in 1968 and was named after Section 8(a) of the Small Business Act.

The purpose of the program is to foster business ownership for disadvantaged entrepreneurs, promote their competitive viability, and encourage the procurement by federal government departments of products and services from such disadvantaged companies.

To be eligible for the Section 8(a) Program, the applicant must prove that he or she owns at least 51 percent of the company for

FACT SHEET NO. 17

U.S. Small Business Administration

LOANS TO SMALL GENERAL CONTRACTORS

THE PROGRAM

The Small Business Administration (SBA) may make regular business loans to small general contractors to finance construction or renovation of residential or commercial buildings for sale.

ELIGIBILITY

Construction contractors and homebuilders that have demonstrated managerial and technical ability in constructing or renovating projects of comparable size, that are small by SBA size standards, and meet the other credit criteria are eligible for this program.

AMOUNT, TERMS AND INTEREST RATES

SBA may guarantee up to $500,000 or 85 percent of the loan, whichever is less. (The maximum guaranty for loans up to $155,000 is 90 percent.) Direct and Immediate Participation (IP) loans, when funds are available, have administrative ceilings of $150,000 on SBA's share of the loan.

The maturity cannot exceed 36 months plus a reasonable estimate of the construction or renovation period. Principal repayment may be required as a single payment at the time of sale. Interest payments, however, are required at least semi-annually and must be paid from the applicant's own resources, not from loan proceeds.

The interest rates charged or permitted by SBA for these loans are the same as for regular business loans.

USE OF PROCEEDS

Loan proceeds are to be used solely for the direct expenses of acquisition, immediate construction, and/or significant rehabilitation (costing more than one-third of the purchase price or fair market value at time of loan application) of residential or commercial structures for sale. Cost of vacant land is eligible as long as it does not exceed 20 percent of the loan proceeds. Not more than five percent of this loan may be used for streets, curbs and other developmental costs that benefit more than the property being constructed or rehabilitated with SBA financial assistance.

SPECIAL APPLICATION REQUIREMENTS

In addition to the application requirements of SBA's regular business loan program, the applicant must submit three letters to SBA (or to the participating lender).

(1) A letter is required from a mortgage lender doing business in the area to advise whether permanent mortgage financing is normally available to qualified purchasers of comparable real estate at the project location.

(2) A letter is required from an independent licensed real estate broker with three years experience in the project area advising whether a market for the proposed structure exists and that it is compatible with other structures in the neighborhood.

(3) A letter is required from an independent architect, appraiser or engineer to confirm the availability of construction inspection and certification as needed to support interim disbursement. This person must not be affiliated with the applicant in any way. The cost of construction inspections are to be paid by the applicant and may, if desired, be included in the use of proceeds.

COLLATERAL

Loans will be secured by not less than a second lien on the property to be constructed or renovated. The total amount of the first and second liens on a property cannot exceed 80 percent of the contractor's selling price and the first lien must contain provisions for the transfer of clear title to the purchaser of each parcel. SBA will not take a second position in a subdivision subordinate to a lien that requires the entire loan be paid in full before any property is released. The applicant must have an adequate investment in the property to show that the loan can be repaid from the sale of the property.

ADDITIONAL INFORMATION

Detailed information can be obtained from the nearest SBA office in your area.

Issued by:
Office of Public Communications
December 1986

Figure 6. Fact Sheet No. 17

which assistance is sought, be a citizen of the United States, and be able to prove ethnic prejudice or cultural bias that places his or her business at a disadvantage. Fact Sheet 36, available from any local SBA office, explains this special situation in detail.

Financial assistance is available to Section 8(a) participants on a direct basis—including advance payments for labor and material that might be needed to complete a government procurement contract.

Loans for Veterans

While Vietnam-era veterans and disabled veterans are not considered to be disadvantaged under Section 8a, some special considerations are given to them. For one, each SBA office has a veterans' counselor who will go over the applicant's case in fine detail and help him expedite the application.

Loans may be made to establish a small firm or assist in the operation or expansion of an existing one. The administrative ceiling for a veteran's loan is $150,000. Quarterly adjusted interest rates on veterans' loans are whatever the current SBA direct loans call for. Collateral is required as for all other loans.

To be eligible, the veteran must have served for a period of more than 180 days, between August 5, 1964 and May 7, 1975; been honorably discharged; or have a 30 percent or greater service-connected disability.

PUBLICATIONS: LOW-COST FINANCIAL AIDS FROM THE SBA

The U.S. Small Business Administration publishes a baker's dozen of financial pamphlets, priced from 50¢ to $1.00. Below is a complete list, with order numbers and costs. They are available from the U.S. Small Business Administration, P.O. Box 15434, Fort Worth, TX 76119.

FM 1   ABC's OF BORROWING
Some small business people cannot understand why a lending institution refused to lend them money. Others have no trouble getting

funds but are surprised to find strings attached to their loans. Learn the fundamentals of borrowing . . . $1.00.

FM 2   PROFIT COSTING AND PRICING FOR MANUFACTURERS
Uncover the latest techniques for pricing your products profitably . . . $1.00.

FM 3   BASIC BUDGETS FOR PROFIT PLANNING
This publication takes the worry out of putting together a comprehensive budgeting system to monitor your profits and assess your financial operations . . . $0.50.

FM 4   UNDERSTANDING CASH FLOW
In order to survive, a business must have enough cash to meet its obligations. Learn how to plan for the movement of cash through the business and thus plan for future requirements . . . $1.00.

FM 5   A VENTURE CAPITAL PRIMER FOR SMALL BUSINESS
This best-seller highlights the venture capital resources available and how to develop a proposal for obtaining these funds . . . $0.50.

FM 6   ACCOUNTING SERVICES FOR SMALL SERVICE FIRMS
Sample profit/loss statements are used to illustrate how accounting services can help expose and correct trouble spots in a business's financial records . . . $0.50.

FM 7   ANALYZE YOUR RECORDS TO REDUCE COSTS
Cost reduction IS NOT simply slashing any and all expenses. Understand the nature of expenses and how they inter-relate with sales, inventories and profits. Achieve greater profits through more efficient use of the dollar . . . $0.50.

FM 8   BUDGETING IN A SMALL BUSINESS FIRM
Learn how to set up and keep sound financial records. Study how to effectively use journals, ledgers and charts to increase profits . . . $0.50.

FM 9   SOUND CASH MANAGEMENT AND BORROWING
Avoid a "cash crisis" through proper use of cash budgets, cash flow projections and planned borrowing concepts . . . $0.50.

FM 10   RECORDKEEPING IN A SMALL BUSINESS
Need some basic advice on setting up a useful record keeping system? This publication describes how . . . $1.00.

FM 11   BREAKEVEN ANALYSIS: A DECISION MAKING TOOL
Learn how "breakeven analysis" enables the manager/owner to make

better decisions concerning sales, profits and costs . . . $1.00.

FM 12 A PRICING CHECKLIST FOR SMALL RETAILERS
The owner/manager of a small retail business can use this checklist to apply proven pricing strategies that can lead to profits . . . $0.50.

FM 13 PRICING YOUR PRODUCTS AND SERVICES PROFITABLY
Discusses how to price your products profitably, how to use the various techniques of pricing and when to use these techniques to your advantage . . . $1.00.

SBA FIELD OFFICES

All contact between entrepreneurs and the SBA takes place through its field offices. The government divides the United States into ten regions. Each region has from 6 to 16 SBA offices that you can visit for information about loans or just about any other small-business problems.

In addition, the subsidiary organization SCORE (Service Corps of Retired Executives) can always be located through these offices. There are more than 750 locations where volunteer SCORE counselors can be consulted. Many are in SBA offices; others have offices in local chambers of commerce or community colleges. SCORE counselors will help you make contact with the proper bank or SBA loan officer, and they will give you advice on starting your business and keeping it going successfully. There is no charge for these counseling services, although workshops and seminars sponsored by either SBA or SCORE usually cost a nominal $10 to $25.

In addition to the 112 regional, district and branch offices, SBA also maintains four special offices to handle emergency disaster loans at the following locations:

1501 Broadway, Fairlawn, NJ 07410 (201)794-8195
120 Ralph McGill St., Atlanta, GA 30308 (404)347-3771
2306 Oak La., Grand Prairie, TX 75051 (214)767-7571
1825 Bell St., Sacramento, CA 95825 (916)978-4578

Hopefully, you will never need them. The 112 regular SBA offices follow as Figure 7.

CITY	ST	ZIP	ADDRESS	PUBLIC PHONE
			Region I	
BOSTON	MA	02110	60 BATTERYMARCH STREET	(617) 451-2030
BOSTON	MA	02114	10 CAUSEWAY STREET	(617) 565-5590
AUGUSTA	ME	04330	40 WESTERN AVENUE	(207) 622-8378
CONCORD	NH	03301-1257	55 PLEASANT STREET	(603) 225-1400
HARTFORD	CT	06106	330 MAIN STREET	(203) 240-4700
MONTPELIER	VT	05602	87 STATE STREET	(802) 828-4474
PROVIDENCE	RI	02903	380 WESTMINISTER MALL	(401) 528-4586
SPRINGFIELD	MA	01103	1550 MAIN STREET	(413) 785-0268
			Region II	
NEW YORK	NY	10278	26 FEDERAL PLAZA	(212) 264-7772; (212) 264-4355
ALBANY	NY	12207	445 BROADWAY	(518) 472-6300
CAMDEN	NJ	08104	2600 MT. EPHRAIN AVE.	(609) 757-5183
ROCHESTER	NY	14614	100 STATE STREET	(716) 263-6700
ST. CROIX	VI	00820	4C & 4D ESTE SION FRM	(809) 778-5380
ST. THOMAS	VI	00801	VETERANS DRIVE	(809) 774-8530
HATO REY	PR	00918	CARLOS CHARDON AVE.	(809) 753-4002
NEWARK	NJ	07102	60 PARK PLACE	(201) 645-2434
SYRACUSE	NY	13260	100 S. CLINTON STREET	(315) 423-5383
BUFFALO	NY	14202	111 W. HURON STREET	(716) 846-4301
ELMIRA	NY	14901	333 E. WATER STREET	(607) 734-8130
MELVILLE	NY	11747	35 PINELAWN ROAD	(516) 454-0750

Region III

City	State	ZIP	Address	Phone
KING OF PRUSSIA	PA	19406	475 ALLENDALE ROAD	(215) 962-3750; (215) 962-3846
BALTIMORE	MD	21202	10 N. CALVERT STREET	(301) 962-4392
CLARKSBURG	WV	26301	168 W. MAIN STREET	(304) 623-5631
PITTSBURGH	PA	15222	960 PENN AVENUE	(412) 644-2780
RICHMOND	VA	23240	400 N. 8TH STREET	(804) 771-2617
WASHINGTON	DC	20036	1111 18TH STREET, NW	(202) 634-4950
CHARLESTON	WV	25301	550 EAGAN STREET	(304) 347-5220
HARRISBURG	PA	17101	100 CHESTNUT STREET	(717) 782-3840
WILKES-BARRE	PA	18701	20 N. PENNSYLVANIA AVE.	(717) 826-6497
WILMINGTON	DE	19801	920 KING STREET	(302) 573-6294

Region IV

City	State	ZIP	Address	Phone
ATLANTA	GA	30367-8102	1375 PEACHTREE ST., NE	(404) 347-2797
ATLANTA	GA	30309	1720 PEACHTREE RD, NW	(404) 347-2441
STATESBORO	GA	30458	52 N. MAIN STREET	(912) 489-8719
TAMPA	FL	33602	700 TWIGGS STREET	(813) 228-2594
W. PALM BEACH	FL	33407	5601 CORPORATE WAY S.	(305) 689-3922
BIRMINGHAM	AL	35203-2398	2121 8TH AVE. N.	(205) 731-1344
CHARLOTTE	NC	28202	222 S. CHURCH STREET	(704) 371-6563
COLUMBIA	SC	29202	1835 ASSEMBLY STREET	(803) 765-5376
CORAL GABLES	FL	33146	1320 S. DIXIE HIGHWAY	(305) 536-5521
JACKSON	MS	39269-0396	100 W. CAPITOL STREET	(601) 965-4378
JACKSONVILLE	FL	32202	400 W. BAY STREET	(904) 791-3782
LOUISVILLE	KY	40202	600 M. L. KING, JR. PL.	(502) 582-5976
NASHVILLE	TN	37219	404 JAMES ROBERTSON PKWY	(615) 736-5881
GULFPORT	MS	39501-7758	ONE HANCOCK PLAZA	(601) 863-4449

Figure 7. SBA Field Offices

(*Figure continues on p. 86.*)

CITY	ST	ZIP	ADDRESS	PUBLIC PHONE
			Region V	
CHICAGO	IL	60604-1593	230 S. DEARBORN STREET	(312) 353-0359
CHICAGO	IL	60604-1779	219 S. DEARBORN STREET	(312) 353-4528
EAU CLAIRE	WI	54701	500 S. BARSTOW COMMO	(715) 834-9012
CLEVELAND	OH	44199	1240 E. 9TH STREET	(216) 522-4180
COLUMBUS	OH	43215	85 MARCONI BLVD.	(614) 469-6860
DETROIT	MI	48226	477 MICHIGAN AVE.	(313) 226-6075
INDIANAPOLIS	IN	46204-1584	575 N. PENNSYLVANIA ST.	(317) 269-7272
MADISON	WI	53703	212 E. WASHINGTON AVE.	(608) 264-5261
MINNEAPOLIS	MN	55403-1563	100 N. 6TH STREET	(612) 370-2324
CINCINNATI	OH	45202	550 MAIN STREET	(513) 684-2814
MARQUETTE	MI	49885	300 S. FRONT ST.	(906) 225-1108
MILWAUKEE	WI	53203	310 W. WISCONSIN AVE.	(414) 291-3941
SPRINGFIELD	IL	62704	511 W. CAPITOL STREET	(217) 492-4416
			Region VI	
DALLAS	TX	75235-3391	8625 KING GEORGE DR.	(214) 767-7643
DALLAS	TX	75242	1100 COMMERCE STREET	(214) 767-0605
AUSTIN	TX	78701	300 E. 8TH STREET	(512) 482-5288
MARSHALL	TX	75670	505 E. TRAVIS	(214) 935-5257
SHREVEPORT	LA	71101	500 FANNIN STREET	(318) 226-5196
ALBUQUERQUE	NM	87100	5000 MARBLE AVE., NE	(505) 262-6171
EL PASO	TX	79902	10737 GATEWAY W.	(915) 541-7586
HARLINGEN	TX	78550	222 E. VAN BUREN ST.	(512) 427-8533

City	State	Address	ZIP	Phone
HOUSTON	TX	2525 MURWORTH	77054	(713) 660-4401
LITTLE ROCK	AR	320 W. CAPITOL AVE.	72201	(501) 378-5871
LUBBOCK	TX	1611 TENTH STREET	79401	(806) 743-7462
NEW ORLEANS	LA	1661 CANAL STREET	70112	(504) 589-6685
OKLAHOMA CITY	OK	200 N. W. 5TH STREET	73102	(405) 231-4301
SAN ANTONIO	TX	7400 BLANCO ROAD	78216	(512) 229-4535
CORPUS CHRISTI	TX	400 MANN STREET	78401	(512) 888-3331
FT. WORTH	TX	819 TAYLOR STREET	76102	(817) 334-3613

Region VII

City	State	Address	ZIP	Phone
KANSAS CITY	MO	911 WALNUT STREET	64106	(816) 426-2989
KANSAS CITY	MO	1103 GRAND AVE.	64106	(816) 374-3419
CEDAR RAPIDS	IA	373 COLLINS ROAD NE	52402-3118	(319) 399-2571
DES MOINES	IA	210 WALNUT STREET	50309	(515) 284-4422
OMAHA	NB	11145 MILL VALLEY RD.	68154	(402) 221-4691
ST. LOUIS	MO	815 OLIVE STREET	63101	(314) 539-6600
WICHITA	KS	110 E. WATERMAN ST.	67202	(316) 269-6571
SPRINGFIELD	MO	620 S. GLENSTONE ST.	65802-3200	(417) 864-7670

Region VIII

City	State	Address	ZIP	Phone
DENVER	CO	999 18TH STREET	80202	(303) 294-7001
DENVER	CO	721 19TH STREET	80202-2599	(303) 844-2607
CASPER	WY	100 EAST B. STREET	82602-2839	(307) 261-5761
FARGO	ND	657 2ND AVE. N.	58108-3086	(701) 239-5131
HELENA	MT	301 S. PARK	59626	(406) 449-5381
SALT LAKE CITY	UT	125 S. STATE STREET	84138-1195	(801) 524-5800
SIOUX FALLS	SD	101 S. MAIN AVE.	57102-0527	(605) 336-2980

Figure 7. (Continued)

(Figure continues on p. 88.)

CITY	ST	ZIP	ADDRESS	PUBLIC PHONE
Region IX				
SAN FRANCISCO	CA	94102	450 GOLDEN GATE AVE.	(415) 556-7487
SAN FRANCISCO	CA	94105-1988	211 MAIN STREET	(415) 974-0642
RENO	NV	89505	50 S. VIRGINIA ST.	(702) 784-5268
TUCSON	AZ	85701	300 W. CONGRESS ST.	(602) 629-6715
FRESNO	CA	93721	2202 MONTEREY ST.	(209) 487-5189
HONOLULU	HI	96850	300 ALA MOANA BLVD.	(808) 541-2990
LAS VEGAS	NV	89125	301 E. STEWART ST.	(702) 388-6611
GLENDALE	CA	91203	330 N. GRAND BLVD.	(213) 894-2956
PHOENIX	AZ	85004	2005 N. CENTRAL AVE.	(602) 261-3732
SAN DIEGO	CA	92188	880 FRONT STREET	(619) 557-5440
AGANA	GM	96910	PACIFIC DAILY NEWS BDG	(671) 472-7277
SACRAMENTO	CA	95814-2413	660 J STREET	(916) 551-1426
SANTA ANA	CA	92703	901 W. CIVIC CTR DR	(714) 836-2494
VENTURA	CA	93003-4459	6477 TELEPHONE RD.	(805) 642-1866
Region X				
SEATTLE	WA	98121	2615 4TH AVENUE	(206) 442-5676
SEATTLE	WA	98174-1088	915 SECOND AVE.	(206) 442-5534
ANCHORAGE	AK	99501	8TH & C STREETS	(907) 271-4022
BOISE	ID	83702	1020 MAIN STREET	(208) 334-1696
PORTLAND	OR	97204-2882	1220 S. W. THIRD AVE.	(503) 326-2682
SPOKANE	WA	99210	W. 920 RIVERSIDE AVE.	(509) 456-3783

Figure 7. (*Continued*)

STATES AND LOCALITIES

9

States are actively helping local entrepreneurs in five areas that usually include business development, procurement assistance, minority/women opportunities, international trade, and financial assistance.

In this book we are primarily interested in those states that are sources of financial assistance.

There are several reasons why states go out of their way to make seed money or expansion funds available: (1) to encourage local employment, (2) to aid existing business expansion, (3) to help increase the local tax base, (4) to attract out-of-state businesses, or (5) simply to act as regional conduit for federal funds.

Some states offer unique or special programs that we have detailed on the following pages. In addition to financial assistance, these might include technical and management training, workshops, and counseling. In other states tax incentives are offered as indirect financial aid, usually in what is called enterprise zones, which most often are federally sponsored but are run by state, county, or municipal administrations.

For a complete list of state business-assistance offices, see the Appendix.

SPECIAL STATE PROGRAMS

In addition to the state programs described below, Texas and North Carolina are working on franchise investment programs, and Louisiana entered a similar program into its legislature.

Numerous states have taken the route of providing tax incentives, such as tax holidays for a number of years, tax reductions, or tax credits for taking on certain employees. (See Figure 8.) Other direct or guaranteed loan programs have been developed in the following states:

COLORADO: A program connected with the SBA's 7a loan program guarantees loans for five to seven years at low fixed interest. There is no minimum loan amount, which is helpful when banks will not accept small business loans under $50,000, and a ceiling of $750,000.

CONNECTICUT: A Small Manufacturing Loan Program helps those whose annual sales run under $5 million. The money is to be used for fixed assets or working capital; loans are in amounts of up to $300,000, payable in seven to ten years at only 6 percent interest.

DELAWARE: This state encourages research and development of new products and services with loans of up to $50,000, to be used as interim seed money until a larger, federal grant materializes. It also sponsors an interesting Entrepreneur's Forum, through which participants can network innovative ideas.

DISTRICT OF COLUMBIA: A joint public-private Economic Development Finance Corporation provides $50,000 to $300,000 risk-oriented financing for start-ups and expanding businesses. A related fund provides between $350,000 and $750,000 to businesses that are expanding, while a third program has up to $300,000 in debt capital for businesses that want to buy their own facilities.

FLORIDA: The Industrial Development Authority and private sector investors have created a taxable bond fund that makes $750,000 to $8 million available for manufacturing expansion.

IOWA: A business owned at least 51 percent by a woman or minority can get a guaranteed, low-interest loan through the applicant's bank. Up to $100,000 may be borrowed for working capital and up to $250,000 for fixed assets.

State	Business Loan Program	Tax Incentives	Venture Capital
Alabama	×	×	
Alaska	×	×	
Arizona		×	
Arkansas	×		
California	×	×	
Colorado	×	×	×
Connecticut	×	×	×
Delaware	×	×	
D.C.	×	×	×
Florida	×	×	×
Georgia			
Hawaii	×	×	×
Idaho	×	×	
Illinois	×	×	×
Indiana	×	×	×
Iowa	×	×	×
Kansas	×	×	×
Kentucky	×	×	×
Louisiana	×	×	×
Maine	×	×	×
Maryland	×		×
Massachusetts		×	×
Michigan	×	×	×
Minnesota	×		×

Figure 8. State Development Services Chart

State	Business Loan Program	Tax Incentives	Venture Capital
Mississippi	×		×
Missouri	×	×	×
Montana	×		×
Nebraska	×	×	×
Nevada		×	
New Hampshire	×	×	×
New Jersey		×	×
New Mexico	×	×	
New York	×	×	
North Carolina			×
North Dakota	×	×	×
Ohio	×	×	
Oklahoma			
Oregon	×	×	×
Pennsylvania	×	×	×
Puerto Rico	×		
Rhode Island	×	×	×
South Carolina	×	×	×
South Dakota		×	×
Tennessee	×	×	×
Texas	×	×	×
Utah	×	×	×
Vermont	×	×	×
Virginia	×		
Washington	×	×	×
West Virginia	×	×	×
Wisconsin	×		×
Wyoming	×		

Figure 8. (*Continued*)

KANSAS: The Kansas Venture Capital Company Act has certified 13 venture capital companies so far, to make $20 million available for business start-ups and expansions. The fund is targeted toward small manufacturers needing upward of $50,000.

KENTUCKY: Craftspeople who want to produce and market their output commercially can submit their products to the Kentucky Department of the Arts. Once these are approved, the artisans can get loans of $2,000 to $20,000, as well as SBDC assistance.

LOUISIANA: The Economic Development Commission was funded with $14.7 million to administer grants, loans, and venture capital programs, as well as minority programs of up to $250,000. Other loan programs guarantee private bank loans up to 75 percent.

MAINE: If you start a business that is labor intensive, you might be able to get help from the Governor's Contingency Fund for Job Training. Up to $1500 for training is provided. In addition, the Finance Authority of Maine allows state tax credits if you invest up to $50,000 of equity funds in a small Maine business doing less than $200,000 annually.

MARYLAND: This state has both a Small Business Development Financing Authority and a comprehensive $3 million annual program for entrepreneurs who want to buy a franchise or expand an established business. The latter, named the Equity Participation Investment Program (EPIP), is designed especially for minorities, women, and handicapped or socially disadvantaged people; in the past year, it invested $1.7 million in 28 franchise deals.

MISSISSIPPI: Up to $500,000 can be guaranteed to support a bank loan under the Certified Development Company program for a term of up to 20 years. A separate land and building fund makes loans for up to 10 years.

NORTH CAROLINA: The Entrepreneur Council acts as an intermediary between small businesses with high-growth potential and venture capital investors. The capital-based Council sponsors an annual Venture Fair where start-up entrepreneurs can meet investors willing to put up $50,000 to $300,000, and expanding companies attract sums in excess of $300,000. Funding offers have been received by 60 percent of participating companies.

RHODE ISLAND: A state program provides up to $2500 to fund applications to Phase I (start-ups) and up to $25,000 for R&D until federal funds materialize in the Small Business Innovative Research (SBIR) program.

SOUTH CAROLINA: Certified businesses owned and controlled by women or minorities may obtain a secondary grant—up to an additional $50,000—to a bank loan. The requirements are that for each $10,000 put up by the state, one new job must be created, and half of the newly created jobs must go to low- to moderate-income employees.

SOUTH DAKOTA: The state's Rural Economic Development Initiative raised $40 million to provide small businesses with one- to five-year loans at a mere 3 percent interest, to be used for fixed assets or working capital. The program, designed to bolster the state's economy, also encourages companies moving into South Dakota.

WASHINGTON: A system has been developed of encouraging local companies to raise up to $1 million annually through securities sold to the public. Corporations filing under these state regulations are exempt from federal regulations. Apply to the Securities Division, Washington Department of Licensing.

WEST VIRGINIA: An 11-community organization called The Main Street Revitalization Program helps small new businesses, light manufacturing, and crafts incubators to locate in these towns.

WYOMING: The Wyoming Economic Development Loan Program has a $15 million fund available for businesses within the state. Loans and loan guarantees range from $40,000 to $2 million, at below-market interest rates and terms of up to 10 years.

CERTIFIED DEVELOPMENT COMPANIES

Throughout the United States are more than 400 private financing companies that are certified by the government to make fixed loans available to companies with fixed assets—property and machinery with an assured life of at least 10 years.

The loans bear an interest rate pegged to U.S. Government T-bills. Successful applicants are expected to put up about 10 percent of the money; private sources, such as banks, will put up about 50 percent; and the U.S. Small Business Administration guarantees the 40 percent balance. The bank advancing most of the loan gets first lien on all collateral, while the SBA takes a secondary position. Loans are made for 10 years or more and are similar to government-backed mortgages called Ginnie Maes; they are guaranteed debentures, handled by one of these certified development companies.

The basic purpose of such a debenture loan is to stimulate the local economy. CDCs, therefore, operate in a circumscribed local area; they are a conduit that allows private funds, guaranteed by the SBA, to flow into community businesses. Their support is supposed to be structured to provide one new job for every $15,000 of the debenture. The maximum of $750,000, therefore, should open up 30 new jobs in the local sector.

Besides that, there are certain debenture criteria. If you qualify to apply to one of these CDCs for a long-term loan, loan proceeds must be used for the financing of the following:

- Plant acquisition
- Construction
- Conversion
- Expansion
- Land purchase and/or improvement
- Machinery and equipment (with an expected life of at least 10 years)
- Leasehold improvement
- Approved projects
- Approved short-term financing
- Closing costs

In order to become a CDC, a finance company must negotiate at least two such loans a year. During one recent year almost 50 CDCs were decertified because of inactivity. On the other hand, the SBA has renewed certification with about 449 others, of which 175 have 10 or more loans active at this time (some have over 200).

A city-by-city list, in alphabetical order, can be found in the Appendix and will enable you to locate the city nearest you in which there is a CDC.

Section IV

Cash Flow, Costs, and Savings

Triple Truism
Work expands to the time allowed; success expands to the planning allowed;
inventory expands to the space allowed.

CASH FLOW AND ACCOUNTING $\boxed{\textbf{10}}$

DEFINITION

Cash is simply available money. Cash is *not* profits. Cash is *not* capital resources. The way cash comes and goes is called the cash flow. It is the movement of cash in and out of your business within a certain time period—usually a week or a month.

In *The Annual Report Glossary* (Annandale, VA: FIPS Publishers, 1988), Richard B. Loth says, "Some experts believe that cash flow is a better indicator of a company's operating performance than earnings." He adds this commentary:

> Of the three sources of cash flow, *operations*, financing and investment, conservative analysis would consider the first named as the only truly dependable source of cash. While outside sources of funds, debt and equity, enable a company to grow, a company that cannot generate strong internal cash flow will gradually weaken its balance sheet. It is important for the shareholder (*and entrepreneur*) to recognize that adequate cash flow is the single most important element in a company's survival.

THE IMPORTANCE OF KNOWING YOUR CASH FLOW

You can have a lot of cash coming over the counter and still not have a profitable business. You can have little cash coming in and still have a profitable business—because the cash might be tied up in new inventory or in accounts receivable. You can easily see that if that cash is tied up somewhere (even though it will *eventually* come in!), you can't pay bills with it.

By tracking the way cash flows in and out of your business, you can make projections for the weeks and months ahead to find out how much money you are going to need at any time. You have to know this no matter what kind of a business you want to run. If you don't know how much money you are going to need, you could run short—and that could make it impossible to pay your vendors, your employees (maybe yourself!), or the landlord. You might not be able to make your loan payments on time. Running short could force you into a financial bind that causes terminal illness—bankruptcy.

Further, if you are going to borrow money to start your business, or to operate it, you will want to determine the amount you need pretty accurately. Some start-up businesspeople try to borrow as much as possible. They think it's a badge of honor to have a high credit rating. Sure, that sounds good, but loans have to be paid back—plus interest.

Why borrow more than you need? It only increases the cost of doing business and reduces the profit *you* make. It is more important to have an open line of credit with the bank, or wherever you get capital. By having accurate and continual cash-flow projections, you can tell quite correctly how much you need, and then you can draw on your credit and pay interest only on what you actually borrow. It's really not that difficult. It's only difficult when you *don't* take the time to make those projections.

Regard a cash-flow chart as a map. It tells you where you are going and how much "gas" you need to get there. Most small businesses use the "cash method" of accounting, which works this way: Expenses are recorded when they are paid. Income is recorded when it is received. It's the bird-in-hand method: Don't count it till you've got it.

It's nice to deal with achievable sales, true operating expenses, and reasonable profits. But life, and business, don't always work as they should. Sales have a way of varying all over the map. Your trade association, trade journals, U.S. Department of Commerce, Dun & Bradstreet, and many other excellent sources give you figures—but they are *averages*. Sometimes unforeseen circumstances occur in your area that affect sales; there is no way that you can anticipate excessive rain or snow, floods, labor layoffs, strikes, sudden shifts in fashion trends or tastes, etc. All these fluctuations can change the best-intentioned cash-flow projections.

Operating expenses, too, can jump up and down like a scared kangaroo. What to do? Put some elasticity into your cash-flow projections! Remember, too, that a budget is not a monolithic object. It is subject to changes—your changes. You can restructure it, shift amounts; juggle all you want, as long as you make it work for you and don't let it catch you by surprise at the end of the year. An example follows that will illustrate the kinds of figuring you will have to do to know where you are going, and the paperwork you will be expected to bring to the bank.

CASH-FLOW EXAMPLE: THE REFERENCE

A married couple plan to open a bookstore. They will call their new enterprise THE REFERENCE, An Information Bookshop. The location they've chosen is between the campus of a major university and some downtown apartment complexes that house thousands of government and private-industry workers.

The store will specialize in reference and research books, dictionaries, books on art and travel, and all kinds of calendars; on the second floor, beside the foreign-language books, it will have a small café, where an international variety of pastries and coffees will be featured. Basically, the husband-and-wife owners will run the store; however, part-time help will be used from the university during after-class hours, and it will be open Saturdays to take advantage of the nearby highrise-apartment dwellers, as well as the university students and professors.

Financial Projections

The owners project a first-year gross of $200,000, with a 20 to 25 percent annual growth factor for the first three years. Planning for a four-time turnover annually, a $200,000 gross demands a $50,000 inventory, which, at cost, should amount to $30,000, allowing for some overlap and slow-moving titles. They have that much money in personal funds but need an equal amount in the form of a loan to take care of operating expenses during the initial year.

Figure 9 shows the way they worked out their cash-needs projections and estimated profits, and Figure 10 gives a projected one-month budget for the same business. At the end of this chapter are some sample blank worksheets including Figure 14, corresponding to Figure 9; Figure 15, a worksheet for equipment that is needed for the store prior to the opening, offering options of outright purchases or leasing; and Figure 16, a standard SBA month-by-month cash-flow form.

Explanation of Cash-Flow Projections for THE REFERENCE (Figure 9)

Rent: The owners signed a three-year lease at a fixed $1200 per month. A $2500 security deposit was demanded, on which they were able to obtain 6 percent interest, to be repaid at the conclusion of the lease. No security deposit will be demanded upon renewal at 10 percent above current level.

Planned depreciation: This is not so much on fixtures (which are minimal) and equipment (most of which will be leased and include service contracts), but on inventory, to be taken in markdowns and pilferage. Some increases are expected for Years Two and Three.

Interest on loan and annual loan-principal repayment: An interest rate of 14 percent was charged on unpaid balance over a period of five years, which decreases year by year. While interest is $4200 in Year One, it will be $3360 in Year Two and $2520 in Year Three, etc.

Leasehold improvements and fixtures: Improvements will not need to be repeated for three years, although some additional fixtures will be desired as inventory expands. Year Two is allotted $1500 and Year Three $1000.

	Year One	Year Two	Year Three
Gross Sales	$200,000	$250,000	$300,000
Cost of Sales	$120,000	$150,000	$180,000
Gross Profit	$ 80,000	$100,000	$120,000

Fixed Expenses

	Year One	Year Two	Year Three
Rent	$ 14,400	$ 14,400	$ 14,400
Planned depreciation	1,500	2,500	3,500
Insurance	900	1,000	1,200
Tax and license	300	300	300
Interest on loan (14% on $30,000)	4,200	3,360	2,520
Utility deposits	300	—	—
Rent deposits	2,500	—	—
Leasehold improvements and fixtures	3,300	1,500	1,000
Equipment deposits	1,300	—	—
Signage	400	3,500	300
Subtotal	$ 29,100	26,560	23,220

Variable Expenses

	Year One	Year Two	Year Three
Part-time salary	6,000	13,500	15,000
Employment taxes	850	1,700	2,000
Security	600	700	800
Automobile	5,000	5,000	5,000
Advertising, promotion	5,000	7,000	8,000
Dues and subscriptions	350	500	500
Legal and accounting	5,000	3,000	3,000
Office supplies	600	800	1,000
Utilities	3,000	3,500	4,000
Telephone	500	600	700
Equipment leases	1,400	2,000	3,000
Travel and entertainment	1,200	1,500	2,000
Petty cash (miscellaneous)	1,200	1,800	2,400
Subtotal	$ 30,700	$ 41,600	$ 47,400
Total	$ 59,800	$ 68,160	$ 70,620

(Annual loan principal repayment set-aside: $6,000)

Figure 9. Three-Year Expense Projection for THE REFERENCE

Year One: Projected Sales $200,000

Month: January 19 ___

	Actual	Actual Year to Date	Comments
Planned Cash Receipts			
Cash sales, books	$ 15,000		
Accounts receivable	1,500		
Other income (miscellaneous goods; taxes)	1,000		
Total receivables	17,500		
Planned Cash Payments			
Rent, utilities, insurance	1,500		
Telephone, equipment	160		
Administration	700		
Payroll (part-time salary)	500		
Taxes	70		
Advertising, promotion	500		
Automobile	500		
Loan amortization	500		
Loan interest	350		
Inventory purchases	4,000		
Personal (net)	1,220		
Total payments	10,000		
Cash balance EOM*	$ 7,500		

* End-of-Month

Figure 10. Budget for One Month for THE REFERENCE

Signage: First-year expenditures are for painted signs; an illuminated sign might be installed in Year Two, depending on cash flow and zoning.

Part-time salary: Because student assistance will probably change annually, this item might increase in subsequent years due to (1) hourly rate increase, (2) longer store hours, and (3) employment of *two* assistants.

Legal and accounting: Year One includes initial setup of the operation, and this expense is expected to be higher than in succeeding years. It is hoped that $3000 will be sufficient for accounting services in each of Years Two and Three.

Other costs are expected to vary only moderately. Advertising has risen proportionately; *petty cash* (miscellaneous) has increased to account for more unforeseen items.

Adding projected fixed and variable expenses together, plus $6000 in each year for loan amortization, leaves the proprietors with $14,200 in Year One ($80,000 gross profit–[$59,800 total expenses + $6000]); $25,840 in Year Two ($100,000–[$68,160 + $6000]); and $43,380 in Year Three ($120,000–[$70,620 + $6000]) for personal disposition. This is probably a typical progression for small businesses.

Explanation of Sample Budget for THE REFERENCE (Figure 10)

The sample budget shown in Figure 10 continues the example of THE REFERENCE, a bookstore. It is primarily a cash business (90 percent) with only a few corporate accounts that pay monthly (10 percent). The owners had sufficient equity in a $100,000 home to borrow $30,000 with which to acquire inventory. This was a five-year (long-term) loan at 14 percent. In addition, they borrowed $10,000 for 12 months (short-term) at 15 percent. Some of the items from the budget are detailed as follows:

Payroll: The payroll appears very low; initially, the only employee will be a part-time student two afternoons and Saturdays. As business increases, this item should rise sharply.

Loan amortization and loan interest: As noted above, the short-term loan is a 12-month commitment at 15 percent, and the long-term loan is a 60-month (five-year) commitment at 14 percent. Repayments and interest payments are made monthly and have been rounded off to the nearest dollar.

Inventory purchases: The starting inventory of $30,000 will be supplemented monthly with an "open-to-buy" of $4000. This will vary with the seasons, of course. Purchases will slow down during the summer months but accelerate in the fall.

Note: There are numerous ways of keeping records. Any budget that the new entrepreneur can understand is all right. If a budget is used in a loan application, the services of a CPA are desirable for several reasons: (1) The budget will be more accurate; (2) it can serve as a model for future record keeping; and (3) it has increased credibility in the eyes of a loan officer.

THE INCOME STATEMENT

Accountants frequently call the income statement a "profit and loss statement" (P&L) or an "operating statement." Its purpose is to show your net income or net loss for a particular period of time. The income statement can give you the information on your business operation for the preceding month, for a quarter, and for the entire year. It is like a picture taken of your business at a specific time. A simple formula for the income statement is

$$\text{Total Income} - \text{Total Expenses} = \text{Net Income}$$

The income statement for a service business is quite simple. For a merchandise business, it is more complicated, however. The latter is generally divided into three sections:

- Gross profit on sales
- Total operating expenses
- Net income (or net profit)

If you are already in business, the figures for this statement are readily available. If you are just starting out and need to prepare an income statement for the loan application, then you need to call on your imagination, research, and experience. A sample income, or operating, statement appears as Figure 11.

Using the Income (P&L) Statement Long-Range

The SBA's Form 1099 is a convenient 12-month worksheet for figuring your actual or potential profits and losses. Hopefully, there will be few or none of the latter; in any business, however, there will be months when you are operating on a negative cash flow. It is then that you need back-up capital—either short-term bank loans or financial resources of your own.

In retailing, it is axiomatic to "beat last year's figures." That is, when you get the sales totals for a specific day or week or month, you compare them with the same day or week or month last year—hoping to have bettered last year's figures. This is an exercise in frustration. You can discern *trends* from last year's figures, but it would be impossible always to match, let alone beat, last year's figures for that exact date. There are many variables that will affect the figures, including weather, the dates when holidays fall, fashion trends, local and national economic patterns, politics and strikes, and all the man-made influences or acts of God that you personally cannot control.

So consider the P&L statement primarily in today's context, and only secondarily as a barometer of comparison with last year's sales.

THE BALANCE SHEET

The balance sheet shows the relationship between your *assets* (anything of value owned by the business) and *liabilities* (a debt or something your business owes). It is another picture of your business.

The balance sheet reveals your business decisions for the past year. It records how the lifeblood, your cash position or liquidity, looks at that time. It tells you, and your accountant and banker, what your actual equity is.

Month _____ 19

Sales 100%	Percentage	Amount	Total
Total sales			$19,940
Opening inventory		$45,900	
Merchandise purchases		12,710	
Total		58,610	
Less closing inventory		45,396	
Cost of merchandise sold	66.3%	13,214	
Plus freight in	1.1	212	
Cost of sales	67.3		13,426
Gross profit	32.7		6,514
Operating expenses			
Salaries	12.6	2,508	
Advertising	2.6	514	
Delivery	.4	88	
Supplies	1.1	214	
Rent	2.3	450	
Utilities	1.1	216	
Telephone	.2	42	
Insurance	.5	104	
Maintenance	.4	82	
Depreciation	1.2	238	
Miscellaneous	.9	182	
Total operating expenses	23.3		4,638
Net operating income	9.4		1,876
Other income			
Interest earned	.1	24	
Discounts taken	.2	36	60
Net income		1,936	
Less estimated federal including tax	2.9		581
Net income (after tax)	6.8%		$ 1,355

[*Note:* The income statement, or profit and loss statement, shows the relationship between sales and costs. This sample might be for a small wholesale business or distributor that operates out of a 1000 sq. ft. garage-style warehouse or incubator facility.]

Figure 11. Sample Income (Operating) Statement

PROJECTED PROFIT & LOSS

	Start-up or Prior to Loan	1st Month	2nd Month	3rd Month	4th Month	5th Month	6th Month	7th Month	8th Month	9th Month	10th Month	11th Month	12th Month	Total for Year
1. Total sales (Net)														100%
2. Cost of sales														
3. Gross profit (Line 1 minus line 2)														
4. Expenses (operating)														
5. Salaries (other than owner)														
6. Payroll taxes														
7. Rent														
8. Utilities (including phone)														
9. Insurance														
10. Professional service (i.e., acct.)														
11. Taxes & licenses														
12. Advertising														
13. Supplies (for business)														
14. Office supplies (forms, postage, etc.)														
15. Interest (loans, contracts, etc.)														
16. Depreciation														
17. Travel (incl operating costs of veh)														
18. Entertainment														
19. Dues & subscriptions														
20. Other														
21.														
22. Total expenses (add lines 5 thru 21)														
23. Profit before taxes (line 3 minus 22)														

Figure 12. Sample SBA Form 1099

(*Figure continues on p. 110.*)

FORECAST OF CASH FLOW

	Start-up or Prior to Loan	1st Month	2nd Month	3rd Month	4th Month	5th Month	6th Month	7th Month	8th Month	9th Month	10th Month	11th Month	12th Month	Total for Year
24. Income (cash received)														
25. Cash sales														
26. Collection of accts. receivable														
27. Other														
28. Total income (add lines 25, 26, & 27)														
29. Disbursements (cash paid out)														
30. Owner's draw														
31. Loan repayments (principal only)														
32. Cost of sales (line 2)														
33. Total expenses (minus line 16)														
34. Capital expenditures (equip., bldgs., veh., leasehold improvements)														
35. Reserve for taxes														
36. Other														
37. Total disbursements (add 30 thru 36)														
38. Cash flow monthly (line 28 − 37)														
39. Cash flow cumulative (ln 38 + ln 39)														

Figure 12. (*Continued*)

_____ , 19 _____

	YEAR I	YEAR II
Current Assets		
Cash	$ _____	$ _____
Accounts receivable	_____	_____
Inventory	_____	_____
Fixed Assets		
Real estate	_____	_____
Fixtures and equipment	_____	_____
Vehicles	_____	_____
Other Assets		
License	_____	_____
Goodwill	_____	_____
TOTAL ASSETS	$ _____	$ _____
Current Liabilities		
Notes payable (due within one year)	$ _____	$ _____
Accounts payable	_____	_____
Accrued expenses	_____	_____
Taxes owed	_____	_____
Long-Term Liabilities		
Notes payable (due after one year)	_____	_____
Other	_____	_____
TOTAL LIABILITIES	$ _____	$ _____
NET WORTH (ASSETS minus LIABILITIES)	$ _____	$ _____

TOTAL LIABILITIES plus NET WORTH should equal ASSETS

Figure 13. Sample Balance Sheet

	Year One	Year Two	Year Three
Gross Sales	$ _____	$ _____	$ _____
Cost of Sales	$ _____	$ _____	$ _____
Gross Profit	$ _____	$ _____	$ _____

Fixed Expenses

Rent	$ _____	$ _____	$ _____
Planned depreciation	_____	_____	_____
Insurance	_____	_____	_____
Tax and license	_____	_____	_____
Utility deposits	_____	_____	_____
Rent deposits	_____	_____	_____
Leasehold improvements and fixtures	_____	_____	_____
Equipment deposits	_____	_____	_____
Signage	_____	_____	_____
Subtotal	_____	_____	_____

Variable Expenses

Salaries	_____	_____	_____
Employment taxes	_____	_____	_____
Security	_____	_____	_____
Automobile(s)	_____	_____	_____
Advertising, promotion	_____	_____	_____
Dues and subscriptions	_____	_____	_____
Legal and accounting	_____	_____	_____
Office supplies	_____	_____	_____
Utilities	_____	_____	_____
Telephone	_____	_____	_____
Equipment leases	_____	_____	_____
Travel and entertainment	_____	_____	_____
Miscellaneous	_____	_____	_____
Subtotal	$ _____	$ _____	$ _____
Total	$ _____	$ _____	$ _____

Loan repayment: $ _____
Owner(s)' net: $ _____

Figure 14. Your Start-up Shop: Three-Year Expense Projection Worksheet

MONTHLY CASH FLOW PROJECTION

Form Approval:
OMB No. 3245-0019
Expires 8-31-91

See Reverse Side for Instructions and Public Comment Information

NAME OF BUSINESS

ADDRESS

OWNER

TYPE OF BUSINESS

PREPARED BY

DATE

MONTH		Pre-Start-up Position		1		2		3		4		5		6		7		8		9		10		11		12		TOTAL Columns 1—12	
YEAR		Estimate	Actual	Estimate	Actual	Estimate	Actual	Estimate	Actual	Estimate	Actual	Estimate	Actual	Estimate	Actual	Estimate	Actual	Estimate	Actual	Estimate	Actual	Estimate	Actual	Estimate	Actual	Estimate	Actual
1. CASH ON HAND (Beginning of month)	1.																									
2. CASH RECEIPTS	2.																									
(a) Cash Sales	(a)																									
(b) Collections from Credit Accounts	(b)																									
(c) Loan or Other Cash injection (Specify)	(c)																									
3. TOTAL CASH RECEIPTS (2a + 2b + 2c = 3)	3.																									
4. TOTAL CASH AVAILABLE (Before cash out) (1 + 3)	4.																									
5. CASH PAID OUT	5.																									
(a) Purchases (Merchandise)	(a)																									
(b) Gross Wages (Excludes withdrawals)	(b)																									
(c) Payroll Expenses (Taxes, etc.)	(c)																									
(d) Outside Services	(d)																									
(e) Supplies (Office and operating)	(e)																									
(f) Repairs and Maintenance	(f)																									
(g) Advertising	(g)																									
(h) Car, Delivery, and Travel	(h)																									
(i) Accounting and Legal	(i)																									
(j) Rent	(j)																									
(k) Telephone	(k)																									
(l) Utilities	(l)																									
(m) Insurance	(m)																									
(n) Taxes (Real estate, etc.)	(n)																									
(o) Interest	(o)																									
(p) Other Expenses (Specify each)	(p)																									
(q) Miscellaneous (Unspecified)	(q)																									
(r) Subtotal	(r)																									
(s) Loan Principal Payment	(s)																									
(t) Capital Purchases (Specify)	(t)																									
(u) Other Start-up Costs	(u)																									
(v) Reserve and/or Escrow (Specify)	(v)																									
(w) Owner's Withdrawal	(w)																									
6. TOTAL CASH PAID OUT (Total 5a thru 5w)	6.																									
7. CASH POSITION (End of month) (4 minus 6)	7.																									
ESSENTIAL OPERATING DATA (Non-cash flow information)																										
A. Sales Volume (Dollars)	A																									
B. Accounts Receivable (End of month)	B																									
C. Bad Debt (End of month)	C																									
D. Inventory on Hand (End of month)	D																									
E. Accounts Payable (End of month)	E																									
F. Depreciation	F																									

SBA FORM 1100 (1–83) REF: SOP 60 10 Previous Editions Are Obsolete

Figure 15. Initial Equipment Cost Worksheet

(Figure continues on p. 114.)

GUIDELINES

GENERAL

Definition: A cash flow projection is a forecast of cash funds* a business anticipates receiving, on the one hand, and disbursing, on the other hand, throughout the course of a given span of time, and the anticipated cash position at specific times during the period being projected.

Objective: The purpose of preparing a cash flow projection is to determine deficiencies or excesses in cash from that necessary to operate the business during the time for which the projection is prepared. If deficiencies are revealed in the cash flow, financial plans **must** be altered either to provide more cash by, for example, more equity capital, loans, or increased selling prices of products, or to reduce expenditures including inventory, or allow less credit sales until a proper cash flow balance is obtained. If excesses of cash are revealed, it might indicate excessive borrowing or idle money that could be "put to work." The objective is to finally develop a plan which, if followed would provide a well-managed flow of cash.

The Form: The cash flow projection form provides a systematic method of recording estimates of cash receipts and expenditures, which can be compared with actual receipts and expenditures as they become known—hence the two columns, Estimate and Actual. The entries listed on the form will not necessarily apply to every business, and some entries may not be included which would be pertinent to specific businesses. It is suggested, therefore, that the form be adapted to the particular business for which the projection is being made, with appropriate changes in the entries as may be required. Before the cash flow projection can be completed and pricing structure established, it is necessary to know or to estimate various important factors of the business, for example: What are the direct costs of the product or services **per unit**? What are the monthly or yearly costs of the operation? What is the sales price per unit of the product or service? Determine that the pricing structure provides this business with reasonable breakeven goals (including a reasonable net profit) when conservative sales goals are met. What are the available sources of cash, other than income from sales; for example, loans, equity capital, rent, or other sources?

Procedure: Most of the entries for the form are self-explanatory; however, the following suggestions are offered to simplify the procedure:

(A) Suggest even dollars be used rather than showing cents.

(B) If this is a new business, or an existing business undergoing significant changes or alterations, the cash flow part of the column marked "Pre-start-up Position" should be completed. (Fill in appropriate blanks only.) Costs involved here are, for example, rent, telephone, and utilities deposits before the business is actually open. Other items might be equipment purchases, alterations, the owner's cash injection, and cash from loans received before actual operations begin.

(C) Next fill in the pre-start-up position of the essential operating data (non-cash flow information), where applicable.

(D) Complete the form using the suggestions in the partial form below for each entry.

CHECKING

In order to insure that the figures are properly calculated and balanced, they must be checked. Several methods may be used, but the following four checks are suggested as a minimum:

CHECK #1: Item #1 (Beginning Cash on Hand—1st Month) plus Item #3 (Total Cash Receipts — Total Column) minus Item #6 (Total Cash Paid Out—Total Column) should be equal to Item #7 (Cash Position at End of 12th Month).

CHECK #2: Item A (Sales Volume—Total Column) plus Item B (Accounts Receivable—Pre-start-up Position) minus Item 2(a) (Cash Sales—Total Column) minus Item 2(b) (Accounts Receivable Collection—Total Column) minus Item C (Bad Debt—Total Column) should be equal to Item B (Accounts Receivable at End of 12th Month).

CHECK #3: The horizontal total of Item #6 (Total Cash Paid Out) is equal to the vertical total of all items under Item #5 (5(a) through 5(w)) in the total column at the right of the form.

CHECK #4: The horizontal total of Item #3 (Total Cash Receipts) is equal to the vertical total of all items under #2 (2(a) through 2(e)) in the total column at the right of the form.

ANALYZE the correlation between the cash flow and the projected profit during the period in question. The estimated profit is the **difference** between the estimated change in assets and the estimated change in liabilities before such things as any owner withdrawal, appreciation of assets, change in investments, etc. (The change may be positive or negative.) This can be obtained as follows:

The **change in assets** before owner's withdrawal, appreciation of assets, change in investments, etc., can be computed by adding the following:

(1) Item #7 (Cash Position—End of Last Month) minus Item #1 (Cash on Hand at the Beginning of the First Month).

(2) Item #5(t) (Capital Purchases—Total Column) minus Item F (depreciation—Total Column).

(3) Item B. (Accounts Receivable—End of 12th Month) minus Item B (Accounts Receivable—Pre-start-up Position).

(4) Item D, (Inventory on Hand—End of 12th Month) minus Item D (Inventory on Hand—Pre-start-up Position).

(5) Item #5 (w) (Owner's withdrawal—Total Column) or dividends, minus such things as an increase in investment.

(6) Item #5 (v) (Reserve and/or Escrow—Total Column).

The **change in liabilities** (before items noted in "change in assets") can be computed by adding the following:

(1) Item 2(c) (Loans—Total Column) minus 5(s) (Loan Principal Payment—Total Column).

(2) Item E (Accounts Payable—End of 12th Month) minus E (Accounts Payable—Pre-start-up Position).

ANALYSIS

A. The cash position at the end of each month should be adequate to meet the cash requirements for the following month. If too little cash, then additional cash will have to be injected or cash paid out must be reduced. If there is too much cash on hand, the money is not working for your business.

B. The cash flow projection, the profit and loss projection, the breakeven analysis, and good cost control information are tools which, if used properly, will be useful in making decisions that can increase profits to insure success.

C. The projection becomes more useful when the estimated information can be compared with actual information as it develops. It is important to follow through and complete the actual columns as the information becomes available. Utilize the cash flow projection to assist in setting new goals and planning operations for more profit.

Please Note: Public reporting burden for this collection of information is estimated to average 1 hour per response, including the time for reviewing instructions, searching existing data sources, gathering and maintaining the data needed, and completing and reviewing the collection of information. Send comments regarding this burden estimate or any other aspect of this collection of information, including suggestions for reducing this burden, to: Chief, Administrative Information Branch, William A. Cline, Room 200 U.S. Small Business Administration, 1441 L St., NW Washington, DC 20416; and to the Office of Information and Regulatory Affairs, Office of Management and Budget, Washington, DC 20503.

_____
* Cash funds, for the purpose of this projection, are defined as cash, checks, or money order, paid out or received.

1. **CASH ON HAND** (Beginning of month)	Cash on hand same as (7), Cash Position Previous Month
2. **CASH RECEIPTS**	
(a) Cash Sales	All cash sales. Omit credit sales unless cash is actually received
(b) Collections from Credit Accounts	Amount to be expected from all credit accounts.
(c) Loan or Other Cash injection	Indicate here all cash injections not shown in 2(a) or 2(b) above. See "A" of "Analysis"
3. **TOTAL CASH RECEIPTS** (2a + 2b + 2c = 3)	Self-explanatory
4. **TOTAL CASH AVAILABLE** (Before cash out) (1 + 3)	Self-explanatory
5. **CASH PAID OUT**	
(a) Purchases (Merchandise)	Merchandise for resale or for use in product (paid for in current month)
(b) Gross Wages (Excludes withdrawals)	Base pay plus overtime (if any)
(c) Payroll Expenses (Taxes, etc.)	Include paid vacations, paid sick leave, health insurance, unemployment insurance, etc. (this might be 10 to 45% (1F 5b)
(d) Outside Services	This could include outside labor and/or material for specialized or overflow work, including subcontracting
(e) Supplies (Office and operating)	Items purchased for use in the business (not for resale)
(f) Repairs and Maintenance	Include periodic large expenditures such as painting or decorating
(g) Advertising	This amount should be adequate to maintain sales volume—include telephone book yellow page cost
(h) Car, Delivery, and Travel	If personal car is used, charge in this column—include parking
(i) Accounting and Legal	Outside services, including, for example, bookkeeping
(j) Rent	Real estate only (See 5(p) for other rentals)
(k) Telephone	Self-explanatory
(l) Utilities	Water, heat, light, and/or power
(m) Insurance	Coverages on business property and products e.g. fire, liability; also workman's compensation, fidelity, etc. Exclude "executive" life (include in "5W")
(n) Taxes (Real estate, etc.)	Plus inventory tax—sales tax—excise tax, if applicable
(o) Interest	Remember to add interest on loan as it is injected (See 2(c) above)
(p) Other Expenses (Specify each)	Unexpected expenditures may be included here as a safety factor
	Equipment expenses during the month should be included here (Non-capital equipment)
	When equipment is rented or leased, record payments here
(q) Miscellaneous (Unspecified)	Small expenditures for which separate accounts would not be practical
(r) Subtotal	This subtotal indicates cash out for operating costs
(s) Loan Principal Payment	Include payment on all loans, including vehicle and equipment purchases on time payment
(t) Capital Purchases (Specify)	Non-expensed (depreciable) expenditures such as equipment, building, vehicle purchases, and leasehold improvements
(u) Other Start-up Costs	Expenses incurred prior to first month projection and paid for after the "start-up" position
(v) Reserve and/or Escrow (Specify)	Example: insurance, tax, or equipment escrow to reduce impact of large periodic payments
(w) Owner's Withdrawal	Should include payment for such things as owner's income tax, social security, health insurance, "executive" life insurance premiums, etc.
6. **TOTAL CASH PAID OUT** (Total 5a thru 5w)	Self-explanatory
7. **CASH POSITION** (End of month) (4 minus 6)	Enter this amount in (1) Cash on Hand following month—See "A" of "Analysis"
ESSENTIAL OPERATING DATA (Non-cash flow information)	This is basic information necessary for proper planning and for proper cash flow projection. In conjunction with this data, the cash flow can be evolved and shown in the above form.
A. Sales Volume (Dollars)	This is a very important figure and should be estimated carefully, taking into account size of facility and employee output as well as realistic anticipated sales (Actual sales performed—not orders received)
B. Accounts Receivable (End of month)	Previous unpaid credit sales plus current month's credit sales, less amounts received current month (deduct "C" below)
C. Bad Debt (End of month)	Bad debts should be subtracted from (B) in the month anticipated
D. Inventory on Hand (End of month)	Last month's inventory plus merchandise received and/or manufactured current month minus amount sold current month
E. Accounts Payable (End of month)	Previous month's payable plus current month's payable minus amount paid during month
F. Depreciation	Established by your accountant, or value of all your equipment divided by useful life (in months) as allowed by Internal Revenue Service

SBA FORM 1100 (1-83)

☆ U S G P O : 1985 — 219-382/89257

Figure 15. (*Continued*)

A balance sheet should be prepared monthly once you are operating, and again at the end of the year. If you are about to embark on a brand new business, however, you can hardly look back upon the last year in order to come up with the necessary figures. This is when you have to look into your very own crystal ball—your imagination and experience.

Accounts receivable, for example, will be impossible to predict with any accuracy if you have not started operating. Also, some businesses will be conducted strictly on a cash basis, or by charge cards, and thus will not have any "A/Rs" on their books.

Liabilities also will be projected if you are still in the planning or loan-application stage. However, if you are already in business, then all liabilities should be listed, one by one. It is not always done, but we suggest including the *number of days old* of the listed liabilities. If a liability or debt is only 30 days old, put (30) after the name of that supplier; if 60 days, then (60). It might give you a little nudge to pay off the older creditors.

START-UP AND OTHER COSTS | 11

AVERAGE INITIAL COSTS OF SELECTED BUSINESSES

Initial costs to set up a new business are all over the map. So much depends on the location or neighborhood, the level of merchandise or services you plan to offer, the needs of your customers or clientele, your own business philosophy and training—even the demands of your lease and competition.

The SBA has prepared several sample cost-comparison charts (Figures 16–20), showing suggested cost averages for retailers, wholesalers, and small manufacturers, each doing approximately $100,000 during the initial year. For higher annual volumes, increase start-up costs proportionately, although certain initial costs such as leasehold improvements, fixturing, and some equipment might remain the same.

OPERATING RATIOS THAT AFFECT YOUR MONEY REQUIREMENTS

Making the kind of fiscal projections that can serve as a guide to your future, and that seem credible to a loan officer, is a very difficult

| Description of item you must have for the opening of your business | Full cash cost | If leasing, the deposit; if purchasing on installments, the payments | | | Cash required |
		Price	Downpmt.	Mo. Pmt.	
Show cases	$	$	$	$	$
Storage shelves	$				
Counters	$				
Display stands, tables, shelves	$				
Window display fixtures	$				
Customer lounge/reception	$				
Administrative office	$				
Employee facility	$				
Cash register(s)	$				
Delivery equipment	$				
Lighting	$				
Signs	$				
Wrapping/shipping fixtures	$				
Others	$				

Total cash or financing need: $ _____   Monthly payments: $ _____

Figure 16. Monthly Cash-Flow Projection Worksheet

Average Costs		Your Comparative Figures
Cash deposits	$ 5,000	_____
Fixtures, equipment	$ 25,000	_____
Transportation	$ 15,000	_____
Property improvements	$ 15,000	_____
Professional services	$ 2,000	_____
Advertising, promotions	$ 3,000	_____
Inventory	$ 35,000	_____
Working capital	$ 15,000	_____
Total	$115,000	_____

[*Note*: The above transportation figure assumes one personal automobile or one delivery vehicle. Property improvements might or might not be necessary, depending upon whether the new business takes over from an established one in good condition, or whether the landlord will make improvements and amortize them into the lease. The inventory figure assumes a four-time annual turnover with a $10,000 cushion for slow merchandise or special manufacturers' closeout offers, etc.]

Figure 17. Cost-Comparison Chart—Retailer

Average Costs		Your Comparative Figures
Cash deposits	$ 5,000	_____
Furniture, equipment	$10,000	_____
Property improvements	$ 2,000	_____
Professional services	$ 2,000	_____
Advertising	$ 1,000	_____
Inventory (supplies)	$ 2,000	_____
Working capital	$20,000	_____
Total	$42,000	_____
Transportation	$18,000	_____
Total	$60,000	_____

[*Note*: Much of the equipment for a service business can be leased—such as a computer, cash register, photocopy machine, etc.—thus minimizing the need for up-front cash. For transportation, a prestigious personal car or better van might be desired as optional equipment. Most office improvements will be performed by the landlord and incorporated in the monthly rent payments.]

Figure 18. Cost-Comparison Chart—Service Business

Average Costs		Your Comparative Figures
Cash deposits	$ 5,000	_____
Furniture, equipment	$ 5,000	_____
Warehouse equipment	$ 25,000	_____
Transportation	$ 30,000	_____
Property improvements	$ 5,000	_____
Professional fees	$ 2,000	_____
Advertising, promotion	$ 2,000	_____
Inventory	$ 25,000	_____
Working capital	$ 21,000	_____
Total	$120,000	_____

[*Note*: Transportation could include one heavy-duty vehicle or two van-type delivery vehicles, although it might be preferable to lease them and conserve start-up working capital. Inventory is a highly variable figure, depending on whether small products or major products like appliances, machinery, etc., are handled. In the latter case, the expected gross would also rise sharply above the minimal, assumed $100,000 opening volume.]

Figure 19. Cost-Comparison Chart—Wholesaler

Average Costs		Your Comparative Figures
Cash deposits	$ 10,000	_____
Furniture, equipment	$ 25,000	_____
Machinery, equipment	$ 10,000+	_____
Transportation	$ 30,000	_____
Property improvements	$ 15,000	_____
Advertising, professional fees	$ 5,000	_____
Inventory (parts)	$ 15,000+	_____
Working capital	$ 15,000	_____
Total	$125,000+	_____

[*Note*: Some of the equipment can be leased or bought on installment contracts— thus reducing the immediate up-front cash need. Obviously there are variables, especially in machinery required and in the amount of raw material or parts inventory. In a labor-intensive manufacturing business, working capital requirements may be elevated, because it can take from a couple of weeks to several months before a noticeable cash flow comes in.]

Figure 20. Cost-Comparison Chart—Small Manufacturer

job. Trade organizations, such as the National Retail Merchants Association, have been compiling performance guidelines (average operating ratios) for more than fifty years. Dun & Bradstreet, National Cash Register Company (NCR), and pertinent trade magazines also compile useful fiscal data.

We have selected a few categories of retail businesses for which fairly complete national averages are available (Figures 21–25). Although there are regional and seasonal variations to be considered, these standards will help you determine your own cash requirements. For the most part, we have selected small enterprises, with the kind of figures you might project during your start-up phase.

HOW MUCH SHOULD YOU PAY FOR A BUSINESS?

Buying a business is like shooting craps. But it may be less of a gamble than starting your own. Perhaps the choice can be compared to creating your own baby versus adopting one. The entrepreneur surely has the drive and self-confidence to believe that he or she could start a business, and yet the idea of buying somebody else's is worth considering—as long as the conditions are right.

In this book's companion volume we have discussed some pros and cons of buying an existing business—calling the latter somebody else's boon or headache. Figure 26 is a chart showing fair and average prices to pay for a variety of businesses that you might be considering. The advantages of buying are obvious: (1) You can get started on the day you pass papers. (2) Fixtures, inventory, personnel, permits, licenses, signs, lease, and even customers/clients, are "go." (3) If all's well, you save time, money, and the many headaches involved in any start-up.

HOW MUCH DOES A LOAN *REALLY* COST YOU?

A thorough analysis of your start-up needs reveals that in addition to the $150,000 you have available from private and family resources you will need another $150,000. While your personal financing takes care of nonrepeat start-up costs (deposits on your lease and utilities, purchase of fixtures, accounting and legal costs, insurance payment, Chamber of Commerce and Better Business Bureau dues, printing

These operating ratios are for typical small electronic products (1), hardware (2), and furniture stores (3). While there will be local variations, depending on competitive and economic factors, these are national averages as determined by trade associations and financial services. Percentages are based on an approximate volume of $500,000.

	(1)*	(2)**	(3)***
Cost of sales	70 %	63.64 %	57.4 %
Salespeople	2.7	11.43	7.1
Office salaries	1.7	(incl.)	.7
Owner/manager salary	4.6	5.91	8.0
Service salaries	1.3	(incl.)	2.5
Payroll taxes	1.2	1.09	.8
Other taxes	.6	(incl.)	.7
Rent or mortgage	1.8	3.93	2.7
Building maintenance	.3	.26	.2
Utilities	.9	1.25	.8
Telephone	.6	.34	.4
Insurance (group health)	.9	.53	.4
Insurance (other)	1.3	1.13	.8
Travel and entertainment	.2	.21	.2
Accounting and legal	.3	.54	.2
Advertising and promotion	2.8	2.3	3.7
Service shop	.4	1.7	—
Service truck	.7	.57	.3
Delivery wages	.6	—	3.3
Motor vehicle	.5	—	.9
Dues and donations	.2	.11	.2
Collection expense	—	—	—
Office supplies	.6	.49	.5
Training	.1	—	—
Depreciation	1.1	.76	.5
Miscellaneous	.4	.39	.6
Bad debts	.3	.16	1.9
Interest	1.5	1.97	1.0
Federal, state taxes	.6	.34	2.4
Net profit	2.1	2.85	4.1
After tax income	1.5	2.51	1.7

* Electronic appliance store
** Hardware store
*** Furniture store

Figure 21. Operating Ratios—Electronic Appliance, Hardware, and Furniture Stores

Medium-sized fashion, clothing, and shoe stores, often referred to as specialty stores, exhibit the following average performance or operating ratios. Some of these stores have departments that are leased out to other even more specialized companies; hence the categories "sales, owned departments" and "sales, leased departments." In the national sample shown here, leased departments amount to 12.39 percent of total sales. The percentages are for about $1,000,000 annual gross.

	%
Property costs (rent/mortgage)	5.62
Management	5.81
Accounting and legal	1.44
Credit and A/Rs	1.10
Advertising and sales promotion	6.06
Services	2.91
Personnel (nonsales)	2.56
Receiving, warehousing	1.36
Selling and support services	11.52
Merchandising	3.37
Salespeople	9.23
Buyers	2.30
Supplies	2.30
Returns and allowances	6.4
Sales, owned departments	87.61
Sales, leased departments	12.39
Cash sales	55.23
Credit sales	38.68
Third part credit cards	6.09
Sales per square foot	212.15
Initial markup	51.97
Markdowns	19.62
Stock shrinkage (shortages)	1.59
Alteration cost	0.31
Gross margin (owned departments)	42.30
Gross margin return per dollar of inventory	3.05
Stock turnover	3.61
Gross margin	38.63
Net operating expense	36.92
Other income	0.36
Pretax earnings	2.07*

* Pretax earnings on net working capital: 5.78%

Figure 22. Operating Ratios—Specialty Stores

These statistics are for relatively small businesses that have less than 75 rooms and usually no food or cocktail-lounge accommodations, other than vending machines.

	%
Payroll and related costs	24.8
Rooms and telephone	8.2
General administrative	4.7
Marketing	.9
Heating, A/C, water	7.7
Property maintenance	4.0
Rent/mortgage	12.3
Property taxes	2.6
Insurance	1.1
Interest	1.9
Depreciation	6.8
Revenue from rooms	97.4
Telephone income	2.1
Other income	.5
Income before taxes	16.8

[*Note*: Income in lodging establishments over 75 rooms rises sharply, averaging 25 to 27.4 percent.]

Figure 23. Operating Ratios—Hotel/Motel/Bed and Breakfast Establishments

of stationery, finishing of premises, signs and, most important of all, enough money to pay yourself for the first six months), the loan proceeds will make sure you can pay for your operating costs: inventory payments, salaries, tax deposits, and other on-going expenses, as well as unexpected ones.

You are able to obtain a favorable loan of $150,000 for seven years at 11¾ percent interest. You are asked to make monthly payments of $3000 over a period of 84 months. This is the amount you figure you can meet with a four-time annual turnover of merchandise. Because you have good relations with the lending institution, you are able to arrange to make your first monthly payment 12 months

The figures below are combined median statistics for men's and women's stores. The differences between the two are remarkably small, although the net income for men's stores tends to be about 0.6 percent higher—due, perhaps, to the lower rate of obsolescence in men's styles.

	%
Total cost of merchandise sold	56.7
Gross margin	43.4
Alteration cost	2.7
(Net alteration cost)	1.9
Owners'/managers' payroll	6.3
Selling payroll	9.4
Nonselling payroll	2.8
Advertising	2.9
State and local taxes	.5
Social security, unemployment taxes	1.5
Supplies	1.4
Utilities	1.2
Factoring of A/Rs	1.0
Data processing	0.6
Credit-card service fees	0.3
Other services (cleaning, security, buying office, legal)	0.4
Travel	0.6
Telephone	0.5
Pension plan	0.7
Insurance (all types)	1.5
Depreciation	1.0
Professional services	0.4
Contributions	0.1
Bad-debt write-offs	0.2
Equipment costs	0.4
Rent/mortgage	3.8
Interest on loans	1.2
Other miscellaneous expenses	1.0
Net profit before federal taxes	2.7

Figure 24. Operating Ratios—Men's and Women's Wear

The statistics below are averages for small pharmacies doing about $250,000 to $300,000 in annual gross sales. Of this gross, normally 65 percent comes from prescriptions and 35 percent from miscellaneous goods. The average pharmacy fills about 10,000 new prescriptions and an equal number of renewals. Annual turnover of merchandise should be at least four times. The average store had 1,549 square feet of selling space, of which only a little more than 20 percent was devoted to the prescription department. While the value of pharmaceuticals and miscellaneous convenience goods was about the same, the pharmaceuticals returned almost twice as much net profit as the other merchandise.

	%
Proprietor/manager salary	9.1
Employees' wages	9.3
Rent	2.5
Utilities	0.9
Accounting, legal	0.5
Taxes and licenses	1.4
Insurance	1.0
Interest on loans	1.0
Maintenance	0.3
Delivery	0.6
Advertising	1.0
Depreciation	1.0
Bad-debt write-offs	0.2
Telephone	0.5
Miscellaneous	2.4
Net profit before taxes	3.9
Average worked by proprietor	48 hours
Employed pharmacist	21 hours

Figure 25. Operating Ratios—Pharmacies

Type of Business	Price Multipliers
Fashion/clothing/apparel shops	.75–1.5 × net plus equipment and inventory
Beauty salons	.25 to .75 × gross plus equipment and inventory
Automobile agencies	1.25–2 × net plus equipment
Employment agencies	.75–1 < gross, including equipment
Fast food groceries	1–1.25 × net
Gas stations	$1.25–$2/gallon/per month pumped, including equipment
Grocery stores (larger)	¼–⅓ × gross, including equipment
Insurance agencies	1–2 × annual renewal commissions
Manufacturers	1.5–2.5 × net plus inventory, including equipment
Newspapers, magazines	.75–1.25 × gross, including equipment
Real estate brokerages	.75–1.5 × gross, including equipment
Restaurants	.25–.50 × gross, including equipment
Retail stores	.75–1.5 × net plus equipment and inventory
Travel agencies	.04–.10 × gross, including equipment

[*Note*: Obviously, each category has a lot of variables built into the final price. Among these might be: shopping patterns, parking facilities, public transportation, traffic count, age of inventory, employee turnover, age of establishment, competition, three-year trend of gross and net, lease terms, servicing and access areas, number of customers/clients, previous history (failures), area demographics, product or service trends, and seller's financing assistance.]

Figure 26. Formulas for Determining How Much to Pay for a Business

after you open for business. This will give you a little elasticity and will allow you to start payments out of income.

How much will this loan actually cost you? It will be revelatory to find out, even though you might not be able to do anything about it. After all, if you want to do the business you have projected, you will need the capital, and an outside, matching loan is the only way—short of taking in a partner.

Calculation

Monthly payments are a straight $3000. Starting 12 months after you receive the loan, you will actually make 70 payments. Right up front, you have to pay finance charges of $1500 and legal costs of $500. That takes $2000 off your receipts.

Initially your interest in proportion to the amortization of the principal is quite steep. At first, $1531.25 goes to reduce the principal, and a whopping $1468.75 goes for interest on the balance. However, each month the interest goes down while the principal contribution goes up. Seven years after you have opened your business, including six years of paying off the loan, you are free and clear. Your interest payments over these seven years have totaled $58,558.53.

The interest payments, however, have been a tax-deductible item on your annual taxes, which should have reduced the "pain" considerably.

You may consider an alternative: Had you kept $150,000 (providing you had that extra $150,000) in the banks at, let's say, 8 to 10 percent interest, that money would have earned you between $12,000 and $15,000. To borrow an equal amount at, let's say, 13 percent, would cost you $19,500. You might feel that the net interest cost of $7500 to $4500 makes it more economical to have those cash assets in the bank for quick use or unexpected emergencies. Either way, the most important factor is that you have sufficient working capital to make a hoped-for success of your business. If you have taken a loan and repaid it on time, you have a fine credit rating with the bank for any future needs.

HOW TO SAVE MONEY ON A LEASE | 12

For many small businesses, the lease is the major expenditure. While some annual leases are available, most leases for prime locations are for periods of five or ten years. This, of course, is a two-way saw. For the property owner (lessor), the advantage is being assured of a paying tenant for a specific period of time—and the fact that the lease can then be translated into a bank loan on the property, should this be necessary. For the business owner (lessee), having a lease in a good location at a fixed rate presents security that can be built on.

However, leases do not always operate as simply as this. The variations are endless and could take a team of Philadelphia lawyers to unscramble. As with everything in life, the party dealing from a position of strength has the greatest leverage. The owners and promoters of a large shopping mall at a prime intersection might have tenants standing on line to get into their emporium. The lease they present to you will be IT, and except for a triple-A-rated tenant, like a prestigious chain store or major department store, it is doubtful that they will condone many changes.

PITFALLS

Regardless of whether you are going to rent a garage, a warehouse, a 500-square-foot boutique, a 3000-square-foot luxury-office suite, or a 30,000-square-foot supermarket or specialty store, your lease represents a major commitment and investment. What are some of the problems that can crop up, and what can you do about them?

The Site

Realtors often list the three major reasons for a property's value as location, location, and location. *Where* your enterprise is located and how it meets your needs is indeed of prime consideration. You can change fixturing, inventory, windows and doors, signage, and advertising, but you cannot change the location. This first decision might well be the biggest money saver of your business start-up. So here is a quick checklist to use before you commit any money. While not all of these factors pertain specifically to the site, they are upfront considerations:

- Traffic-flow pattern
- Parking capacity
- Accessibility for customers and employees
- Community demographics
- Signage and zoning
- Street and traffic exposure
- Storage feasibility
- Sanitation
- Competition
- Local laws/taxation
- Loading/receiving facility
- Utility capabilities
- Shipping ease
- Load factors (if there is heavy equipment)
- Local labor market
- Security of premises
- Public transportation
- Telecommunication access

- Cost per square foot
- Maintenance
- Rent/tax escalators

Suppose you are not sure that this location is what you want, but you want to secure the premises until you decide. You can offer the landlord one month's rent, nonrefundable, in return for a 60- or 90-day option. One good reason for this approach is to use the address of this location in your business plan and loan application. It demonstrates greater seriousness on your part than not having an address and will help to secure that loan. Another reason is that you now have a firm expense item of a major proportion to use in your projection. Further, by optioning these premises, you might keep them away from a potential competitor. This is especially applicable in seeking a prime retail location.

Parties to the Lease

If your business is a closely held entity or a start-up business, your landlord undoubtedly will demand a personal guaranty on the lease. Try to avoid this personal commitment, especially if you are planning to incorporate. Your personal liability in case of an unplanned default could jeopardize your home and other personal assets. If you can't avoid the condition, offer a compromise—such as a one- or two-year personal guaranty. By that time, hopefully, your business will have matured and become profitable.

Physical Ambiguity

It is easy to run into conflicts at some future time regarding the exact boundaries of your leased premises. This is particularly likely in renting an entire building. You might want to erect a fence, a sign, or a temporary structure, only to find that the addition to the premises is not covered or permitted in your lease. The costs involved in rewriting the lease or in pursuing litigation could drain your fiscal resources.

Duration of the Lease

The duration of your lease is the period during which you have exclusive right of possession to the premises—as well as the obligation to pay rent and maintain it in the agreed condition. If your lease calls for rent payment as of a certain date, but the premises are not completely constructed or renovated according to the terms of your lease, who's stuck with the bill? Be sure to clarify the final occupancy date in relation to readiness of the premises, and to make it part of the lease, or you could wind up paying dollars for an unusable site.

Percentage Lease

Many modern retail leases, especially in shopping centers, contain a clause calling for a specific percentage of rent payment over and above the base rent. Let's say that you agree to pay $10 per square foot for the 3000 square feet of your premises. That comes to $30,000 for the year or $2500 per month. This figure is projected as 10 percent of your gross income and is, therefore, based on your doing $300,000 worth of business. If you go over that amount—let's say you do $350,000—the landlord will commonly demand a 6 percent override on that extra $50,000. At the end of the fiscal year and upon an audit of your books (a right that is also demanded in the lease), you owe the landlord an additional $3000.

Commercial or retail leases usually do not have percentage clauses, because there is hardly any way an office tenant or manufacturing tenant can be audited to ensure an honest percentage return. Usually leased office and manufacturing facilities are easier to obtain. The potential tenant has options not always accorded the retail entrepreneur who is seeking entry into a prestigious mall.

There are, however, some pluses to the percentage lease. Because the landlord has a specific vested interest in the profitability of the lessee's business, he or she will make sure that the premises are in optimum condition, that they are fully leased, and that they are promoted to attract continuous business. To ensure such performance, the landlord usually will make financial contributions toward the promotion and management of the center, which tend to reduce the contributions that have to be made by you (the tenant) and the merchants' association.

OTHER MONEY-SAVING CAUTIONS

Several other clauses either should be written into the lease, or if already present, examined closely, because a default on any one of them could cost you dearly. The following are cautionary points in leasing:

- Make sure the premises you lease are free from restrictions and encumbrances not of your own making, such as suits against the landlord or zoning violations unknown to you.
- Protect yourself against unwarranted competition by stating what other enterprises may or may not be located on the same premises.
- Provide a clause for your possible expansion, or for taking options on adjacent property that is or might become available in the future.
- Specify that under a change in ownership of the premises there will be a continuance by the new owner(s) of your lease clauses and privileges. This will be an important selling point if you want to get out of the business.
- The rights of the landlord should be balanced by your rights as a tenant. These could include your right to withhold rent or percentage payments unless the services agreed to in the lease are fulfilled.
- If any default occurs that is not your fault but is the responsibility of the landlord, you should be able to claim compensation for loss of business, or your insurance carrier should have the right to do so. This, too, should be spelled out in your lease.

The time to tighten up these potentially troublesome issues is at the beginning *before* you sign. A good lawyer and accountant, and your own knowledge of what leases can and cannot do, will help save you thousands of dollars from potential conflicts, whether in or out of court. In lease negotiations, prevention is always cheaper than cure.

INCREASING YOUR CAPITAL ONCE YOU'RE IN BUSINESS

13

While the major part of this book is devoted to raising outside capital, it was pointed out in an earlier chapter that the costs of borrowing are substantial. There are several commonsense measures you can take to minimize your need for outside loans.

First of all, don't rush into any business until you have sufficient working capital—whether it's yours or somebody else's. It would be better to postpone opening your business than to risk skating on the thin ice of inadequate capital. There will be enough problems in running a business under adequately financed conditions. Why create problems through your own impatience?

THE BUSINESS BANK ACCOUNT

Now you are ready and you want to open a business account at the local bank. How much will you need for operating expenses? Can you put all or some of the money into an interest-bearing account? Surplus capital investment is an obvious savings opportunity. Every $1000 that you can put into short-term CDs or into an interest-bearing account will earn your business $5.00 to $8.00 in interest each month. A comfortable surplus nestegg can cut outside financing for which you are paying 12 to 20 percent interest.

The account you open is subject to some scrutiny. If you use a fictitious or contrived name, or if you are incorporated, the bank will want to see a Fictitious Name Certificate or copies of your corporate papers. It might be annoying, but those are the rules by which a bank must operate.

The business account you open should be used only for business. Don't dip into it for personal expenses. Once you open the account, you might look at all that money and decide that this is the time to buy yourself some long-awaited status: a big new car, a computer, a new wardrobe, a bigger desk, a horizontal filing cabinet or two. The list can be endless when the checkbook is fat. As many start-up businesspeople have discovered, this is the quickest route to oblivion. Be tempted neither by yourself nor by vendors, advertising media representatives, insurance agents, and all those other folks who want to live off your money. One of the start-up entrepreneurs greatest assets is the ability to say "no."

Another way of increasing your capital is to watch for available discounts. If you have the money for immediate payment, then you can find suppliers, wholesalers, and manufacturers who offer 2 percent, or even more, off the purchase price.

INTERNAL SOURCES

Internal accumulation of wealth—the most accessible means—depends squarely on your management and self-discipline. Perhaps you can add to the following list of 10 operational areas that are under your control—all of which can mean savings:

- Time management
- Proper cost accounting
- Accurate inventory control
- Production efficiency
- Accounts receivable collections
- Auto expense control
- Travel and entertainment control
- Internal security

- Advertising/promotion cost analysis
- Budget discipline

Time management. Your own executive management time is a precious, constant commodity—possibly the most important one. A wasted dollar can be recouped; an hour wasted is lost forever. Too many small entrepreneurs have been conditioned to be jacks-of-all-trades. This is nourishing and satisfying at the beginning, but after a while your skills are needed more in managing the business than in the hands-on work, which should be delegated to others. Your most important tasks will be idea creation, supervision of others, analysis of various business procedures, internal and external public relations, and sales generation.

Another, subtler benefit of proper time management is the health of your family relationships. Too many marriages and relationships with children suffer when breadwinners lose perspective on their personal lives. It is easy to give in to the lures of money and prestige. They are, of course, necessary to a successful enterprise, but there is a point of temperance, when it is time to say to yourself: Isn't my family life one of the fruits of success? If you ignore the fruit and don't enjoy its sweetness, why bother fertilizing the tree?

Proper cost accounting. Cost accounting is an ornery item that can get away from you. This writer recalls the period, some 30 years ago, when he struck out on his own. Well into the third year of a close relationship with his first client, a problem arose. The client was demanding more and more time, yet demurred at any increase in the price of the service it received. Finally this entrepreneur presented evidence that he was working for $5.00 an hour for the client. When there was no possibility of give—no reduction in service, no increase in remuneration—the account was resigned. From that moment on, every client was costed out, and the young business began to flourish.

Here is the formula that was put into practice at that time and became a rule of thumb for this entrepreneur: Figure out as accurately as possible what you want to earn from your efforts. Then double the figure. This is what you must charge to come out of the situation profitably, because somehow 50 percent of your time will be spent in nonprofitable activities. The latter may include research and reading, prospecting, travel time, bookkeeping, relevant social/professional meetings, etc.

Accurate inventory control. An insidious fact of business life is the easy accumulation of "dogs and cats." These are merchandise and other accoutrements of business that at one time were irresistible bargains, but that nobody else bought or desired. These items were purchased with hard dollars, but their value has gone soft. Turn them into money as fast as you can, or donate them to charities and take a tax deduction. That way you can put the money to work again and utilize the space these "dogs" had taken up for something more worthwhile.

Production efficiency. An increase in efficiency often comes from the very employees who have been doing things inefficiently. With some incentives and some morale boosting, people can be quite ingenious. Have periodic meetings to explore finding more effective and efficient procedures; have an open-door policy for seeing management; provide monetary incentives for cost-saving suggestions; have a suggestion box available for such contributions; be in touch with your trade peers and with government innovators like the U.S. Bureau of Standards or the Department of Commerce, which make new ideas and methods available to the private sector, often at no charge.

Accounts receivable collections. Accounts receivables grow precipitously as you go forward in your business. Little accounts can accumulate big sums. The sad part is that when a customer gets too far behind in payments, he or she will no longer buy. Resentment builds up, and you lose both former profits and future ones. Make it plain from the outset that your terms are 30-60-90 days, or whatever you decide to make them. Explain the need for a relationship that is mutually advantageous. When it appears the customer/client will no longer be a viable client, start collection proceedings promptly. Consider turning such accounts over to a factor, a bank, or a collection agency after you have exhausted all your own efforts.

Auto expense control. These expenses can be analyzed from your monthly financial statement, where abuses will show up glaringly. It might be a bagatelle in the total expense picture, but when you have several vehicles, and when some are used by employees, this item can mount up. Both a high rate of accidents and an unusually high mileage of one user when compared with others, are two common indicators of privilege abuse. See below for the advantages of leasing over ownership.

Travel and entertainment control. The potential for abuse is obvious. The IRS is taking an increasingly jaundiced look at this item, so make sure you get guidelines from the IRS or your accountant.

Internal security. Watch anybody who handles your cash or inventory. The temptation to pocket some loose money coming in, or to set aside merchandise that is delivered in or out of your premises is too great not to check. You'll have to temper your idealism with reality; the figure of 20 percent has been mentioned for the number of small businesses that have gone bankrupt due to internal theft.

Advertising/promotion cost analysis. This is another one of those subtle, sneaky categories with which few entrepreneurs are familiar. As soon as it is known that you are opening a business—your trade license is filed, your sign goes up, your premises are leased, the local newspaper makes the announcement—you will be deluged with well-meaning but hungry salespeople. Be assured that the representatives from local newspapers, magazines, radio and TV stations, billboard companies, imprinted novelty outfits, and the Yellow pages will be calling on you. They will offer you dozens of benefits of our capitalistic world, from insurance and investment opportunities to new merchandise and leases. The seductions are formidable. Your knowledge of these media, your analysis, and your resistance must be equally astute. Work against your own budget and not any of theirs. Use either a specific sum that you know you can afford and that, in your opinion, will do the expected job, or a customary percentage of your expected sales. If you have any doubt about your ability in this field, hire an advertising agency, either by the job or for a contractual time period. Don't forget local and trade publicity. Properly handled, they are a real boon and are the most cost-effective approaches.

Budget discipline. Stick to your budget. Keeping within projected expenditures could translate into more profits for you and less money that needs to be borrowed. Your budget includes not only routine expenditures, but also contracts for leasing real estate, equipment, and rolling stock. The sharper you can deal, the less the pressure to seek a loan.

LEASING OPTIONS

Today you can lease just about anything. Property, offices, automobiles and trucks, office equipment, machinery, even personnel. Somebody is making money on leasing what you need to you, so why not do it yourself? Some well-to-do entrepreneurs actually buy property or even equipment, then lease the places or items to their own corporations, taking the depreciation allowances themselves. For most of us, however, leasing property and equipment is not a source of profit but a way of *reducing* capital needs.

Generally, leasing is limited to items that have a long-term use and can easily be repossessed in case of default. Basic equipment and rolling stock (automobiles) are prime examples. In many leasing situations, you have the option to purchase the item at the conclusion of the lease, at a favorable, predetermined price.

At start-up, leasing makes sense for several reasons:

1. If you lease a property rather than buy it, you don't tie up money in the downpayment. The property (or equipment) itself is the collateral.

2. When you lease equipment, you won't need to expend your short-term funds on long-term assets. You can preserve your company's credit line for other needs, and if you are already heavily indebted, leasing may offer the only way to get that equipment or rolling stock. Your accountant can structure your equipment lease so that lease payments become an operating expense that does not show up on your balance sheet—giving you a better debt-to-payment ratio.

3. At start-up you need everything, and money is limited, but leasing allows you to have the kind of *quality* equipment you otherwise could not afford.

4. Related to the above, leasing makes sense with equipment that is subject to quick obsolescence. Examples are computers, robotic machinery, or any highly sophisticated items that go through development changes every year—even cars and trucks.

One of the latest wrinkles in leasing is personnel. There are now personnel management companies that will hire your employees, make sure they perform, replace them if previous ones leave, screen and even help train them, pay all taxes and other withholdings, and send you one bill each week or each month. If hiring and firing are not your strong suits, and keeping all those records required in today's labor market is not to your taste, then this personnel-leasing option is something to investigate.

You are advised to check with your accountant, who can analyze your income and usage and advise you whether leasing or purchasing is more advantageous for you in various situations.

FINANCIAL AND OPERATING PITFALLS

14

FIFTEEN PROBLEMS AND SOLUTIONS

1. *Problem*: You figure to sell stock to the public. According to your projections, you can use $100,000 and keep the majority of the stock for yourself and your family. Should you do it?

Solution: $100,000 is a pittance in the public financing field. It will cost you that much in legal and accounting fees. The experts say that if you go for a public stock offering, make it $200,000 or more by doubling or tripling your expenses and projections.

2. *Problem*: Start-up capital is difficult to project and to get. How should you project your expenses for your loan application?

Solution: When you make your expense projections, increase your expenses or reserves at least another 25 percent for those unforeseen expenses that are sure to crop up and set your collections at 15 to 30 days later than you anticipate. It's Murphy's Law, and it works virtually every time.

3. *Problem*: Greater sales are not always the answer to having more money. It costs money to make sales, which require more time, help, commissions, and inventory. What should you do about this?

Solution: If you plan to expand your sales efforts, you will probably need an infusion of capital. Plan your cash flow and get a short-term bank loan to permit you to increase your business.

4. *Problem*: You like to be a big fish in a little pond, and that's why you put all your money into one bank. But when you apply for a line of credit, you find that your bank won't lend you enough. What should you do?

Solution: If you have enough of those dollars to spread around, or sufficient earnings, open accounts in several banks. Then get a number of small loans to build up greater loan capacity. This way, you can also make comparisons of various banks' interest rates and find out which ones give the best terms.

5. *Problem*: Doing business with Uncle Sam can require a lot of paper work, and you hate red tape. Should you forgo doing business with the world's largest customer?

Solution: If you have a product or service that you can sell to the U.S. Government, consider it seriously. One important reason is that, while banks lend money on your ordinary accounts receivable, it is usually only 75–80 percent; but on A/Rs from Uncle Sugar, you get 100 percent loans.

6. *Problem*: Retained earnings from small businesses that turn out to be profitable can either go back into your pocket or go out in taxes. How can you minimize your tax bite?

Solution: Discuss the possibility of retained earnings with your accountant. Can you change the legal character of your enterprise? Buy additional equipment? Investment in income-producing property? Have a personal-income distribution? You should know the answers at the beginning of the year. If you wait until tax time, it will be too late to do anything about the situation.

7. *Problem*: Running a small cash-based business—like a restaurant, news store or taxi service—imposes great temptations to tap the till. What's so bad about this? After all, it's your money, isn't it?

Solution: If you rob your left pocket to pay your right pocket, you'll soon wear out your pockets. How you keep accounts is your business, but fooling yourself in order to short-change the tax collector is a short-cut to bankruptcy. You need a set of accurate records, if only for yourself.

8. *Problem*: You run a service business that allows certain "good" customers to pay at the end of the month. But some of those "good" folks forget or run short of cash. How long should you go along with them? You've found that when they owe you a lot of money, they don't call anymore.

Solution: It is axiomatic that deadbeats, even nice ones, cease being customers. Make it a policy to have friendly collection reminders that go out at specific periods. If this doesn't work, turn the accounts over for collection by a professional organization. You've lost the business anyway, and at least you'll get some of your money.

9. *Problem*: Your policy is to allow exchange of merchandise if the customer is unhappy—even months later. Should you continue this practice, even though there are some customers who will take advantage of the courtesy? Isn't it, as you feel, good public relations?

Solution: Yes on both counts. Exchanges rarely amount to more than 1 or 2 percent. If you have a prestigious business with a high markup, a 2 percent "add-on" can easily take care of such exchanges.

10. *Problem*: Timing is all-important in opening a business and starting promotions. How should you incorporate this factor in opening a bed-and-breakfast or an ice-cream shop, or in starting any kind of business?

Solution: Consult industry associations, trade magazines, other people in that line. Know the cyclical sales curves, for virtually all businesses have them. Don't go belly-up because you got caught at the bottom of a traditional sales curve.

11. *Problem*: You know that you alone are responsible for the success or failure of your business, but how hard should you work? Should you take time off regularly, even though you could make more money by working?

Solution: The old Horatio Alger story might apply to some people with unlimited energy and the vigor of youth, but the majority of start-up entrepreneurs are in their 40s and up. In your business planning, be sure to build in adequate help and some time for family and leisure activities. Remember that your body is not a machine. You'll lose more money if you get sick or burn out.

12. *Problem*: What should you do about high fixed costs?

Solution: At the beginning you should remain as liquid as possible. Consider using leasing or lease-backs rather than making outright purchases. Variable costs are always more than you anticipate. Believe it!

13. *Problem*: How can you avoid waste?

Solution: Wasting dollars on little things, especially when you first start out, or when employees are free to place orders, is the quickest way to go broke. Make sure you see each purchase order; make price comparisons; ask whether this purchase was needed in the first place. At the end of the year those "little" savings could buy you a "big" vacation.

14. *Problem*: You know that most employees work below their capacity. Should you hire more workers than are actually needed to compensate for this fact?

Solution: No. While it's true that most employees don't work up to their capacities, you can consider hiring part-time employees, who will work 20 hours a week or less. Chances are that they'll provide the equivalent of a 30- to 40-hour worker. You can also look for "leaks" in the employees' workday—too many coffee and cigarette breaks, a steady toilet caravan, a very busy water cooler, etc. Set a policy, set parameters. Your employees will work better if they know you mean "business."

15. *Problem*: You look at your current balance sheet and discover to your horror that your assets (the money that you actually have or will have) are less than your liabilities (what you owe to others). What should you do?

Solution: You are in trouble. If you delay taking action, you can bet that the problem will get worse. Arrange to postpone payments to some of your creditors; call up a few good customers who owe you money and ask whether they can accelerate their payment; transfer some money from your private funds; see if you have assets that can be used as collateral for a short-term bank loan; tighten your own belt until the deficit balances. After all that is done, analyze the problem honestly and take steps to ensure that you won't get into such a bind again.

HOW TO COPE WITH OR AVOID AN IRS AUDIT

Somewhere in the back of an entrepreneur's mind there always lurks that specter—an audit by the Internal Revenue Service. It can happen to anyone, but if you keep your records accurately and pay your estimated and year-end taxes promptly, going through an audit should be routine. Your accountant should be with you to answer questions as only a professional can.

The IRS has some rarely published "inside tips" on what can trigger an audit. They may help you avoid being audited. If not, knowing about them and being prepared can take some of the tension out of this procedure. Here is what the IRS looks for in selecting business returns for an audit:

- Lack of detailed schedules for each unit in a consolidated return
- The sudden incorporation of a new business with good will and accelerated depreciation
- International deals and foreign tax credits
- Starting out your business with the last-in, first-out accounting method
- Sizable outside income, such as rents, royalties, investments, etc.
- Sizable deviations from the industry "norms"
- Unusual changes in inventories from the last report
- Asset sales without comparable gain/loss schedules
- Large bad-debt reports
- Premature write-offs, especially of "good will"
- Unreported interest from A/Rs, when interest is charged
- Loans to and from stockholders
- Expenses that are well above industry "norms"
- Stock issues for "services rendered"
- Schedules M (reconciling income per books with income per return), which are generally scrutinized under any circumstances

EMPLOYMENT PITFALLS

A small entrepreneur who did not want to be bothered with a lot of employees, bookkeeping, taxes, and all the problems inherent in a fluctuating business, hired his workers with the understanding that they were "independent contractors" and would report and pay their own taxes.

He went along like this until, one year, the IRS came after him with a whopping bill for full back taxes, plus penalties and interest.

The IRS claimed that this entrepreneur's employees were *his* responsibility and were not "independent contractors." The ramifications of such an onerous bill could put a small businessperson out of business.

The IRS has named a figure of $3.7 billion in delinquent payroll taxes owed by entrepreneurs—and they are going after that money with every means at their disposal. A clear understanding of exactly what "independent contractor" means in the eyes of the law is vital to your future financial health. This is especially true in industries like construction and home improvement, agriculture and homework or piecework. In brief, the rules for distinguishing employees from independent contractors are as follows: Employee status is indicated if

- you train the worker and furnish tools and a place where he or she will work;
- you pay the worker by the hour, week, or month.

Independent contractor status is shown if:

- the worker can make a profit or loss from his or her efforts;
- payment is made by straight commission or by the job;
- the worker has a personal investment in the facility used to make the product;
- the worker has the right to determine the services he or she is to perform;
- the worker sets his or her own hours for doing the job.

To get further clarification, read or have your attorney and CPA read IRS Publication 539 (available by calling 1-800-424-FORM). You can also get the U.S. Department of Labor Regulations, Part 530, "Employment of Homeworkers in Certain Industries," as well as the Labor Department's "Homeworker Handbook" (Form WH-75). Since the court decisions have clarified and stratified the rules under which an employer can hire contract labor, the labels by which these workers are called have become unimportant. A person required to comply

INDEPENDENT CONTRACTOR'S AGREEMENT

Date: _____

Name: _____ Social Security No.: _____

Address: _____

Name and address of nearest of kin: _____

_____

Reference: _____

_____

I, _____ , hereby acknowledge
to _____ (company) _____ that I am acting as an outside independent contractor in regard to the services I am supplying. I
understand that I will be issued a government tax information
form No. 1099 reflecting my earnings for the calendar year
_____ . I further represent that I am being engaged by
_____ (company) _____ on a job-by-job basis to perform various
services. The arrangements under which I work for the above
company are determined on a job-by-job basis. I understand that
I am not an employee of the above company, and I am personally
responsible for my own personal income tax and other benefit
payments.

Signed: _____

Date: _____

Witnessed: _____

Date: _____

Figure 27. Independent Contractor's Agreement

with instructions about where, when, and how to do the assigned job is ordinarily called an employee.

To guard against such repercussions, one small contractor was advised to have each of her part-time and occasional workers sign a statement like the one shown in Figure 27.

There is another option: Draw your occasional or part-time employees from a temporary agency that will pay the employees' social security and workmen's compensation contributions, make proper withholdings, give them the pertinent receipts and forms, and take care of all the headaches required by the bureaucracy. Of course, you are going to pay for this service one way or another, but at least you will be getting *one* bill—and no invitation from the IRS for a meeting about this subject. You will also have all advertising for and preselection of the employees taken care of. Further, the total bill from the temp agency becomes an expense item.

Section V

Innovations and Innovators

*Curiosity is one of the permanent and certain characteristics
of a vigorous intellect.*

Samuel Johnson

INTRODUCTION TO SECTION V

It is said that if you can build a better mouse trap, the public will beat a path to your door. Chances are that investors will do likewise. Innovating is one of the best ways to attract capital.

One reason that small businesses innovate more than large corporations (at least in our capitalistic society) is that the individual entrepreneur has some special incentives. Beyond the desire for money, which motivates both corporate types and entrepreneurs, there is the desire for freedom of thought and action. Corporate workers are stymied by rules and regulations, fiscal restrictions, jealousies that keep them working at the level of the lowest common denominators. They mustn't rock the boat. They shouldn't stand out too much (there are often even wardrobe restrictions).

Unless, of course, the company has a research and development (R&D) department, and the worker is given time, money, and facilities with which to innovate. This relatively new trend within corporations has created a class of *intrapreneurs*. But on the whole, it is the little independent person who comes up with the gadget, the novelty, and the restructuring of old products or procedures into an exciting new format.

On the following pages are more than two dozen case histories based on real-life situations—successful small businesses launched by innovators. Any one of them could be you.

You will note certain common threads: All of the following examples develop and market an idea—involving some creation of a product or service that had not been in existence before, or some improvement on an existing product or service. They also started with no or very little outside financing. And they all demonstrate persistence and hard work.

Business success is often a state of mind. You have to be open to doing things differently. You have to be adventurous. You have to be willing to learn new ways and procedures. You have to be an *imagineer*—someone who goes beyond current limitations and restrictions. You also have to be organized. When and if you show these qualities, you can be confident that you will succeed. Ideas and, equally important, their implementation, is what sets us off from the animals. Or from those who become failure statistics.

So let's take a look around the country and see what has been done recently in the way of creating new products and services, or just fresh and innovative packaging and marketing of the old ones. The successes of these individuals prove that there is always room for one more entrepreneur on the American scene.

ENTREPRENEURIAL SUCCESS STORIES | 15

ANTIQUES

Hardly a day goes by that some dusty discovery does not make the news: It is discovered, cleaned up, and put up at an auction; it brings thousands and even millions of dollars by a wealthy bidder. This trend was not lost on two brothers in New Hope, Pennsylvania, a picturesque little town along the Delaware River that is famous for its many antique shops and art galleries.

The brothers' father had been in the business of restoring and selling antiques since 1955. But once they took over from their father, the dealers really became big and profitable. From their father they had inherited a supply of good will built up over the years, and a good location—being close to Philadelphia and within driving distance of New York City, Baltimore, and Washington, New Hope gets a constant stream of tourists and antique hunters. To those assets they added good taste and diligent work, and more sophisticated advertising.

Today their "objets" sell for $1000 to $40,000. The brothers' liking for the antique business and their skills in it have combined to ensure their success.

BABY FOOD

Two other brothers in a little town in Vermont got a brainstorm in health foods for babies. "If there is a health market for pets, why not for babies?" they mused. They searched and researched in the vast baby-food industry, investigating the market, trends, manufacturing, licensing, packaging, pricing, and selling. They did not give up their regular income-producing activities until they had raised enough money to get started on a modest scale.

After three years of research and preparation they were ready and started shipping out the first cases of organically grown, pesticide-free baby foods. They called this product **Earth's Best**, and today it can be found in health-food stores and selected grocery stores from coast to coast.

The brothers discovered a need. Then they took their time; prepared themselves; did lots of research, both on the product and the market. They amassed enough knowledge to convince a lender that theirs was a sound proposition. They started the business—and succeeded. Their products might be for babies, but their earnings are hardly kids' stuff.

BILLBOARDS

This is not a story about a brand new start-up business. It is about a business that has been in existence, and has been prospering, for 20 years. However, it is a good example of one of the most important ingredients in entrepreneurial success—perseverance.

In the late sixties two electronics engineers in Brookings, South Dakota, had the idea of producing a computer-programmable billboard. They literally had a garage start, working on their idea after hours over nearly a decade while holding down their regular jobs.

Once they got a prototype working, they were able to borrow some seed money and began to translate their long research into practical products. They left their jobs and started in earnest developing their new electronic billboard company.

That was twenty years ago. Today their company employs 350 full- and part-time people. At the 1988 Winter Olympics in Calgary, Canada, one of their illuminated, computer-programmed billboards announced events and results. All this from a garage beginning and a good idea.

BLACKSMITHING

You wouldn't think that in this era of high-tech production a craft as ancient as blacksmithing would provide a viable living. But there is a very noticeable ground swell of "back-to-the-pioneers" enterprise. Old-fashioned food products, handmade fabrics, recycled attic fashions, and antique furnishings are gaining in popularity and value.

In the small town of Mountain View, Arkansas, 10 years ago, a man read a mail-order catalog that showed a number of wrought-iron, hand-forged pieces. That was just what this entrepreneur wanted to do: blacksmithing.

He acquired the necessary smithing tools, an anvil, a forge, and set to work making fireplace accessories; he added some planters, kitchen equipment, and whatever else took his fancy—and people bought.

Soon he needed help; then more and more. Naturally, as he grew, he also needed more money, and the local bank saw the potential in the enterprise. Today he gives employment to more than 80 people from the area. His shop sells to nearly 2000 retail shops throughout the United States and Canada, and 20 catalog houses feature his products. He even exports to Japan. This entrepreneur forged a great future by looking backward.

BOATING

How many Sunday boaters dream of being able to turn their weekend avocation into a paying business? For some enterprising sailors, the sea has provided both pleasure and a good income. In Hawaii a triumvirate of boating aficionados revived an old twin-hulled catamaran, seeing some potential in the tremendous growth of tourism.

Back in 1970 they started taking tourists out on "sunset dinner cruises." They provided food, local lore, and an open bar, and nature provided the rest with spectacular sunsets coloring the sky and sea. Gradually they built up a full-time business that became exceptionally successful. Today, their company, which was financed primarily with their own internally generated resources, handles about 200,000 paying passengers a year.

A related business was started in St. Thomas, Virgin Islands, some years ago. An ex-Navy officer bought an old boat with his discharge pay, installed a "window" in the bottom, and daily took dozens of visitors out to gaze at fish and coral reefs. In a few years he sold it for a handsome profit and retired again.

CHILD CARE

The surrogate caretaking of children of working parents has become a very big business. Mothers who work in offices and factories, including single mothers whose numbers are growing each year, need places for their preschool tots during the school day and after-school supervision and entertainment for older children.

On federal, state, and municipal levels, the government has set up training and financial-support divisions so that more child-care facilities can be established. Many corporations, singly or jointly with other companies, also have set up "kiddie co-ops" operated by trained child-care specialists.

This means there is an opportunity for people with training to tap into the money available on all four levels of government to support the day care of children. In a creative twist on this service, in Omaha, Nebraska, an alert expert saw the need for a private training and consulting service. After 10 years of operation, Janet W. Phelan's child-care consulting service is flourishing and doing a valuable job for a growing industry—with a minimum of financial investment but a maximum of imagination and know-how.

CHIMNEY SWEEPING

It would be difficult to think of a more prosaic business than sweeping the sooty chimneys of suburban homeowners. But back in 1977, when the energy crisis suddenly made fireplaces more important, a young man in Fairfield, Iowa, Robert Daniels, saw an opportunity and started a chimney-sweeping business.

The innovative "Sooty" Daniels could not rest on his smoky laurels, however. He thought about the profession itself, saw the need for a cap that chimney sweeps could wear, had some made up, and sold them to his fellow soot-busters.

Then he realized that there were other accessories that chimney sweeps could use—and beyond that, that they could sell fireplace products to their customers. He formed a wholesale company that handled such supplies. With money saved gradually from his business, he developed a catalog of products and a mailing list.

Today virtually all of this country's 5000 chimney sweeps are on Daniels' mailing list, and many are his customers. He has added a newsletter and marketing literature to his line of chimney products. In the process of helping America's chimney sweeps, "Sooty" is turning the industry into a respected profession, while turning a good buck for himself.

COMMUNICATIONS EQUIPMENT

In this age of communication and information, many a small consulting and distribution business has been spawned by former employees of the big communications corporations. Out in Medway, Ohio, a husband-and-wife team in this category decided that, sink or swim, they were going into business for themselves selling and installing custom communication equipment.

They started with more enthusiasm than money, having literally $40 to invest, plus a lot of confidence and experience in the business. There was indirect outside financing, however: the husband's parents, who had the couple over for dinner on many an evening. The first job they sold enabled them to put food on their own table.

It should be mentioned that this Medway couple forged a strong bond between themselves, as well as making a go of their business. It is not always easy to "make it" in a husband-and-wife enterprise, but if it works, it can be one of the most productive partnerships in existence.

COMPUTER SOFTWARE

The annals of modern American business are studded with success stories from the new computer generation. Perhaps Fargo, North Dakota, seems an unlikely place to back a large computer software company—especially when the head of the company is only 32 years old. But a group of investors saw an opportunity they could support in **Great Plains Software**. Stanford University graduate Doug Bergum, then 27, came to the attention of this investment group, and with the young man serving as active head of the group, they purchased the Fargo company, which had 40 employees.

Bergum's skills and abilities have expanded the firm sixfold in the five years of the new group's management. When asked the secret of his success, the intrepid young executive said it wasn't money, location, uniqueness of product, or price—but something far more precious. The "secret," Doug Bergum was quick to point out, was a steady supply of intelligent, hard-working employees. Money helps, but people make a company.

DRAPERIES

From rags to ruffles to riches is the story of Dorothy Noe of Wilmington, North Carolina. Starting in her garage with nothing, she built up a business making drapery and bedding accessories—all with ruffles—that in 1989 will gross $20 million!

The impetus that made Mrs. Noe a success was necessity, the well-known mother of invention. She wanted a certain kind of ruffled drapery to accent her home's antique decor. The area's stores were unable to supply her, so she made her own. Friends and neighbors saw the results, and their oohs and aahs turned Dorothy Noe into an entrepreneur.

Year by year, **Dorothy's Ruffled Originals, Inc.** added new products and acquired more internal working capital; at the same time, she expanded her operation. Today the company provides work for 300 employees.

If all it routinely took were 16 years, building at a pace of more than $1 million-a-year increase, everybody would go into businesses of their own. It doesn't happen often, but such success stories are still possible, even without big-money start-up capital.

EMPLOYMENT AGENCIES

Two trends have made the employment-agency business more interesting and lucrative. One is the greater use of temporary employees, resulting in part from the nearly full employment in some cities, and the other is specialization.

A combination of both trends is exemplified by a business in Golden, Colorado, where Swiss-born Hans Amstein, a former chef, started **Chef Temps**. Given the proliferation of restaurants across the country and a scarcity of good chefs, this new enterprise took off immediately. Ninety experienced chefs were found and assigned the first year Amstein was in business.

In Maitland, Florida, **Parsons Associates**, a personnel agency specializing in engineers, decided to expand into temporary placement of high-tech executives. At the same time a vice president of the local Martin Marietta aerospace company retired. The personnel agency and the vice president got together and formed a joint venture, setting up a separately incorporated high-tech division. With the new associate's experience, additional operating capital, and contacts in the technology industry, the new business got off the ground like a rocket.

A brother-and-sister team in Washington, DC, took advantage of their city's saturated, high-priced labor market by creating **Temps & Co.** Starting in 1981 with little money of their own, they built the business into a $40 million success by concentrating on strong employee relationships.

FARMERS' MARKETS FOR CITY ENTREPRENEURS

If you don't have resources to open a million-dollar supermarket, you might consider renting a stall in an urban farmers' market. They are proliferating all over the country.

Outside of Washington, DC, in Burtonville, Maryland, the **Dutch Farmers' Market** attracts buyers from a 30-mile radius. The entrepreneurs, who sell produce and pretzels, garden products and gift-wares, do a land-office business each Thursday, Friday, and Saturday. The rest of the time they tend to their farms, small businesses, or avocations.

At the **DeKalb Farmers' Market** near Atlanta, Georgia, 45,000 shoppers fill the aisles of this 116,000-square-foot structure each week. They buy mountains of fresh produce and pick from among 125 varieties of fish and seafood.

Baltimore's venerable **Lexington Market** is a huge in-city affair that has been bringing suburban housewives downtown for more than two centuries—by bus, car, train, and even chauffeured limousine. The market's Chesapeake seafood selection is legendary. Another well-known example is the **Pike's Street Market** in Seattle, with its mouth-watering fish and fruit selections. It keeps stretching out year by year.

Hilary Baum, director of New York City's nonprofit Public Market Collaborative, says, "These markets support the local agricultural base by providing farmers with a direct retailing opportunity." She estimates that there are many thousands of business opportunities in the more than 2000 farmers' markets in the United States. Increasing crowds of urban shoppers come to these facilities for variety, value, freshness—and a festival ambience, which is nothing like that of the traditional supermarket.

While the retailing appeal of these markets is primarily to farmers and those who produce or process their own meat and fish, in many markets, small restaurants do a huge business. Novelty, jewelry, and crafts tables and booths also fare respectably.

The marketplace concept goes back to ancient times (the Greek name is the *agora*), but the American adaptation is as varied in size and composition as the numbers of markets available. If this is the kind of business you want to get into, you may also want to visit the following:

Reading Terminal Market, Philadelphia, PA

Public Market Collaborative, New York, NY

Eastern Market, Detroit, MI

Farmers' Market, Dallas, TX

Farmers' Market, Los Angeles, CA
Findlay Market, Cincinnati, OH
West Side Market, Cleveland, OH
The Public Market, Aurora (Denver), CO
El Mercado & Farmers' Market, San Antonio, TX
Soulard Market, St. Louis, MO

FOOT FASHIONS

Five years ago an attractive Indian maiden with the lyrical name of Melody Lightfeather was busy running the American Indian Marketing Services. The place was Albuquerque, New Mexico; the year, 1984.

Many native artisans were making belts and trims of colorful glass beads; however, no one was making any truly stylish beaded shoes and fashions. Melody's first pair of beaded shoes were for her own pleasure. When she went out in them, people commented and wanted to buy a pair for themselves. Melody accommodated them—at $500 or more a pair, which did not prevent more and more customers from seeking her out.

Soon she was employing a hundred beaders, most of whom were kept busy making intricately executed **Lightfeather Line** beaded shoes. Recently, fashions have been added—bead designs on denim.

It is truly a home-grown business—and even the financing of it was by the slow-grow method. Melody proved that, even today, if you build a better mousetrap, the people will find a way to your door.

GUEST HOUSES AND SMALL RESORTS

Running a resort hotel or even a guest house is the dream of many entrepreneurs. As with restaurant operation, accommodating the traveler is interesting, and it can be lucrative. Because you are dealing with property, a loan is more easily obtained than many other businesses, requiring less concrete collateral.

On Orcas Island, in Puget Sound off the Washington coast, one couple bought a five-bedroom home with a good-sized mortgage.

For a year they worked on turning it into a neat-as-a-pin showplace. The rooms were decorated in that classic style, "early Salvation Army"; each one was different from the others and very charming. The publicity went out, and the inn started filling up. It was a natural in an area in which tourist traffic was growing steadily.

An older couple created their own "retirement" pension plan by purchasing a run-down guest house. They renovated it themselves, furnishing it with proceeds from an equity loan. In the area around Newport, Rhode Island, where the establishment was located, the market could bear prices of $65 to $95 per night per room, which helped to make the project successful. They opened just in time for a major, highly advertised seasonal event, and the higher prices they were able to charge during the opening remained—as did the crowds.

Not too far from Atlanta, Georgia, stood a typical southern mansion, nestled among 16 beautiful acres. A young executive in the area had heard that the property was up for sale, and she had an idea. She took it to the bank, where an alert loan officer recognized the opportunity—and the would-be entrepreneur made an offer on the property. It was accepted, and work was begun immediately to turn the mansion into a health resort for women executives. The new owner installed a sauna, work-out equipment, and exercise rooms; established classes in gourmet cooking and stress reduction; leased space to a beauty shop that also provided facials and massages—and made a success of a handsome but much underutilized property.

Up in Maine, another executive came across an old inn and country club. It had 60 rooms and stood amid 90 acres that included a usable swimming pool and a golf course. He took a chance and made a low-ball offer of $450,000. It was accepted, and the bank saw the immense potential when the marketing-wise new proprietor presented his business plan. A decade later, the resort has expanded to 140 guest rooms, and the business has grown from $350,000 gross to $4 million. How did the entrepreneur do it? He redirected the property's appeal away from an elderly leisure class to a mobile professional clientele by changing a dowdy old facility into an upbeat country club that was already within easy driving range of several large cities.

Spotting a sleeping opportunity and awakening it to a new potential, getting the right bank loan, and having a little luck combined in all four of these cases to create success with a capital $.

INVESTMENT ENTREPRENEURSHIP

It's amazing how in the American society so many successful entrepreneurs started and succeeded with very little training for their specific operation. However, those we hear and read about are the survivors. The ones who failed, the majority, become unknown statistics.

Sometimes, in a relatively small town, an entrepreneur catches the brass ring, learning to operate OPM style—i.e., with "other people's money." In Charleston, West Virginia, a young man did just that by building, not houses, but credit. He started or bought small local businesses by borrowing small sums of money from local banks against equity. He paid back quickly and promptly. Soon he became known as a go-getter and a reliable kind of a guy who made things happen.

Before he was out of his 20s, Joe Minardi owned a residential property, a bar and grill, a catering business, an optical store, and a tanning salon. Besides being financed by bank loans, each was supported by I.F. (intestinal fortitude), hard work, and shrewdness. Only in America!

JANITORIAL SERVICE

When you're one of 25 children, you cannot expect too many advantages. One thing Mary Winston of Indianapolis learned early in life was to do housecleaning, and so she turned that to advantage.

When she grew older and got married, she and her husband decided to start a side business of their own. For 10 years, when they got through with their regular jobs, they cleaned offices. As they got more clients, they decided to take a plunge and started **Winston Janitorial Services** with a little money they had saved up. After her husband died, Mrs. Winston carried on, doing the kind of conscientious job that made for recommendations. Today she has a payroll of over 270 people, 70 corporate clients, and a gross income of $3 million. She is, indeed, cleaning up—and without any loans, without debts.

PACKAGE SERVICE FOR CAMPERS

In 1984 a different Mrs. Winston—Julie, of Rockville, Maryland—had an idea. Her kids, and those of most of her friends and neighbors, went to summer camps. The parents wanted to keep in touch with their youngsters, and one way of doing that was to send packages. Mrs. Winston's brainstorm was to start a package service, called, appropriately enough, **Sealed with a Kiss (SWAK)**.

The contents were Winston-selected. Every package contained lots of surprises—items Julie "discovered"—and each was different in some way from the others. Children loved getting these packages, and the SWAK enterprise rapidly spread through word of mouth.

Her husband got involved, and the little garage business expanded into a five-times-larger warehouse. In five years the Winstons' efforts grew to a part-time payroll of 15 to 20 high-school and college students, working two shifts. In 1989 they sent out 10,500 packages at $20 apiece, plus postage, with campers across the United States and in Canada on the receiving end.

Financing? It started with some personal seed money and then paid for itself. No outside financing was ever needed. All transactions were prepaid. There were no receivables, no returns, no inventory losses. Next: packages for travelers, birthdays, college kids.

POTTERY BUSINESSES

"Going to pot" can be a very satisfying and even lucrative process—when it means creating earthenware and porcelain objects that are both artistic and utilitarian. A pottery business requires some skills, of course. Investments include a pottery wheel, possibly a commercial kiln (unless you can rent space in one), and the glazing compounds to decorate your output.

In Springfield, Illinois, Ellen Matlins, a potter, decided to make a porcelain tea set for her little girls. The children helped her decorate the pieces. Then she made others to sell. While on a trip to New York, she showed one of her tea sets to the buyer of a large, prestigious chain of toy stores and she got an order for a sample quantity. This beginning led to a large order and inclusion in the company's mail-order catalog. A personal investment of less than $5000 was turned into a sale of $15,000—and a national business for **Ellen Matlins Pottery** was launched.

In Costa Mesa, California, a decade ago, partners Lucyann Cameron and Elizabeth Smoot made 50 bright red dinner plates, inscribing the legend, "You are special today," around the edges. They took their product to a trade show, and by the end of the day they had orders for 2000 plates. With virtually no outside financing, a part-time hobby has grown into a sizable business, **The Original Red Plate Co.**, that last year turned out about 100,000 items. Among their customers, Cameron and Smoot can even count former president Ronald Reagan.

A different but nevertheless successful approach to being in the ceramics business was taken by Nancy Ward and her husband, Clyde, a store manager, in Dover, Delaware. Nancy had been making pottery as a hobby, but when a local ceramics studio became available, the Wards put their savings together and bought the business. They upgraded the items carried—mostly "green ware" that is already formed and ready for painting and baking—and promoted ceramics classes. Having started with six or seven students, Mrs. Ward now instructs 120 a week. Between Nancy's creative talents and Clyde's business skills, **J&J Ceramics Studio** is now a successful retail/wholesale/supply operation.

PUBLICATIONS

Next to opening a restaurant, starting a publication is perhaps the most popular business start-up. As with a restaurant, a publication is also one of the most vulnerable businesses. The reason is hard to pin down with accuracy: Perhaps it is because the business end of a newspaper or magazine is so full of booby traps, and business management skills are incompatible with the creative nature of the founder. A special problem is that neither the local bank nor the SBA, as guarantor, is likely to come up with any financing. To start a publication you have to have your own capital or be able to raise considerable sums through private subscriptions.

The approximately 2500 existing trade publications, 2200 magazines, 1800 daily newspapers, and 8000 weeklies seem to belie the difficulty. Actually, these figures underscore the siren call of this business. Here are some recent examples of how publications were started—and kept running.

In the Orlando, Florida, area a young couple working for the Disney enterprises saw a need for a news conduit to bring the many young talents in the area to the attention of local impresarios, and vice versa. After a year of research and economizing, they had enough money and know-how for the first couple of issues, and a slick newspaper named **"Celebrity"** was born. The need *was* there, and it became successful enough to allow the publishers to retire from their full-time jobs with Disney and devote themselves to the development of the newspaper.

The northern outpost of Anchorage, Alaska, might not strike you as the ideal place to launch a publication, especially by a woman. But Susie Carter was the right person in the right place with the right idea. The magazine she started is called **"Alaska Men."** A commodity that Alaska has plenty of is men, but there is a definite shortage of women. Ms. Carter's idea was to publish physical descriptions and addresses of men featured in each month's issue, and it worked. Interest has reached to the four corners of the world, and mail piles in from everywhere, along with subscriptions and advertising—the backbones of any publication business. Good research and a calculated risk created an instant success for this magazine matchmaker.

In Kenosha, Wisconsin, two aspiring journalists had yet another idea: The Barbie doll has been around as a favorite of girls and almost a national symbol for 30 years; why not a publication for it? They talked with the makers and patent holders, cleared the legal decks, pooled their resources, and produced **"Barbie Bazaar."** The magazine is supported by the many distributors of Barbie accessories and by a legion of fans. With more than 7000 subscriptions, the two publishers have a small but profitable and satisfying business going.

REAL ESTATE

This story is about a small independent real estate broker who developed a new strategy for selling houses. The expansion of this Redmond, Washington, Realtor's business actually took no money at all.

Having been in business for many years, he knew that an empty house is harder to sell than an occupied one. He also knew that an unoccupied house constitutes a security hazard for the owners. Thus, Brian Graves' idea was to find a reliable person or couple who would occupy the house after its owners had moved. He called the business **America's Home Caretakers**.

The approach has several advantages. The temporary residents are able to live in a home that is usually well beyond their means, paying only nominal rent in return for their promise to maintain, clean, and help show the property to prospective buyers. The absentee owners, meanwhile, are assured of the protection of their property and the likelihood of a better, faster sale. This is a perfect symbiosis, and the only investment required was for some promotional material.

SAFETY DEVICES FOR BABIES

Most innovations were probably developed because a problem was encountered by a human being ingenious enough to discover a solution. Out in Ada, Oklahoma, a young mother saw a definite need for a safety harness to keep her active baby boy securely in his chair.

Of course, there were devices on the market, such as fancy high chairs, car seats, and various belts and straps. But none of them were the kind of effective, economical, and simple device this woman envisioned—something that could be taken along on visits and trips and used in virtually any seating situation.

After some at-home experimenting with soft cloths, Mrs. Jamie Leach came up with a satisfying, workable, quick-closing device that she called **Wiggle Wrap**. Her husband, Clyde, became equally enthusiastic about his wife's invention and got into the act. They found a manufacturer that could produce and market the device, and now the company sells nearly 2500 Wiggle Wraps a month; these keep

30,000 babies a year safely and snuggly in any type of seat, and out of harm's way.

There was little financing involved in the business, proving that human ingenuity often is more important than a lot of money.

TRUNKS FOR TOTS

A young mother in Texas remembered her childhood pastime of dressing up in her mother's hats and shoes when she saw her little daughter enjoying the same activity. The woman brought her own mother in on a plan to buy the child a little trunk for her birthday and fill it with dress-up clothes. There was only one problem: They could not find a child-sized trunk.

To solve the problem, they had a small trunk made, and then they carried out their plan in time for the youngster's birthday. In the process, a business was born! The next steps were to arrange a price and time schedule with the maker of the model trunk, prepare a flyer and order form, make up a sample list of toy distributors and major toy stores throughout the country, and send out the literature. The final price of each package depended on the fantasy clothes that filled the trunk.

Orders kept coming in, and mother, grandmother, and the trunk manufacturer were kept busy filling them. It's only been a few years, but the business is growing apace with its first customer—the young daughter who inspired it all. Internal financing was able to accommodate gradual growth.

WOODEN BRIEFCASE BUSINESS

In Aiken, South Carolina, a business was sparked when Beverly Booth saw someone carrying a wooden briefcase and fell in love with it. Its rosewood grain was a thing of beauty, and at first Beverly just wanted one for herself. She found out the name of the manufacturer and tracked him down, only to discover that he had gone out of business. She searched for other makers of this case but could not locate anyone in the United States. Still undaunted, she perused export catalogs and found a manufacturer overseas.

The only hitch now was that it would be impossible to purchase and import a single case from this source. So she invested in the minimum quantity. Lo and behold, Beverly Booth was in business.

Within three years she developed a brisk, mostly word-of-mouth business, selling oak or rosewood briefcases. As profits materialized, she added other selected business gifts to her line, until **B. Booth Ltd.** grew so large it had to be moved out of the owner's home and into a commercial space.

By keeping her eyes open and recognizing an opportunity when she saw one, this entrepreneur created a new business. Her success is literally an open and shut case.

WORKERS' COMPENSATION CONSULTANTS

A few years ago two friends in the Boston area pooled their skills and financial resources to start a business for which they perceived a need—consulting with companies on workers' compensation problems.

The main ingredient these partners had to offer was strong background experience. Bonnie Brook was an industrial relations director, and Anne Stephenson was an occupational health and safety manager. Their one up-front expense was an office—requiring good furniture, a library of impressive reference books, and first-class stationery. They hung out a shingle in the suburb of Marblehead as **Stephenson & Brook Co., Inc.** and started calling on prospective clients. What they found was that most businesses did not know they had problems. It was a tough selling job, but the partners had a strong case to make: Their analyses could save clients money. And they did. Enough companies realized the value of the service to sign up.

Acquired skills, confidence, hard work, and persistence combined to spell success for these two savvy entrepreneurs.

APPENDIX

SAMPLE SBA LOAN FORMS

The various SBA forms that follow will be available from your own bank or any other SBA-cooperating financial institution. According to an official at the U.S. Small Business Administration: "Due to limited personnel and a government policy that calls for optimum private-sector utilization, we suggest that all loan applications are processed through the banks." These forms, therefore, are for your information and guidance only. Should you require any assistance in filling out these forms, or any additional information, contact your nearest SBA loan officer (see list of SBA offices in Chapter 8) or the closest SCORE chapter (you will find it listed in the blue government section of your telephone book, under Small Business Administration; there are more than 750 SCORE locations throughout the United States).

OMB Approval No. 3245-0016
Expiration Date: 10-31-87

U.S. Small Business Administration

Application for Business Loan

Applicant	Full Address	

Name of Business	Tax I.D. No.

Full Street Address	Tel. No. (Inc. A/C)

City	County	State	Zip	Number of Employees (Including subsidiaries and affiliates)

Type of Business	Date Business Established	At Time of Application _____

Bank of Business Account and Address	If Loan is Approved _____

Subsidiaries or Affiliates _____
(Separate from above)

Use of Proceeds: (Enter Gross Dollar Amounts Rounded to Nearest Hundreds)	Loan Requested	SBA USE ONLY
Land Acquisition		
New Construction/ Expansion/Repair		
Acquisition and/or Repair of Machinery and Equipment		
Inventory Purchase		
Working Capital (Including Accounts Payable)		
Acquisition of Existing Business		
Payoff SBA Loan		
Payoff Bank Loan (Non SBA Associated)		
Other Debt Payment (Non SBA Associated)		
All Other		
Total Loan Requested		
Term of Loan		

Collateral

If your collateral consists of (A) Land and Building, (D) Accounts Receivable and/or (E) Inventory, fill in the appropriate blanks. If you are pledging (B) Machinery and Equipment, (C) Furniture and Fixtures, and/or (F) Other, please provide an itemized list (labeled Exhibit A) that contains serial and identification numbers for all articles that had an original value greater than $500. Include a legal description of Real Estate offered as collateral.

	Present Market Value	Present Loan Balance	SBA Use Only Collateral Valuation
A. Land and Building	$	$	$
B. Machinery & Equipment			
C. Furniture & Fixtures			
D. Accounts Receivable			
E. Inventory			
F. Other			
Totals	$	$	$

PREVIOUS SBA OR OTHER GOVERNMENT FINANCING: If you or any principals or affiliates have ever requested Government Financing, complete the following:

Name of Agency	Original Amount of Loan	Date of Request	Approved or Declined	Balance	Current or Past Due
	$			$	
	$			$	

SBA Form 4 (2-85) Previous Editions Obsolete

Figure 28. Sample SBA Loan Application Form

INDEBTEDNESS: Furnish the following information on all installment debts, contracts, notes, and mortgages payable. Indicate by an asterisk (*) items to be paid by loan proceeds and reason for paying same (present balance should agree with latest balance sheet submitted).

To Whom Payable	Original Amount	Original Date	Present Balance	Rate of Interest	Maturity Date	Monthly Payment	Security	Current or Past Due
	$		$			$		
	$		$			$		
	$		$			$		
	$		$			$		

MANAGEMENT (Proprietor, partners, officers, directors and all holders of outstanding stock — <u>100% of ownership must be shown</u>). Use separate sheet if necessary.

Name and Social Security Number	Complete Address	% Owned	*Military Service From	To	*Race	*Sex

* This data is collected for statistical purposes only. It has no bearing on the credit decision to approve or decline this application.

ASSISTANCE   List the name(s) and occupation(s) of any who assisted in preparation of this form, other than applicant.

Name and Occupation	Address	Total Fees Paid	Fees Due
Name and Occupation	Address	Total Fees Paid	Fees Due

Signature of Preparers if Other Than Applicant

THE FOLLOWING EXHIBITS MUST BE COMPLETED WHERE APPLICABLE. ALL QUESTIONS ANSWERED ARE MADE A PART OF THE APPLICATION.

For Guaranty Loans please provide an original and one copy (Photocopy is Acceptable) of the Application Form, and all Exhibits to the participating lender. For Direct Loans submit one original copy of application and Exhibits to SBA.

Submit SBA Form 1261 (Statements Required by Laws and Executive Orders). This form must be signed and dated by each Proprietor, Partner, Principal or Guarantor.

1. Submit SBA Form 912 (Personal History Statement) for each person e.g. owners, partners, officers, directors, major stockholders, etc.; the instructions are on SBA Form 912.

2. Furnish a signed current personal balance sheet (SBA Form 413 may be used for this purpose) for each stockholder (with 20% or greater ownership), partner, officer, and owner. Social Security number should be included on personal financial statement. Label this Exhibit B.

3. Include the statements listed below: 1, 2, 3 for the last three years; also 1, 2, 3, 4 dated within 90 days of filing the application; and statement 5, if applicable. This is Exhibit C (SBA has Management Aids that help in the preparation of financial statements.) All information must be signed and dated.

1. Balance Sheet   2. Profit and Loss Statement
3. Reconciliation of Net Worth
4. Aging of Accounts Receivable and Payable
5. Earnings projections for at least one year where financial statements for the last three years are unavailable or where requested by District Office.
   (If Profit and Loss Statement is not available, explain why and substitute Federal Income Tax Forms.)

4. Provide a brief history of your company and a paragraph describing the expected benefits it will receive from the loan. Label it Exhibit D.

ALL EXHIBITS MUST BE SIGNED AND DATED BY PERSON SIGNING THIS FORM.

SBA Form 4 (2-85) Previous Editions Obsolete

Figure 28. (*Continued*)

(*Figure continues on p. 178.*)

5. Provide a brief description of the educational, technical and business background for all the people listed under Management. Please mark it Exhibit E.

6. Do you have any co-signers and/or guarantors for this loan? If so, please submit their names, addresses and personal balance sheet(s) as Exhibit F.

7. Are you buying machinery or equipment with your loan money? If so, you must include a list of the equipment and cost as quoted by the seller and his name and address. This is Exhibit G.

8. Have you or any officers of your company ever been involved in bankruptcy or insolvency proceedings? If so, please provide the details as Exhibit H. If none, check here: ☐ Yes ☐ No

9. Are you or your business involved in any pending lawsuits? If yes, provide the details as Exhibit I. If none, check here: ☐ Yes ☐ No

10. Do you or your spouse or any member of your household, or anyone who owns, manages, or directs your business or their spouses or members of their households work for the Small Business Administration, Small Business Advisory Council, SCORE or ACE, any Federal Agency, or the participating lender? If so, please provide the name and address of the person and the office where employed. label this Exhibit J. If none, check here: ☐ Yes ☐ No

11. Does your business, its owners or majority stockholders own or have a controlling interest in other businesses? If yes, please provide their names and the relationship with your company along with a current balance sheet and operating statement for each. This should be Exhibit K.

12. Do you buy from, sell to, or use the services of any concern in which someone in your company has a significant financial interest? If yes, provide details on a separate sheet of paper labeled Exhibit L.

13. If your business is a franchise, include a copy of the franchise agreement and a copy of the FTC disclosure statement supplied to you by the Franchisor. Please include it as Exhibit M.

CONSTRUCTION LOANS ONLY

14. Include a separate exhibit (Exhibit N) the estimated cost of the project and a statement of the source of any additional funds.

15. File the necessary compliance document (SBA Form 601).

16. Provide copies of preliminary construction plans and specifications. Include them as Exhibit O. Final plans will be required prior to disbursement.

DIRECT LOANS ONLY

17. Include two bank declination letters with your application. These letters should include the name and telephone number of the persons contacted at the banks, the amount and terms of the loan, the reason for decline and whether or not the bank will participate with SBA. In cities with 200,000 people or less, one letter will be sufficient.

EXPORT LOANS

18. Does your business presently engage in Export Trade?
Check here ☐ Yes ☐ No

19. Do you plan to begin exporting as a result of this loan?
Check here ☐ Yes ☐ No

20. Would you like information on Exporting?
Check here ☐ Yes ☐ No

AGREEMENTS AND CERTIFICATIONS

Agreements of Nonemployment of SBA Personnel: I/We agree that if SBA approves this loan application I/We will not, for at least two years, hire as an employee or consultant anyone that was employed by the SBA during the one year period prior to the disbursement of the loan.

Certification: I/We certify: (a) I/We have not paid anyone connected with the Federal Government for help in getting this loan. I/We also agree to report to the SBA office of the Inspector General, 1441 L Street N.W., Washington, D.C. 20416 any Federal Government employee who offers, in return for any type of compensation, to help get this loan approved.

(b) All information in this application and the Exhibits are true and complete to the best of my/our knowledge and are submitted to SBA so SBA can decide whether to grant a loan or participate with a lending institution in a loan to me/us. I/We agree to pay for or reimburse SBA for the cost of any surveys, title or mortgage examinations, appraisals etc., performed by non-SBA personnel provided I/We have given my/our consent.

I/We understand that I/We need not pay anybody to deal with SBA. I/We have read and understand Form 394 which explains SBA policy on representatives and their fees.

If you make a statement that you know to be false or if you over value a security in order to help obtain a loan under the provisions of the Small Business Act, you can be fined up to $5,000 or be put in jail for up to two years, or both.

If Applicant is a proprietor or general partner, sign below:

By: _____
                                                    Date

If Applicant is a Corporation, sign below:

_____
Corporate Name and Seal   Date

By: _____
                        Signature of President

Attested by: _____
                   Signature of Corporate Secretary

ALL EXHIBITS MUST BE SIGNED AND DATED BY PERSON SIGNING THIS FORM.

SBA Form 4 (2-85) Previous Editions Obsolete

⋆U.S.GPO:1986-0-623-058/281

Figure 28. (*Continued*)

United States of America

SMALL BUSINESS ADMINISTRATION

STATEMENT OF PERSONAL HISTORY

Please Read Carefully - Print or Type

Each member of the small business concern requesting assistance or the development company must submit this form in TRIPLICATE for filing with the SBA application. This form must be filled out and submitted by:

1. If a sole proprietorship by the proprietor.
2. If a partnership by each partner.
3. If a corporation or a development company, by each officer, director, and additionally by each holder of 20% or more of the voting stock.
4. Any other person including a hired manager, who has authority to speak for and commit the borrower in the management of the business.

Name and Address of Applicant (Firm Name) (Street, City, State and ZIP Code)	SBA District Office and City
	Amount Applied for:

1. Personal Statement of: (State name in full, if no middle name, state (NMN), or if initial only, indicate initial. List all former names used, and dates each name was used. Use separate sheet if necessary. First　　　　　Middle　　　　　Last	2. Date of Birth: (Month, day and year) 3. Place of Birth: (City & State or Foreign Country). U.S. Citizen? ☐ YES ☐ NO If no, give alien registration number: ＃

4. Give the percentage of ownership or stock owned or to be owned in the small business concern or the Development Company.	Social Security No.

5. Present residence address:	City	State
From:　　　　To:　　　　Address:		

Home Telephone No. (Include A/C):

Business Telephone No. (Include A/C):

Immediate past residence address:

From:　　　　To:　　　　Address:

BE SURE TO ANSWER THE NEXT 3 QUESTIONS CORRECTLY BECAUSE THEY ARE IMPORTANT.

THE FACT THAT YOU HAVE AN ARREST OR CONVICTION RECORD WILL NOT NECESSARILY DISQUALIFY YOU. BUT AN INCORRECT ANSWER WILL PROBABLY CAUSE YOUR APPLICATION TO BE TURNED DOWN.

6. Are you presently under indictment, on parole or probation?

☐ Yes ☐ No　　If yes, furnish details in a separate exhibit. List name(s) under which held, if applicable.

7. Have you ever been charged with or arrested for any criminal offense other than a minor motor vehicle violation?

☐ Yes ☐ No　　If yes, furnish details in a separate exhibit. List name(s) under which charged, if applicable.

8. Have you ever been convicted of any criminal offense other than a minor motor vehicle violation?

☐ Yes ☐ No　　If yes, furnish details in a separate exhibit. List name(s) under which convicted, if applicable.

9. Name and address of participating bank

The information on this form will be used in connection with an investigation of your character. Any information you wish to submit, that you feel will expedite this investigation should be set forth.

Whoever makes any statement knowing it to be false, for the purpose of obtaining for himself or for any applicant, any loan, or loan extension by renewal, deferment or otherwise, or for the purpose of obtaining, or influencing SBA toward, anything of value under the Small Business Act, as amended, shall be punished under Section 16(a) of that Act, by a fine of not more than $5000, or by imprisonment for not more than 2 years, or both.

Signature	Title	Date

It is against SBA's policy to provide assistance to persons not of good character and therefore consideration is given to the qualities and personality traits of a person, favorable and unfavorable, relating thereto, including behavior, integrity, candor and disposition toward criminal actions. It is also against SBA's policy to provide assistance not in the best interests of the United States, for example, if there is reason to believe that the effect of such assistance will be to encourage or support, directly or indirectly, activities inimical to the Security of the United States. Anyone concerned with the collection of this information, as to its voluntariness, disclosure or routine uses may contact the FOIA Office, 1441 "L" Street, N.W., and a copy of §9 "Agency Collection of Information" from SOP 40 04 will be provided.

SBA FORM 912 (5-87) SOP 9020 USE 6-85 EDITION UNTIL EXHAUSTED　　　　**1. SBA FILE COPY**

Figure 29. Sample SBA Statement of Personal History Form

APPENDIX

SCHEDULE OF COLLATERAL

Exhibit A

Applicant		
Street Address		
City	State	Zip Code

LIST ALL COLLATERAL TO BE USED AS SECURITY FOR THIS LOAN

Section I—REAL ESTATE

Attach a copy of the deed(s) containing a full legal description of the land and show the location (street address) and city where the deed(s) is recorded. Following the address below, give a brief description of the improvements, such as size, type of construction, use, number of stories, and present condition (use additional sheet if more space is required).

LIST PARCELS OF REAL ESTATE					
Address	Year Acquired	Original Cost	Market Value	Amount of Lien	Name of Lienholder

Description(s):

SBA Form 4 Schedule A (8-87) Use 4-87 edition until exhausted.

Figure 30. Sample SBA Schedule of Collateral

SECTION II—PERSONAL PROPERTY

All items listed herein must show manufacturer or make, model, year, and serial number. Items with no serial number must be clearly identified (use additional sheet if more space is required).

Description - Show Manufacturer, Model, Serial No.	Year Acquired	Original Cost	Market Value	Current Lien Balance	Name of Lienholder

All information contained herein is TRUE and CORRECT to the best of my knowledge. I understand that FALSE statements may result in forfeiture of benefits and possible fine and prosecution by the U.S. Attorney General (Ref. 18 U.S.C. 100).

_____   Date _____

_____   Date _____

SBA Form 4 Schedule A (8-87) Use 4-87 edition until exhausted.   *U.S. GPO: 1988-519-129/61911

Figure 30. (*Continued*)

SAMPLE SBA FORM 413 (BANK OF AMERICA FORM CR-2)

Bank of America   **Personal Financial Statement**

Date _____

Instructions

You may apply for credit in your name alone, regardless of marital status. Check your marital status below only if (a) you live in a community property state, such as California, or (b) this is a joint application. You must answer the questions about your spouse only if you're married and (a) you live in a community property state, or (b) this is a joint application with your spouse.

☐ Married   ☐ Unmarried   ☐ Separated

If you're married and live in a community property state, Bank of America NT&SA (the "Bank") will assume that all assets, income, and debts are community property, unless you indicate otherwise in the "Comments Section" on the reverse.

Joint or Individual/Separate Credit (check below):

☐ You are applying for individual credit
☐ You are applying for joint credit

☐ The joint applicant is a person who is not your spouse
(complete two forms). Name_____
☐ The joint applicant is your spouse (complete one form)
Name _____

NAME _____ AGE _____

SOCIAL   HOME
SEC. NO. _____ PHONE _____

STREET
ADDRESS _____

CITY _____ STATE _____ ZIP _____

EMPLOYED BY _____ YEARS _____

EMPLOYER'S
ADDRESS _____
              STREET   CITY   STATE   ZIP

BUSINESS
PHONE _____ POSITION _____

IF EMPLOYED LESS THAN
1 YEAR, PREVIOUS EMPLOYER _____

RECEIVED AT _____ BRANCH   _____

To get and maintain credit with Bank, you furnish the following (and attached, if applicable) full and correct statement of your financial condition. It is the most recent, and Bank may assume it to be a continuing statement of your financial condition as of the date indicated. You will notify Bank immediately, in writing, if your financial condition changes in any important way. You also agree that all of your obligations to Bank, or held by Bank will immediately become due and payable, without demand or notice, if 1) You or any endorser or guarantor of your obligations experience business failure, insolvency or bankruptcy, or any of you die, 2) an attachment or involuntary lien of any kind is issued against your assets or the assets of any endorser or guarantor of your obligations, 3) any information given on your financial statement or credit application proves to be untrue, 4) any important change occurs in your financial condition; 5) you fail to notify Bank of such a change, or 6) your business, or any interest in it, is sold.

ASSETS	AMOUNT (Omit cents)	LIABILITIES	AMOUNT (Omit cents)
Cash in Bank of America (branch)		Notes Payable to Bank of America (Branch)	
Cash in Other (give name)		Notes Payable to Other (give name)	
Accounts Receivable (Schedule C on reverse)		Accounts Payable to (give name)	
Stocks and Bonds (Schedule B on reverse)		1.	
Notes Receivable (Schedule C on reverse)		2	
Cash Surrender Value Life Insurance		3.	
Autos (Year - Make)		4.	
Autos (Year - Make)		Taxes Payable	
Real Estate (Schedule A on reverse)		Real Estate Indebtedness (Schedule A on reverse)	
Household Goods		Other Liabilities (describe)	
Other Assets (describe)		1.	
1.		2.	
2.		3.	
3.		4.	
4.		5.	
5.		TOTAL LIABILITIES $	
		NET WORTH (Total assets minus liabilities) $	
TOTAL ASSETS $		TOTAL LIABILITIES & NET WORTH $	

ANNUAL INCOME		ANNUAL EXPENDITURES	
Salary (Gross) - Applicant		Real Estate payment(s)	
Salary (Gross) - Spouse		Rent/Lease payment(s)	
Securities Income		Income Taxes	
Rental Income		Insurance Premiums (all types)	
Other (describe) (I understand that I need not reveal income from alimony, child support or separate maintenance unless I want the bank to consider it when evaluating this statement.)		Property Taxes	
		Alimony, Child Support or Separate Maintenance	
1.		Other (describe - include installment payments other than real estate)	
2.		1.	
3.		2.	
4.		3.	
TOTAL INCOME $		TOTAL EXPENDITURES $	
LESS - TOTAL EXPENDITURES $		CONTINGENT LIABILITIES (Debts on which you or your spouse is comaker, guarantor, or endorser, and obligations which either of you will have to pay if the person primarily liable does not pay.)	
NET CASH INCOME (Exclusive of ordinary living expenses) $		1. _____	
Is any of this income likely to be reduced or interrupted within the next year?		2. _____	
☐ Yes ☐ No If yes, how long will the interruption last?		3. _____	
		TOTAL $	

CR-2 8-84 (Reprint 3-88)   Bank of America NT&SA · Member FDIC

Figure 31. Sample SBA Form 413

SCHEDULE A - REAL ESTATE

PROPERTY ADDRESS AND TYPE OF IMPROVEMENT	PURCHASE DATE	NAME(S) OF OWNER(S) AND HOW HELD (JOINT TENANTS, TENANTS IN COMMON COMMUNITY PROP., SEPARATE PROP., ETC.)	ESTIMATED VALUE	AMOUNT OWING	TO WHOM PAYABLE

SCHEDULE B - STOCKS AND BONDS

NO. OF SHARES AMT. OF BONDS	DESCRIPTION	NAME(S) OF OWNER(S) AND HOW HELD (JOINT TENANTS, TENANTS IN COMMON COMMUNITY PROP., SEPARATE PROP., ETC.)	CURRENT MARKET ON LISTED OR ESTIMATED VALUE ON UNLISTED

COMMENTS SECTION - If you are married and live in a community property state, here are assets shown on this statement other than those shown in Schedules A and B above, which are NOT held as a community property by yourself and your spouse.

SCHEDULE C - ACCOUNTS/NOTES RECEIVABLE AND TRUST DEEDS (MORTGAGES) OWNED

NAME OF DEBTOR	HOW PAID	BALANCE DUE	FINAL MATURITY DATE	COLLATERAL
	$ per	$		
	$ per			
	$ per			
	$ per			
	TOTAL $			

If additional space is needed for Schedule A, Schedule B or Schedule C, list on separate sheet and attach.

SCHEDULE D - GENERAL INFORMATION ON APPLICANT (AND SPOUSE, IF (a) MARRIED AND LIVE IN A COMMUNITY PROPERTY STATE OR (b) THIS IS A JOINT APPLICATION WITH YOUR SPOUSE.

Are your principal cash deposits held in joint tenancy? ☐ Yes ☐ No   If yes, with whom?

Are any assets encumbered or debts secured except as indicated? ☐ Yes ☐ No   If yes, please itemize by debt and security on a separate sheet.

Are there any suits or unpaid judgements now pending against you? ☐ Yes ☐ No   If yes, please attach a separate sheet and give full details.

Have you ever voluntarily surrendered or had a vehicle, appliance, or any other item repossessed? ☐ Yes ☐ No   If yes, please attach a separate sheet and give full details.

Have you or your spouse ever been the subject of bankruptcy proceedings? ☐ Yes ☐ No   If yes, please attach a separate sheet and give full details.

Have you ever applied for or obtained credit under another name? ☐ Yes ☐ No   If yes, please give other name(s):

Do you have any other business connections? ☐ Yes ☐ No   If yes, please give details:

Are you a U.S. citizen? ☐ Yes ☐ No   If no, please give country of citizenship and visa status:

Number of dependents: Ages:

Life Insurance $	Name of Insured		Name of Company	
Beneficiary's name		Address		Relationship
Life Insurance $	Name of Insured		Name of Company	
Beneficiary's name		Address		Relationship
Automobile Insurance - Public Liability - ☐ Yes ☐ No		Property Damage - ☐ Yes ☐ No	Comprehensive Personal Liability - ☐ Yes ☐ No	

FOR INTERNAL BANK USE ONLY

STATEMENT OF BANK OFFICER:

I have reviewed this financial statement which has been signed by the person whose financial condition is shown above.

Bank of America NT&SA

By: _____
AUTHORIZED SIGNATURE

YOUR SIGNATURE

By signing below, you certify that the statements above and on any attachment(s) are true and complete as of the date given below. You authorize the Bank to verify or check any of the information given, check your credit references, verify employment and obtain credit reports (including your spouse, if you are married and live in a community property state). You also authorize the Bank to provide credit information about you and your accounts to others.

Date: _____ X_____
                          APPLICANT

Date: _____ X_____
                          APPLICANT

Figure 31. (*Continued*)

183

SBA LOAN INSTRUCTIONS

Applying to the SBA, or any government agency, for a loan is a complicated procedure. Read the instructions, rules, and regulations carefully. Be thorough and patient. These instructions might be your only path to entrepreneurial independence. Remember that government agencies and the officials who run them are the custodians of the public's wealth. There are many layers of responsibility—and blame—between the application to these agencies and their actual delivery of a check (or guarantee for a check). At each level of government, from Congress down to the grade 10 clerk, few employees want to stick their necks out. They prefer to go by the rules—because it's safer that way. In the long run, perhaps it is to the taxpayers' advantage. As we said at the outset, be thorough and patient, but be persistent. That pot o' gold could be just around the corner.

SBA *DIRECT* LOAN PACKAGE CHECKLIST

(1)   Two bank declination letters. These letters should include the amount and terms of the loan, the name and telephone number of the persons contacted at the banks, the reason for decline and whether or not the bank will participate with SBA.

(2)   Form DD214, Certificate of Release or Discharge from Active Duty.

(3)   SBA Form 4 (Application for Business Loan). Must be signed and dated with questions answered on back portion.

(4)   SBA Form 1261 (Statements Required by Laws and Executive Orders). This form must be signed and dated.

(5)   SBA Form 912 (Personal History Statement) for each owner, partner, officer, director, and stockholder with 20% or more ownership; instructions are on SBA Form 912.

_____

_____

_____

(6)   A signed current personal balance sheet (SBA Form 413 may be used for this purpose) for each owner, partner, officer, director, and stockholder with 20% or more ownership. Social Security number should be included on personal financial statement.

_____

_____

_____

(7)   A detailed resume for each principal.

(8)   A brief history of company and description of the benefits it will receive from loan.

(9)   Financial Data:
  a. Balance sheet and profit & loss statement no older than 90 days from date submitted.

b. Balance sheet and profit & loss statement for three (3) years, as applicable.

c. Personal tax returns for past three (3) years.

(10) Monthly Cash Flow Projections, and Operating Plan Forecast. (SBA Forms 1100 & 1099, respectively may be used).

(11) An itemized cost estimate of the machinery & equipment to be purchased, if applicable.

(12) An itemized cost estimate for the leasehold improvements, if applicable.

(13) A copy of the franchise agreement and FTC disclosure statement supplied to the franchisee by the franchisor, if applicable.

(14) FOR CONSTRUCTION AND/OR RENOVATIONS OVER $10,000:

(a) Include the estimated cost of the project

(b) Complete SBA Form 601, "Applicant's Agreement of Compliance."

(c) Provide copies of preliminary construction estimates, plans and specifications. Final plans will be required prior to disbursement.

(1) A completed Lender's Application for Guaranty or Participation, SBA Form 4-I.

(2) SBA Form 4 (Application for Business Loan). Must be signed and dated with questions answered on back portion.

(3) SBA Form 1261 (Statements Required by Laws and Executive Orders). This form must be signed and dated.

(4) SBA Form 912 (Personal History Statement) for each owner, partner, officer, director, and stockholder with 20% or more ownership; instructions are on SBA Form 912.

_____

_____

_____

(5) A signed current personal balance sheet (SBA Form 413 may be used for this purpose) for each owner, partner, officer, director, and stockholder with 20% or more ownership. Social

Security number should be included on personal financial statement.

_____

_____

_____

(6)   A detailed resume for each principal.

(7)   A brief history of company and description of the benefits it will receive from loan.

(8)   Financial Data:
          a. Balance sheet and profit & loss statement no older than 90 days from date submitted.
          b. Balance sheet and profit & loss statement for three (3) years, as applicable.
          c. Personal tax returns for past three (3) years.

(9)   Monthly Cash Flow Projections, and Operating Plan Forecast. (SBA Forms 1100 & 1099, respectively may be used).

(10)   An itemized cost estimate of the machinery & equipment to be purchased, if applicable.

(11)   An itemized cost estimate for the leasehold improvements, if applicable.

(12)   A copy of the franchise agreement and FTC disclosure statement supplied to the franchisee by the franchisor, if applicable.

(13)   FOR CONSTRUCTION AND/OR RENOVATIONS OVER $10,000:
          (a) Include the estimated cost of the project
          (b) Complete SBA Form 601, "Applicant's Agreement of Compliance."
          (c) Provide copies of preliminary construction estimates, plans and specifications. Final plans will be required prior to disbursement.

APPENDIX

PART 118

SBA RULES AND REGULATIONS

Filing Instructions: File this Part 118 immediately before Part 119.

This Part 118 establishes regulations to govern Small Business Administration's authority under Section 7(g) of the Small Business Act, as amended, to make Handicapped Assistance Loans.

PART 118—HANDICAPPED ASSISTANCE LOANS

Assistance to Certain Nonprofit Organizations and Small Business Concerns Owned by Handicapped Individuals

A proposal was issued on July 31, 1973 (38 FR 20351), to establish rules and regulations governing financial assistance to certain nonprofit organizations operated in the interests of the handicapped and to small business concerns owned, or to be owned, by handicapped individuals. The proposal established a new Part 118 to set forth guidelines for eligibility, credit terms, and procedures for financial assistance pursuant to section 7(g) of the Small Business Act, as amended. Interested persons were given till August 30, 1973, to submit written statements of facts, opinions, or arguments concerning the proposal. All comments submitted were given due consideration.

As a result of the comments received, the following changes are made:

1. Section 118.1, *Program objectives:* The proposal to limit financial assistance for nonprofit organizations to enable them to perform on Federal contracts under Public Law 92-23 (amended Wagner-O'Day Act), or to fulfill contracts and orders for goods and services from the private sector was considered to be too restrictive. Many workshops market products through their own retail outlets, many workshops have Federal contracts obtained on a competitive basis, and many State and local governments purchase goods and services from workshops and the proposed language appeared to limit this type of activity. The proposed language has, therefore, been revised to broaden the scope of the program objectives for nonprofit organizations to allow for financial assistance to enable these organizations to produce and provide marketable goods and services.

2. Section 118.2, *Definitions:* Many comments were submitted concerning the definition for "handicapped individuals." From the evaluation of the comments, it became apparent that a handicap which in any way limits the selection of employment refers to what is accomplished by employment and training at a workshop but does not apply to "engaging" in a business endeavor. The definition of "handicapped individual" has been modified to allow for this difference and now provides that only for HAL–2 loans should the degree of handicap limit the individual in engaging in normal competitive business practice. Definitions for the "Committee" and for "Central Nonprofit Organization" have been eliminated and the other definitions renumbered accordingly. Under the definition for "nonprofit organization", the word "direct" has been added to clarify production or provision of the commodities or services.

3. Section 118.11(a), Eligibility for HAL–1: The requirement for affiliation with a Central Nonprofit Organization has been eliminated as a result of a general expression that this provision was too restrictive and served no useful purpose in establishing the ability of the applicant organization to meet qualifications for loan assistance. Other new provisions which were recommended were not adopted on the same basis as being too restrictive.

4. Section 118.11(d), Eligibility for HAL–2: The word "professional" has been added to further define a "counselor" and the subparagraph concerning overcoming a handicap has been eliminated. It was pointed out the requirement, as stated in the authorizing legislation, that the handicap be of a permanent nature renders this provision redundant. It was also noted that the suggested provision could rule out for assistance the individual who has a permanent impairment but who has received training to ready him or her for employment or to overcome the handicap. This was not the intention of the proposal as every applicant must still demonstrate that the business can be operated in such a manner as reasonably to assure repayment.

5. Section 118.31, *Terms and conditions*, has been reworded to substitute clarifying language. The intent of the provision remains the same.

6. Section 118.41, *Participations*, has also been reworded to substitute clarifying language. The intent of this provision remain the same.

Many comments dealt with provisions which are of a statutory nature, such as the 75 percent man-hour employment requirement and the need for reasonable assurance of repayment and cannot be eliminated.

Accordingly, with these changes and additions, the proposed amendments are adopted as set forth below:

AUTHORITY: Section 7(g) of the Small Business Act, as amended (sec. 3, Pub. L. 92-595, 86 Stat. 1314; 15 U.S.C. 686(g)).

§ 118.1 Program objectives.

(a) Loans made to public or private nonprofit as defined in § 118.2(e), organizations (HAL–1) will be limited to nonprofit sheltered workshops and any similar organization to enable them to produce and provide marketable goods and services. It is not the purpose of these loans to provide for supportive services to workshops. These supportive services include, but are not limited to, subsidization of wages of low producers, health and rehabilitation services, and management. Usually such supportive services are funded by fees from State or local rehabilitation agencies, community fundraising drives, private donors, grants, bequests, and other Government programs. The Small Business Act prohibits the duplication of the work or activity of any other department or agency of the Federal Government unless expressly provided for.

(b) Loans made to eligible small business concerns owned by handicapped persons (HAL–2) are to assist in the establishment, acquisition, or operation of a small business.

§ 118.2 Definitions.

For purposes of this part:

(a) "Administrator" means the Administrator of the Small Business Administration.

(b) "SBA" means the Small Business Administration.

(c) "Small business concern" means a business concern which would qualify as a small business under § 121.3–10 of this chapter.

(d) The "Act" means the Small Business Act.

(e) "Nonprofit organization" means any public or private organization which is organized under the laws of the United States or of any State, operated in the interest of handicapped individuals, the net income of which does not inure in whole or in part to the benefit of any shareholder or other individual; and which, in the production of commodities and in the provision of services during any fiscal year in which it receives financial asistance under this program, employs handicapped individuals for not less than 75 percent of the man-hours required for the direct production or provision of the commodities or services.

(f) "Handicapped individual" means a person who has a physical, mental, or emotional impairment, defect, ailment, disease, or disability of a permanent nature which in any way limits the selection of any type of employment for which the person would otherwise be qualified or qualifiable and also, in the case of applications for HAL–2, which limits the individual(s) in engaging in normal competitive business practices without SBA loan assistance.

(g) "HAL–1" means a Handicapped Assistance Loan to a nonprofit organization, as defined in Paragraph (e) of this section.

(h) "HAL–2" means a Handicapped Assistance Loan to an eligible small business concern owned, or to be owned, by handicapped individual(s).

HANDICAPPED ASSISTANCE LOANS

§ 118.11 Eligibility.

(a) In order to be eligible to apply for a HAL–1, the nonprofit organization must submit certification that it is organized under the laws of the State, or of the United States, as a nonprofit organization operating in the interests of handicapped individuals. Such certification may include copies of by-laws, incorporation papers, certification of its tax exempt status as determined by the Internal Revenue Service ((501)(3)(c)), and recognition and approval by a State Vocational Rehabilitation Agency. It must provide documentation that it employs during any fiscal year in which it recieves SBA financial assistance, handicapped individuals for not less than 75 percent of the man-hours required for the direct production of commodities or in the provision of services which it renders. In addition it must comply with any applicable occupational health and safety standard which may be prescribed by the Secretary of Labor:

(1) Loans under HAL–1 are not to be used as a substitute for historical sources of funding.

(2) Financial assistance shall not be extended if funds are otherwise available on reasonable terms from private sources or other Federal, State or local programs. It must be demonstrated that:

(i) The applicant's bank account will not make the loan.

(ii) Private credit is not obtainable.

(iii) Grant funds from other Government programs are not available.

(iv) Contributions from foundations, local or state fund raising activities, including tax assessments, donations, and similar historical avenues of funding will not be diminished as a result of the SBA loan.

(b) In order to be eligible to apply for a MAL–2, a business must qualify under Parts 120 and 121 of this chapter, except where inconsistent with specific provisions in this part. In the case of a partnership, corporation, or cooperative, the business must be 100 percent owned by handicapped individuals.

(1) Applications for financial assistance may be considered only when there is evidence that the desired credit is not otherwise available on reasonable terms. The financial assistance applied for shall be deemed to be otherwise available on reasonable terms, unless it is satisfactorily demonstrated that:

(i) Proof of refusal of the required financial assistance has been obtained from

(A) The applicant's bank of account;

(B) If the amount of financial assistance applied for is in excess of the amount that the bank normally lends to any one borrower, then a refusal from a correspondent bank or from any other lending institution whose lending capacity is adequate to cover the financial assistance applied for; and

(C) Not less than 2 financial institutions for direct loans in cities where the population exceeds 200,000.

Proof of refusal must contain the date, amount and terms requested, and the reasons for not granting the desired credit. Bank refusal to advance credit should not be considered the full test of unavailability of credit and, where there is knowledge or reasons to believe that credit is otherwise available on reasonable terms from sources other than such banks, the financial assistance applied for cannot be granted notwithstanding the receipt of written refusals from such banks.

(ii) The financial assistance required does not appear to be obtainable:

(A) On reasonable terms through the public offering or private placing of securities of the applicant;

(B) Through the disposal at a fair price of assets not required by the applicant in the conduct of the existing business or not reasonably necessary to its potential healthy growth; and

(C) Without undue hardship through utilization of the personal credit resources of the owner, partners, management, or principal shareholders of the applicant;

(D) Through other applicable Government financing, including SBA's regular Business Loan Program and its Economic Opportunity Loan Program.

(c) Under HAL-2 financial assistance may be used to acquire a business.

(d) Applicants for assistance under HAL-2 must provide information from a physician, psychiatrist, and/or professional counselor in writing as to the permanent nature of the handicap and the limitations it places on the applicant.

(e) Direct loan assistance is subject to the availability of funds.

§ 118.21 Limitations on use of proceeds.

(a) Loans for nonprofit organizations HAL-1) may not be used for:

(1) Training, education, housing; or other supportive services for handicapped employees of sheltered workshops.

(2) Construction of facilities if a construction grant is available from other Government sources.

(3) Purchase of a building when mortgage insurance through other Federal agencies is available.

(b) Restrictions on use of proceeds for HAL-2 loans are the same as for regular SBA business loans with the exception of acquisition of a business.

§ 118.31 Terms and conditions.

(a) HAL loans shall not be made, participated in, or guaranteed if the total amount of the Government's share of such assistance to a single borrower at any one time exceeds a total outstanding of $350,000. The loan limit applies collectively to all HAL-2 loans to business entities owned or controlled by affiliated ownership and for all HAL-1 loans to the specific applicant nonprofit organization.

(1) The administrative ceiling on a direct loan is $100,000, and $150,000 as the SBA share of an immediate participation loan. Acceptance of such applications is subject to availability of funds.

(b) Interest on direct loans and the SBA share of an immediate participation loan is 3 percent per annum.

(c) Subject to the approval of SBA, the participants share of immediate participation loans and on guaranteed loans prior to SBA's purchase, the interest rate shall be at a legal and reasonable rate. Maximum allowable rates for the bank share of any HAL loan shall be the same as established for business and Economic Opportunity loans which are set forth in Part 120.3(b)(2).

(d) The interest rate on SBA's share of a guaranteed loan after purchase by SBA becomes the same as the rate for direct loans. SBA's payment to the guaranteed participant of accrued interest to the date of purchase shall be at the interest rate established by participant but shall not exceed an effective rate of interest of 8 percent per annum, and without any future adjustment for any unpaid accrued interest in excess of 8 pecent per annum.

(e) Repayment will be required at the earliest feasible Gate giving consideration to the use to be made of the funds and indicated ability to repay with 15 years as the absolute maximum. When deemed necessary, grace periods for payment of principal may be provided. Interest payments must be made as soon after the loan is disbursed as possible and will be required during any grace period. A fluctuating repayment schedule may be established for seasonal businesses or nonprofit organizations.

§ 118.41 Participations.

(a) It is the policy to stimulate and encourage loans by banks and other lending institutions.

(1) An applicant for a direct HAL loan must show that an immediate participation or guaranteed loan is not available. An applicant for any immediate participation loan must show that a guaranteed loan is not available.

(2) SBA's share of immediate participation loans shall not exceed 75 percent of the loan. Exceptions

may be made in cases when the participant's legal lending limit precludes a 25 percent participation. In such cases the participant will be required to share in the loan to the extent of its legal lending limit but in no event less than 10 percent. In guaranteed loans the exposure of SBA under the guaranty may not exceed 90 percent of the unpaid principal balance and accrued interest.

(3) The guaranty fee paid by the bank to SBA on the guaranteed portion of a loan and the service fee charged by the bank to SBA on SBA's share of an immediate participation loan shall be the same as those fees applicable on regular business loans.

(4) No agreement to extend financial assistance under this program shall establish any preferences in favor of a bank or other lending institution.

§ 118.51 Credit requirements.

(a) An applicant must meet certain practical credit requirements established by SBA. Principal requirements are as follows:

(1) An applicant must be of good character as determined by SBA.

(2) There must be evidence that the ability exists to operate the business or the nonprofit organization successfully.

(3) There must be enough capital invested in the business so that, with assistance through SBA, the business will be able to operate on a sound financial basis.

(4) As required by the Small Business Act, as amended, the proposed loan, whether direct, immediate participation, or guaranteed must be "of such sound value or so secured as reasonably to assure repayment."

(i) In those border line cases where a reasonable doubt exists as to repayment ability, the decision shall be resolved in favor of the applicant.

(5) The loan should be secured by collateral of a type, amount, and value which, considered with other factors, such as the character and ability of the management, and of the prospective earnings, will afford the required assurance of repayment.

(i) On loans to be made to finance Federal Government contracts, an assignment of amounts to come due under such contracts may be required.

(ii) Personal guaranties of the officers or directors of nonprofit organizations (HAL–1) shall not be required.

(6) The past earnings record and future prospects of the firm for HAL $ 2 loans must indicate ability to repay the loan out of income from the business.

(i) For loans to nonprofit organizations (HAL–1), evidence that the organization has the capability and experience to perform successfully on the work to be performed must be furnished but it is not necessary that the loan be repaid from the earnings of the organization if repayment ability can be determined on another basis.

§ 118.61 Application procedures.

(a) An applicant desiring to obtain HAL assistance shall apply to the regional, district, or branch office servicing the area where the business or nonprofit organization is located, or to the applicant's bank which in turn will apply for the SBA guaranty to the regional, district, or branch office servicing the area where the business or nonprofit organization is located.

(1) If another SBA office is closer, the applicant may obtain counseling, advice, or assistance in filing an application from that office.

(2) Addresses of SBA offices are listed in Part 101 of this chapter.

(b) After a direct loan application has been submitted to SBA and has been approved or declined, the regional or district office will send a letter of notification to the applicant. In cases of decline, the reasons will be stated. When a bank is participating, the bank will be notified of the final decision.

(1) In the event of decline, the applicant may request a reconsideration from the declining office within six months. A reconsideration request must include new or additional information which will overcome the stated reasons for decline.

§ 118.71 Applicability of other SBA regulations.

(a) All applicable provisions of Parts 120 and 122 of this chapter shall apply to HAL's except where other provision is made in this part.

Published Date: November 6, 1973

Effective Date: November 5, 1973

Cite: 38 F. R. 30546

APPENDIX

U.S. Small Business Administration

AGREEMENT OF COMPLIANCE

In compliance with Executive Order 11246, as amended (Executive Order 11246, as amended prohibits discrimination because of race, color, religion, sex, or national origin, and requires affirmative action to ensure equality of opportunity in all aspects of employment by all contractors and subcontractors, performing work under a Federally assisted construction contract in excess of $10,000, regardless of the number of employees), the applicant/recipient, contractor or subcontractor agrees that in consideration of the approval and as a condition of the disbursement of all or any part of a loan by the Small Business Administration (SBA) that it will incorporate or cause to be incorporated into any contract or subcontract in excess of $10,000 for construction work, or modification thereof, as defined in the regulations of the Secretary of Labor, at 41 CFR Chapter 60, which is paid for in whole or in part with funds obtained from the Federal Government or borrowed on the credit of the Federal Government pursuant to a grant, contract, loan, insurance or guarantee, or undertaken pursuant to any Federal program involving such grant, contract, loan, insurance or guarantee, the following equal opportunity clause:

During the performance of this contract, the contractor agrees as follows:

(1) The contractor will not discriminate against any employee or applicant for employment because of race, color, religion, sex or national origin. The contractor will take affirmative action to insure that applicants are employed, and that employees are treated during employment without regard to their race, color, religion, sex or national origin. Such action shall include, but not be limited to the following: employment, upgrading, demotion or transfer; recruitment or advertising; layoff or termination; rates of pay or other forms of compensation; and selection for training, including apprenticeship. The contractor agrees to post in conspicuous places, available to employees and applicants for employment, notices to be provided setting forth the provisions of this nondiscrimination clause.

(2) The contractor will, in all solicitations or advertisements for employees placed by or on behalf of the contractor, state that all qualified applicants will receive consideration for employment without regard to race, color, religion, sex or national origin.

(3) The contractor will send to each labor union or representative of workers with which he has a collective bargaining agreement or other contract or understanding, a notice to be provided advising the said labor union or workers' representative of the contractor's commitments under Executive Order 11246, as amended, and shall post copies of the notice in conspicuous places available to employees and applicants for employment.

(4) The contractor will comply with all provisions of Executive Order 11246, as amended, and the rules and relevant orders of the Secretary of Labor created thereby.

(5) The contractor will furnish all information and reports required by Executive Order 11246, as amended, and by the rules, regulations and orders of the Secretary of Labor, or pursuant thereto, and will permit access to books, records and accounts by SBA (See SBA Form 793) and the Secretary of Labor for purposes of investigation to ascertain compliance with such rules, regulations and orders. (The information collection requirements contained in Executive Order 11246, as amended, are approved under OMB No. 1215-0072.)

(6) In the event of the contractor's noncompliance with the nondiscrimination clause or with any of the said rules, regulations or orders, this contract may be cancelled, terminated or suspended in whole or in part and the contractor may be declared ineligible for further Government contracts or federally assisted construction contracts in accordance with procedures authorized in Executive Order 11246, as amended, and such other sanctions may be imposed and remedies invoked as provided in the said Executive Order or by rule, regulation or order of the Secretary of Labor, or as otherwise provided by law.

The contractor will include the portion of the sentence immediately preceding paragraph (1) and the provisions of paragraphs (1) through (6) in every subcontract or purchase order unless exempted by rules, regulations or orders of the Secretary of Labor issued pursuant to Executive Order 11246, as amended, so that such provisions will be binding upon each subcontractor or vendor. The contractor will take such action with respect to any subcontract or purchase order as SBA may direct as a means of enforcing such provisions, including sanctions for noncompliance: Provided, however that in the event a contractor becomes involved in or is threatened with litigation with a subcontractor or vendor as a result of such direction by SBA, the contractor may request the United States to enter into such litigation to protect the interest of the United States.

SBA Form 601 (10-85) REF: SOP 9030 Previous editions are obsolete

SBA LOAN INSTRUCTIONS

The Applicant further agrees that it will be bound by the above equal opportunity clause with respect to its own employment practices when it participates in federally assisted construction work.

The Applicant agrees that is will assist and cooperate actively with SBA and the Secretary of Labor in obtaining the compliance of contractors and subcontractors with the equal opportunity clause and the rules, regulations and relevant orders of the Secretary of Labor, that it will furnish SBA and the Secretary of Labor such information as they may require for the supervision of such compliance, and that it will otherwise assist SBA in the discharge of the Agency's primary responsibility for securing compliance. The Applicant further agrees that it will refrain from entering into any contract or contract modification subject to Executive Order 11246, as amended, and will carry out such sanctions and penalties for violation of the equal opportunity clause as may be imposed upon contractors and subcontractors by SBA or the Secretary of Labor or such other sanctions and penalties for violation thereof as may, in the opinion of the Administrator, be necessary and appropriate.

In addition, the Applicant agrees that it if fails or refuses to comply with these undertakings SBA may take any or all of the following actions: cancel, terminate or suspend in whole or in part the loan; refrain from extending any further assistance to the applicant under the programs with respect to which the failure or refusal occurred until satisfactory assurance of future compliance has been received from such applicant; and refer the case to the Department of Justice for appropriate legal proceedings.

In consideration of the approval by the Small Business Administration of a loan to _____
_____ Applicant, said Applicant and _____
the general contractor, mutually promise and agree that the(y) will comply with all nondiscrimination provisions and requirements of Executive Order 11246, as amended.

Executed the _____ day of _____ 19___.

_____
Name, Address, & Phone No. of Applicant

By _____
Typed Name & Title of Authorized Official

Corporate Seal

_____
Signature of Authorized Official

_____
Name, Address, & Phone No. of Subrecipient

By _____
Typed Name & Title of Authorized Official

Corporate Seal

_____
Signature of Authorized Official

SBA Form 601 (10-85) REF: SOP 9030 Previous editions are obsolete

☆ U.S.G.P.O.: 1988 - 518-684/61850

APPENDIX

SMALL BUSINESS ADMINISTRATION

POLICY AND REGULATIONS CONCERNING REPRESENTATIVES AND THEIR FEES

An applicant for a loan from SBA may obtain the assistance of any attorney, accountant, engineer, appraiser or other representative to aid him in the preparation and presentation of his application to SBA; however, such representation is not mandatory. In the event a loan is approved, the services of an attorney may be necessary to assist in the preparation of closing documents, title abstracts, etc. SBA will allow the payment of reasonable fees or other compensation for services performed by such representatives on behalf of the applicant.

There are no "authorized representatives" of SBA, other than our regular salaried employees. Payment of any fee or gratuity to SBA employees is illegal and will subject the parties to such a transaction to prosecution.

SBA Regulations (Part 103, Sec. 103.13-5(c)) prohibit representatives from charging or proposing to charge any contingent fee for any services performed in connection with an SBA loan unless the amount of such fee bears a necessary and reasonable relationship to the services actually performed; or to charge any fee which is deemed by SBA to be unreasonable for the services actually performed; or to charge for any expenses whch are not deemed by SBA to have been necessary in connection with the application. The Regulations (Part 122, Sec. 122.19) also prohibit the payment of any bonus, brokerage fee or commission in connection with SBA loans.

In line with these Regulations SBA will not approve placement or finder's fees for the use or attempted use of influence in obtaining or trying to obtain an SBA loan, or fees based solely upon a percentage of the approved loan or any part thereof.

Fees which will be approved will be limited to reasonable sums for services actually rendered in connection with the application or the closing, based upon the time and effort required, the qualifications of the representative and the nature and extent of the services rendered by such representative. Representatives of loan applicants will be required to execute an agreement as to their compensation for services rendered in connection with said loan.

It is the responsibility of the applicant to set forth in the appropriate section of the application the names of all persons or firms engaged by or on behalf of the applicant. Applicants are required to advise the Regional Office in writing of the names and fees of any representatives engaged by the applicant subsequent to the filing of the application. This reporting requirement is approved under OMB Approval Number 3245-0016.

Any loan applicant having any question concerning the payment of fees, or the reasonableness of fees, should communicate with the Field Office where the application is filed.

SBA FORM 394 (8-83) REF: SOP 50.10 PREVIOUS EDITIONS OBSOLETE   ☆ U.S.G.P.O.: 1987 – 516-451/61576

194

SBA REPRINTS

The following booklets, "The ABC's of Borrowing" and "Sound Cash Management and Borrowing," are publications of the U.S. Small Business Administration. You may make copies of them by photocopying, or order them under Management Aid Number 1.001 and 1.016 by sending $1.50 (to get both) check or money order to U.S. Small Business Administration, P.O. Box 15434, Fort Worth, TX 76119. You can also contact your nearest SBA or SCORE office to obtain the booklets.

U.S. Small Business Administration Management Assistance Support Services Section	Management Aids Number 1.001

SBA

The ABC's of Borrowing

Summary

Some small businesspersons cannot understand why a lending institution refused to lend them money. Others have no trouble getting funds, but they are surprised to find strings attached to their loans. Such owner-managers fail to realized that banks and other lenders have to operate by certain principles just as do other types of business.

This Aid discusses the following fundamentals of borrowing: (1) credit worthiness, (2) kinds of loans, (3) amount of money needed, (4) collateral, (5) loan restrictions and limitations, (6) the loan application, and (7) standards which the lender uses to evaluate the application.

Introduction

Inexperience with borrowing procedures often creates resentment and bitterness. The stories of three small businesspersons illustrate this point.

"I'll never trade here again," Bill Smith* said when his bank refused to grant him a loan. "I'd like to let you have it, Bill," the banker said,"but your firm isn't earning enough to meet your current obligations." Mr Smith was unaware of a vital financial fact, namely, that lending institutions have to be certain that the borrower's business can repay the loan.

Tom Jones lost his temper when the bank refused him a loan because he did not know what kind or how much money he needed. "We hesitate to lend," the banker said, "to business owners with such vague ideas of what and how much they need."

John Williams' case was somewhat different. He didn't explode until after he got the loan. When the papers were ready to sign, he realized that the loan agreement put certain limitations on his business activities. "You can't dictate to me." he said and walked out of the bank. What he didn't realize was that the limitations were for his good as well as for the bank's protection.

Knowledge of the financial facts of business life could have saved all three the embarrassment of losing their tempers. Even more important, such information would have helped them to borrow money at a time when their businesses needed it badly.

*All names in Aids are fictitious

2

This **Aid** is designed to give the highlights of what is involved in sound business borrowing. It should be helpful to those who have little or no experience with borrowing. More experienced owner-managers should find it useful in re-evaluating their borrowing operations.

Is Your Firm Credit Worthy?

The ability to obtain money when you need it is as necessary to the operation of your business as is a good location or the right equipment, reliable sources of supplies and materials, or an adequate labor force. Before a bank or any other lending agency will lend you money, the loan officer must feel satisfied with the answers to the five following questions:

1. What sort of person are you, the prospective borrower? By all odds, the character of the borrower comes first. Next is your ability to manage your business.
2. What are you going to do with the money? The answer to this questions will determine the type of loan, short or long-term. Money to be used for the purchase of seasonal inventory will require quicker repayment than money used to buy fixed assets.
3. When and how do you plan to pay it back? Your banker's judgment of your business ability and the type of loan will be a deciding factor in the answer to this question.
4. Is the cushion in the loan large enough? In other words, does the amount requested make suitable allowance for unexpected developments? The banker decides this question on the basis of your financial statement which sets forth the condition of your business and on the collateral pledged.
5. What is the outlook for business in general and for your business particularly?

Adequate Financial Data Is a "Must."
The banker wants to make loans to businesses which are solvent, profitable, and growing. The two basic financial statements used to determine those conditions are the balance sheet and profit-and-loss statement. The former is the major yardstick for solvency and the latter for profits. A continuous series of these two statements over a period of time is the principal device for measuring financial stability and growth potential.

In interviewing loan applicants and in studying their records, the banker is expecially interested in the following facts and figures.

General Information: Are the books and records up-to-date and in good condition? What is the condition of accounts payable? Of notes payable? What are the salaries of the owner-manager and other company officers? Are all taxes being paid currently? What is the order backlog? What is the number of employees? What is the insurance coverage?

Accounts Receivable: Are there indications that some of the accounts receivable have already been pledged to another creditor? What is the accounts receivable turnover? Is the accounts receivable total weakened because many customers are far behind in their payments? Has a large enough reserve been set up to cover doubtfull accounts? How much do the largest accounts owe and what percentage of your total accounts does this amount represent?

Inventories: Is merchandise in good shape or will it have to be marked down? How much raw material is on hand? How much work is in process? How much of the inventory is finished goods?

Is there any obsolete inventory? Has an excessive amount of inventory been consigned to customers? Is inventory turnover in line with the turnover for other businesses in the same industry? Or is money being tied up too long in inventory?

Fixed Assets: What is the type, age, and condition of the equipment? What are the depreciation policies? What are the details of mortgages or conditional sales contracts? What are the future acquisition plans?

What Kind of Money?

When you set out to borrow money for your firm, it is important to know the kind of money you need from a bank or other lending institution. There are three kinds of money: short term, term money, and equity capital.

Keep in mind that the purpose for which the funds are to be used is an important factor in deciding the kind of money needed. But even so, deciding what kind of money to use is not always easy. It is sometimes complicated by the fact that you may be using some of the various kinds of money at the same time and for identical purposes.

Keep in mind that a very important distinction between the types of money is the source of repayment. Generally, short-term loans are repaid from the liquidation of current assets which they have financed. Long-term loans are usually repaid from earnings.

Short-Term Bank Loans

You can use short-term bank loans for purposes such as financing accounts receivable for, say 30 to 60 days. Or you can use them for purposes that take longer to pay off—such as for building a seasonal inventory over a period of 5 to 6 months. Usually, lenders expect short-term loans to be repaid after their purposes have been served: for example, accounts receivable loans, when the outstanding accounts have been paid by the borrower's customers, and inventory loans, when the inventory has been converted into saleable merchandise.

Banks grant such money either on your general credit reputation with an unsecured loan or on a secured loan.

The unsecured loan is the most frequently used form of bank credit for short-term purposes. You do not have to put up collateral because the bank relies on your credit reputation.

The secured loan involves a pledge of some or all of your assets. The bank requires security as a protection for its depositors against the risks that are involved even in business situations where the chances of success are good.

Term Borrowing

Term borrowing privides money you plan to pay back over a fairly long time. Some people break it down into two forms: (1) intermediate—loans longer than 1 year but less than 5 years, and (2) long-term—loans for more than 5 years.

However, for your purpose of matching the kind of money to the needs of your company, think of term borrowing as a kind of money which you probably will pay back in periodic installments from earnings.

Equity Capital

Some people confuse term borrowing and equity (or investment) capital. Yet there is a big difference. You don't have to repay equity money. It is money you get by selling a part interest in your business.

You take people into your company who are willing to risk their money in it. They are interested in potential income rather than in an immediate return on their investment.

How Much Money?

The amount of money you need to borrow depends on the purpose for which you need funds. Figuring the amount of money required for business construction,

3

198

conversion, or expansion—term loans or equity capital—is relatively easy. Equipment manufacturers, architects, and builders will readily supply you with cost estimates. On the other hand, the amount of working capital you need depends upon the type of business you're in. While rule-of-thumb ratios may be helpful as a starting point, a detailed projection of sources and uses of funds over some future period of time—usually for 12 months—is a better approach. In this way, the characteristics of the particular situation can be taken into account. Such a projection is developed through the combination of a predicted budget and a cash forecast.

The budget is based on recent operating experience plus your best judgment of performance during the coming period. The cash forecast is your estimates of cash receipts and disbursements during the budget period. Thus, the budget and the cash forecast together represent your plan for meeting your working capital requirements.

To plan your working capital requirements, it is important to know the "cash flow" which your business will generate. This involves simply a consideration of all elements of cash receipts and disbursements at the time they occur. These elements are listed in the profit-and-loss statement which has been adapted to show cash flow. They should be projected for each month.

What Kind of Collateral?

Sometimes, your signature is the only security the bank needs when making a loan. At other times, the bank requires additional assurance that the money will be repaid. The kind and amount of security depends on the bank and on the borrower's situation.

If the loan required cannot be justified by the borrower's financial statements alone, a pledge of security may bridge the gap. The types of security are: endorsers; comakers and guarantors; assignment of leases; trust receipts and floor planning; chattel mortgages; real estate; accounts receivables; savings accounts; life insurance policies; and stocks and bonds. In a substantial number of States where the Uniform Commercial Code has been enacted, paperwork for recording loan transactions will be greatly simplified.

Endorsers, Co-makers, and Guarantors
Borrowers often get other people to sign a note in order to bolster their own credit. These **endorsers** are contingently liable for the note they sign. If the borrower fails to pay up, the bank expects the endorser to make the note good. Sometimes, the endorser may be asked to pledge assets or securities too.

A **co-maker** is one who creates an obligation jointly with the borrower. In such cases, the bank can collect directly from either the maker or the co-maker.

A **guarantor** is one who guarantees the payment of a note by signing a guaranty commitment. Both private and government lenders often require guarantees from officers of corporations in order to assure continuity of effective management. Sometimes, a manufacturer will act as guarantor for customers.

Assignment of Leases
The assigned lease as security is similar to the guarantee. It is used, for example, in some franchise situations.

The bank lends the money on a building and takes a mortgage. Then the lease, which the dealer and the parent franchise company work out, is assigned so that the bank automatically receives the rent payments. In this manner, the bank is guaranteed repayment of the loan.

Warehouse Receipts
Banks also take commodities as security by lending money on a warehouse receipt. Such a receipt is usually delivered directly to the bank and shows that the merchandise used as security either has been placed in a public warehouse or has been left on your premises under the control of one of your employees who is bonded (as in field warehousing). Such loans are generally made on staple or standard merchandise which can be readily marketed. The typical warehouse receipt loan is for a percentage of the estimated value of the goods used as securtiy.

Trust Receipts and Floor Planning
Merchandise, such as automobiles, appliances, and boats, has to be displayed to be sold. The only way many small marketers can afford such displays is by borrowing money. Such loans are often secured by a note and a trust receipt.

This trust receipt is the legal paper for floor planning. It is used for serial-numbered merchandise. When you sign one, you (1) acknowledge receipt of the merchandise, (2) agree to keep the merchandise in trust for the bank, and (3) promise to pay the bank as you sell the goods.

Chattel Mortgages
If you buy equipment such as a cash register or a delivery truck, you may want to get a chattel mortgage loan. You give the bank a lien on the equipment you are buying.

4

The bank also evaluates the present and future market value of the equipment being used to secure the loan. How rapidly will it depreciate? Does the borrower have the necessary fire, theft, property damage, and public liability insurance on the equipment? The banker has to be sure that the borrower protects the equipment.

Real Estate

Real estate is another form of collateral for long-term loans. When taking a real estate mortgage, the bank finds out: (1) the location of the real estate, (2) its physical condition, (3) its foreclosure value, and (4) the amount of insurance carried on the property.

Accounts Receivable

Many banks lend money on accounts receivable. In effect, you are counting on your customers to pay your note.

The bank may take accounts receivable on a notification or a nonnotification plan. Under the **notification** plan, the purchaser of the goods is informed by the bank that his or her account has been assigned to it and he or she is asked to pay the bank. Under the **nonnotification** plan, the borrower's customers continue to pay you the sums due on their accounts and you pay the bank.

Savings Accounts

Sometimes, you might get a loan by assigning to the bank a savings account. In such cases, the bank gets an asignment from you and keeps your passbook. If you assign an account in another bank as collateral, the lending bank asks the other bank to mark its records to show that the account is held as collateral.

Life Insurance

Another kind of collateral is life insurance. Banks will lend up to the cash value of a life insurance policy. You have to assign the policy to the bank.

If the policy is on the life of an executive of a small corporation, corporate resolutions must be made authorizing the assignment. Most insurance companies allow you to sign the policy back to the original beneficiary when the assignment to the bank ends.

Some people like to use life insurance as collateral rather than borrow directly from insurance companies. One reason is that a bank loan is often more convenient to obtain and usually may be obtained at a lower interest rate.

Stocks and Bonds

If you use stocks and bonds as collateral, they must be marketable. As a protection against market declines and possible expenses of liquidation, banks usually lend no more than 75 percent of the market value of high grade stock. On Federal Government or municipal bonds, they may be willing to lend 90 percent or more of their market value.

The bank may ask the borrower for additional security or payment whenever the market value of the stocks or bonds drops below the bank's required margin.

What Are the Lender's Rules?

Lending institutions are not just interested in loan repayments. They are also interested in borrowers with healthy profit-making businesses. Therefore, whether or not collateral is required for a loan, they set loan limitations and restrictions to protect themselves against unnecessary risk and at the same time against poor management practices by their borrowers. Often some owner-managers consider loan limitations a burden.

Yet others feel that such limitations also offer an opportunity for improving their management techniques.

Especially in making long-term loans, the borrower as well as the lender should be thinking of: (1) the net earning power of the borrowing company, (2) the capability of its management, (3) the long range prospects of the company, and (4) the long range prospects of the industry of which the company is a part. Such factors often mean that limitations increase as the duration of the loan increases.

What Kinds of Limitations?

The kinds of limitations, which an owner-manager finds set upon the company depends, to a great extent, on the company. If the company is a good risk, only minimum limitations need be set. A poor risk, of course, is different. Its limitations should be greater than those of a stronger company.

Look now for a few moments at the kinds of limitations and restrictions which the lender may set. Knowing what they are can help you see how they affect your operations.

The limitations which you will usually run into when you borrow money are:

(1) Repayment terms.

(2) Pledging or the use of security.

(3) Periodic reporting.

5

A loan agreement, as you may already know, is a tailor-made document covering, or referring to, all the terms and conditions of the loan. With it, the lender does two things: (1) protects position as a creditor (keeps that position in as well a protected state as it was on the date the loan was made and (2) assures himself of repayment according to the terms.

The lender reasons that the borrower's business should **generate enough funds** to repay the loan while taking care of other needs. The lender considers that cash inflow should be great enough to do this without hurting the working capital of the borrower.

Covenants—Negative and Positive

The actual restrictions in a loan agreement come under a section known as covenants. Negative covenants are things which the borrower may not do without prior approval from the lender. Some examples are: further additions to the borrower's total debt, nonpledge to others of the borrower's assets, and issuance of dividends in excess of the terms of the loan agreement.

On the other hand, positive covenants spell out things which the borrower must do. Some examples are: (1) maintenance of a minimum net working capital. (2) carrying of adequate insurance, (3) repaying the loan according to the terms of the agreement, and (4) supplying the lender with financial statements and reports.

Overall, however, loan agreements may be amended from time to time and exceptions made. Certain provisions may be waived from one year to the next with the consent of the lender.

You Can Negotiate

Next time you go to borrow money, thrash out the lending terms before you sign. It is good practice no matter how badly you may need the money. Ask to see the papers in advance of the loan closing. Legitimate lenders are glad to cooperate.

Chances are that the lender may "give" some on the terms. Keep in mind also that, while you're mulling over the terms, you may want to get the advice of your associates and outside advisors. In short, try to get terms which you know your company can live with. Remember, however, that once the terms have been agreed upon and the loan is made (or authorized as in the case of SBA), you are bound by them.

The Loan Application

Now you have read about the various aspects of the lending process and are ready to apply for a loan. Banks

and other private lending institutions, as well as the Small Business Administration, require a loan application on which you list certain information about your business.

For the purposes of explaining a loan application, this **Aid** uses the Small Business Administration's application for a loan (SBA Form 4). The SBA form is more detailed than most bank forms. The bank has the advantage of prior knowledge of the applicant and his or her activities. Since SBA does not have such knowledge, its form is more detailed. Moreover, the longer maturities of SBA loans ordinarily will necessitate more knowledge about the applicant.

Before you get to the point of filling out a loan application, you should have talked with an SBA representative, or perhaps your accountant or banker, to make sure that your business is eligible for an SBA loan. Because of public policy, SBA cannot make certain types of loans. Nor can it make loans under certain conditions. For example, if you can get a loan on reasonable terms from a bank, SBA cannot lend you money. The owner-manager is also not eligible for an SBA loan if he or she can get funds by selling assets which his or her company does not need in order to grow.

When the SBA representative gives you a loan application, you will notice that most of its sections ("Application for Loan"—SBA Form 4) are self-explanatory. However, some applicants have trouble with certain sections because they do not know where to go to get the necessary information.

Section 3—"Collateral Offered" is an example. A company's books should show the net value of assets such as business real estate and business machinery and equipment. "Net" means what you paid for such assets less depreciation.

If an owner-manager's records do not contain detailed information on business collateral, such as real estate and machinery and equipment, the bank sometimes can get it from your Federal income tax returns. Reviewing the depreciation which you have taken for tax purposes on such collateral can be helpful in arriving at the value of these assets.

If you are a good manager, you should have your books balanced monthly. However, some businesses prepare balance sheets less regularly. In filling out your "Balance Sheet as of _____, 19 ___,Fiscal Year Ends _____," remember that you must show the condition of you business within 60 days of the date on your loan application. It is best to get expert advice when working

6

up such vital information. Your accountant or banker
will be able to help you.

Cash Budget

(For three months, ending March 31, 19 _____)

	January		February		March	
	Budget	Actual	Budget	Actual	Budget	Actual
Expected Cash Receipts:						
1. Cash sales						
2. Collections on accounts receivable						
3. Other income						
4. Total cash receipts						
Expected Cash Payments						
5. Raw materials						
6. Payroll						
7. Other factory expenses (including maintenance)						
8. Advertising						
9. Selling expense						
10. Administrative expense (including salary of owner-manager)						
11. New plant and equipment						
12. Other payments(taxes, including estimated income tax; repayment of loans; interest; etc.)						
13. Total cash payments						
14. **Expected Cash Balance** at beginning of the month						
15. Cash increase of decrease (item 4 minus item 13)						
16. Expected cash balance at end of month (item 14 plus item 15)						
17. Desired working cash balance						
18. Short-term loans needed (item 17 minus item 16, if item 17 is larger)						
19. Cash available for dividends, capital cash expenditures, and/or short investments (item 16 minus item 17, if item 16 is larger than item 17)						
Capital Cash:						
20. Cash available (item 19 after deducting dividends, etc.)						
21. Desired capital cash (item 11, new plant equipment)						
22. Long-term loans needed (item 21 less item 20, if item 20 is larger than item 20)						

7

Number 1.001
Previous Designation MA 170

Again, if your records do not show the details necessary for working up profit and loss statements, your Federal income tax returns may be useful in getting together facts for the SBA loan application.

Insurance

SBA also needs information about the kinds of insurance a company carries. The owner-manager gives these facts by listing various insurance policies.

Personal Finances

SBA also must know something about the personal financial condition of the applicant. Among the types of information are: personal cash position; source of income including salary and personal investments; stocks, bonds, real estate, and other property owned in the applicant's own name; personal debts including installment credit payments, life insurance premiums, and so forth.

Evaluating the Application

Once you have supplied the necessary information, the next step in the borrowing process is the evaluation of your application. Whether the processing officer is in a bank or in SBA, the officer considers the same kinds of things when determining whether to grant or refuse the loan. The SBA loan processor looks for:

(1) The borrower's debt paying record to suppliers, banks, home mortgage holders, and other creditors.

(2) The ratio of the borrower's debt to net worth.

(3) The past earnings of the company.

(4) The value and condition of the collateral which the borrower offers for security.

The SBA loan processor also looks for: (1) the borrower's management ability, (2) the borrower's character, and (3) the future prospects of the borrower's business.

Copies of this **Aid** are available free from SBA, P.O. Box 15434, Fort Worth, TX 76119. **Aids** may be condensed or reproduced. They may not be altered to imply approval by SBA of any private organization, product or service. If material is reused, credit to SBA will be appreciated. Use of funds for printing this publication has been approved by the Director of the Office of Management and Budget through June 30, 1985.

8

U.S. Small Business Administration
Office of
Business Development

Management Aids
Number 1.016

SBA

Sound Cash Management and Borrowing

By John F. Murphy
Retired bank executive and member of the Manasota
SCORE Chapter, Sarasota, Florida

Summary

Poor management is the reason why some owner-managers of small firms have trouble when they try to borrow. Those managers often fail to forecast and to plan for cash needs. The resulting business ailment is a "cash crises."

Sound management must be practiced if loans are to be obtained and used profitably. Such management includes: knowing the firm's cash flow, forecasting cash needs, planning to borrow at the appropriate time, and substantiating the firm's payback ability.

This Aid includes examples of the following: a cash budget forecast, a projection of borrowing requirements, and a cash flow schedule for repaying a loan.

In spite of respectable sales volumes, many owners of small businesses run into financial trouble. Some get in so deep that they are barely able to pull their heads back above water. Others find themselves only weeks or months away from tacking "out of business" signs on their doors.

Often these owner-managers have three things in common. First, they know their line of business. Their technical ability is first rate. Second, they are poor managers. In many instances, they fail to plan ahead because of their enthusiasm for the operating side of their business. In the third place, most of them feel that additional money will solve their problems. They think that a loan will pull them out of the red.

Lending Officer's Viewpoint

Often a bank lending officer refuses or "declines" that loan request of such manager-owners. It is not that a banker lacks appreciation for the hard work and long hours which these owners put into their businesses. Nor does the bank question their good intentions.

Foremost in the lender's mind is the question: Can the firm pay back this loan? Thus, in many cases, the lender refuses the loan because the owner-manager hastily and haphazardly prepared the loan application under pressuring circumstances. As a result, the lending officer detects an air of instability and lack of planning in the owner-manager's description of his or her affairs. "How is the borrower really going to repay," the lending officer asks, "if the borrower doesn't actually know how much money is needed and how it is going to be used?"

2

If your request for a loan is turned down, the best bet is to accept the refusal gracefully and look for weaknesses in the presentation. You can correct these weaknesses when applying for a loan in the future.

Pertinent Questions

The lender needs the answers to several pertinent questions to determine whether or not the borrower can repay the loan. One of these questions is: What does the borrower intend to use the money for?

What Kind of Money? When you consider borrowing, determine what kind of money you need. A business uses four basic types of money in its operations. Your purpose in borrowing will determine the type.

1. Trade Credit. This type of "money" is not borrowed. It is money you owe your suppliers who permit you to carry your fast-moving inventory on open account. A good credit experience is proven evidence of your ability to repay borrowed funds.

2. Short-Term Credit. Banks and other lenders will provide this type of money to carry you in your purchases of inventory for special reasons, such as buying inventory for the next selling season. Such loans are self-liquidating because they generate sales dollars. You repay short-term credit in less than a year.

3. Long-Term Credit. Such loans—for more than a year—are used for expansion or modernization of your business. They are repaid out of accumulated profits. Usually, the evidence of this type of loan in a small business is a mortgage or a promissory note with terms.

4. Equity Funds. This type of money is never repaid. You get it by relinquishing a part of your profits to an investor. That is you sell an interest in your business.

Many owner-managers fail to recognize the difference between the four types of money. You should keep in mind that money borrowed for a temporary purpose should be used in the profit producing areas of your business and will be repaid out of that operation. Equity funds are those which remain in the business and increase the net worth for the owner.

Are Your Sales Adequate? Are you asking for a loan to bolster sagging sales volume? To buy additional stocks of high-volume merchandise which you feel has even greater potential? To create a new image by an over-all advertising campaign?

What Is Your Receivables Position? Are your accounts going uncollected and getting old? In effect, do you really need money to carry old accounts?

Is Your Profit Margin Adequate? Are you doing a lot of business and showing a lack of profit thus indicating that expenses are not controlled? Or is your market insufficient? What is your breakeven point for profits?

What Is Your Plan For Repayment? Do you forecast your cash income and expenditures realistically?

The lender scrutinizes the cash flow of the business to determine whether or not the owner-manager is providing sufficient cash to meet the firm's obligations. The lender also has to make sure that cash needed for working capital is not being absorbed by the business into other areas of equity and thereby reducing liquidity.

The "Cash Crisis"

The experience of counsellors, such as members of SCORE (SBA's Service Corps of Retired Executives) volunteers, is that all too often the small business owner feels that his or her needs are financial when they are actually managerial. In such firms, money can ease the pressure temporarily, but further indebtedness only intensifies the basic problem. Money alone cannot provide the sound management needed to continue the business.

Counsellors to small business owners are continually faced with the "cash crisis" problem. This cash deficiency results from the lack of planning.

A mistake many purchasers of a business make is that they buy something beyond their means. They take possession of a business of some value but without one important asset—sufficient operating cash. When a buyer does not put aside working capital (cash), he or she cannot pay current bills and the rest of the story is easy to foretell.

It is the "cash crisis."

Sound management consists of arranging matters so that current liabilities are provided for as they become due and hence paid promptly. When such coordination is not present, the result is a constant "cash crisis."

Without a floating supply of cash, a business will experience occasional convulsions which distort, confuse, embarrass, and alarm everyone concerned with the enterprise. The owner-manager's employees and suppliers are the first to sense the nervousness of the situation. When they do, they begin to consider their futures

in the light of these emergencies.

Lack of cash can drive a firm into bankruptcy even though its products are first rate and its operations are profitable.

Avoid A "Cash Crisis"

To avoid a "cash crisis" you should determine how much cash your firm needs for its normal operations. Then plan your finances to achieve the goal. The amount of cash which a business will need differs because all businesses are not alike. Usually, for comfort, five to ten percent of a firm's working capital should be in cash.

In a sense, financial planning is what you anticipate your financial statements will show on a specific date and how you intend to get there. A cash forecast will indicate whether or not your plan of operation is feasible. A budget will indicate the availability of cash at all points of operations.

Cash Budgeting

When the subject of budgeting comes up, some owner-managers say, "That's for the big fellow. I know what my volume is and my bank account tells me how much money I have." These owners fail to realize that budgeting can help to eliminate errors of judgment made in haste or made on assumptions rather than facts.

The first thing you must know in budgeting is what your anticipated expenses are going to be for the period being budgeted. Then, how much in sales must be generated to pay these expenses? What will be left? You must try to determine the high and low points in your operations in order to provide the adequate amount of cash. A sales analysis of previous periods will indicate when the high and low points occur.

This forecasting helps you to plan for financing the purchase of inventory and for carrying your accounts receivable. Controlling inventory and accounts receivable can help to take the strain off of your working capital.

Uses Of A Cash Budget. The cash budget is the most effective tool for planning the cash requirements and resources of your business. With it you plan your financial operations—the cash you expect to take in and pay out. Your goal in budgeting is to maintain a satisfactory cash position for any contingency. When used to project the cash flow of the business, the cash budget will:

3

Provide efficient use of cash by timing cash disbursements to coincide with cash receipts. These actions may reduce the need for borrowing temporary additional working capital.

Point up cash deficiency periods so that predetermined borrowing requirements may be established and actual amounts determined to reduce excessive indebtedness.

Determine periods for repayment of borrowings.

Establish the practicability of taking trade discounts or not taking them.

Determine periods of surplus cash for investment or purchase of inventory and equipment.

Indicate the adequacy or need for additional permanent working capital in the business.

Be Factual. The important thing to keep in mind in making a cash budget is the word "cash." Be as factual as you can. Try not to over-estimate sales or under-estimate expenses. Your sales forecast must be as accurate as possible because it is the basis for figuring your cash and expenses.

Use your experience to determine your cash sales. In seasonal businesses and those which have high-ticket merchandise, the percent of sales that are for cash will vary from month to month. Account for these ups and downs in each month if they apply to your business.

A format such as that shown in the example below can help you to be factual. This example of a cash budget forecast uses two columns for each month. The second column allows you to insert the actual figures as they occur and helps in correcting mistakes for future forecasts.

Sound Management - Success Story

With sound management a small firm can often achieve a goal by borrowing only a nominal amount. The experience of two partners in a Southeast business provides an example.

They obtained a contract to manufacture and install kitchen cabinets for a large builder. The contract called for installation in 4 months. To meet this deadline, the partners figured that they needed $56,500 in extra working capital.

Because this amount was more than they wanted to borrow, they asked for help from SBA's SCORE program.

The SCORE counselor helped the partners to come up with a borrowing requirement of only $16,000. This solution was arrived at by:

1. Arranging with their supplier to ship and bill for the materials monthly over a 3-month period.

2. Contracting with the builder to make an initial payment and 4 monthly payments.

3. Agreeing not to take any drawings from the business until the cash flow forecast indicated it was free and available.

Based on these facts, the partners estimated that during the 5 months (July through November) the firm should take in $88,000, pay out $56,500, and have a balance of $31,500 at the end of November. However, the problem was in July and August when expenses would run far ahead of the firm's income. To determine how a loan of $16,000 (including interest) could see the firm through these months, the following estimates were made:

**Estimate Of Borrowing Requirements
To Take On Additional Contract**

	July	August	September	October	November
Cash Requirements					
Inventory	$15,000	$10,000	$ 7,000		
Operating Expenses	4,000	6,000	6,000	$ 4,000	$ 2,000
Extra Equipment	2,500				
Total	$21,500	$16,000	$13,000	$ 4,000	$ 2,000
Cash Available					
Cash on Hand	$ 2,000			$ 2,000	$18,000
Collections	10,000	$10,000	$15,000	20,000	31,000
Total	$12,000	$10,000	$15,000	$22,000	$49,000
Excess Cash Over Receipts	0	0	$ 2,000	$18,000	$47,000
Additional Cash Required	$ 9,500	$ 6,000	0	0	0

According to these estimates, at the end of November, the partners would have cash on hand amounting to $47,000. Certain obligations would be outstanding against this cash. The first one would be the repayment of the loan of $16,000. Other obligations would be those which the partners planned to accumulate during the early months of the contract when cash on hand was at a premium, such as reserve for taxes and the partners' draw.

4

These estimates convinced the partners that they could perform the contract if they could get a loan. The next step was to convince the bank that their plan was sound.

For the bank lending officer's benefit, as well as their own, the partners projected the loan funds through a cash flow plan for the entire business. The cash flow schedule that was prepared is shown below. It showed: (1) that the amount of money requested would be adequate for the firm's needs and (2) the margin of cash that was expected to be available both during the contract and at the end of the contract.

Keep in mind that records are a reflection of the quality of a firm's management. Nobody knows this fact better or uses it more often than a banker.

The efficiency of an owner-manager portrays itself on the profit and loss statement (income statement). The P&L of an effective operation will show adequate profits for the particular line of business. Sales, promotion, expense control, merchandise turnover, and net profit application are the points on which you will be judged.

To determine trends, the lender looks at your current financial statement and those for the past several years. The current statement also shows the lender the makeup of your net worth.

Cash Budget Forecast

	January Est.	Actual	February Est.	Actual
(1) Cash in Bank (Start of month)	$1,400	$1,400 *	$1,850	$2,090 *
(2) Cash in Register (Start of Month)	100	100	150	70
(3) Total Cash [add (1) and (2)]	$1,500	$1,500	$2,000	$2,160
(4) Expected Cash Sales	1,200	1,420	900	
(5) Expected Collections	400	380	350	
(6) Other Money Expected	100	52	50	
(7) Total Receipts [add (4), (5) and (6)]	$1,700	$1,852	$1,300	
(8) Total Cash and Receipts [add (3) and (7)]	$3,200	$3,352	$2,200	
(9) All Disbursements (For Month)	1,200	1,192	1,000	
(10) Cash Balance at End of Month in Bank Account and Register [Subtract (9) from (8)]	$2,000	$2,160	$2,300	

*The owner-manager writes in these figures as they become available.

Cash Flow Schedule—Period of Contract to Repayment of Loan

	July	August	Sept.	Oct.	Nov.
Estimated Receipts					
Cash Sales	$ 800	$ 600	$ 700	$ 1,200	$ 2,800
Accounts Receivable	10,000	10,200	15,800	20,000	31,600
Other Income	200	400	200	480	250
Total Receipts	$11,000	$11,200	$16,700	$21,680	$34,650
Estimated Disbursements					
Accounts Payable	17,000	11,000	8,200	2,700	2,200
Payroll & Drawing	2,600	4,200	4,200	7,900	5,800
Expenses	1,200	1,800	2,000	2,700	600
Interest Expense	130	130	130	130	130
Plant & Equipment	2,500	460	600	800	100
Reserve for Taxes				3,800 *	3,800 *
Total Disbursements	$23,430	$17,590	$15,130	$18,030	$12,630
Estimated Excess Receipts over Disbursements	($12,430)	($ 6,390)	$ 1,570	$ 3,650	$22,020
Estimated Cash Balance at Start of Month	$ 4,200	$ 7,770	$ 1,380	$ 2,950	$ 6,600
Borrowings	$16,000				
Loan Repayment					$16,000
Estimated Cash Balance at End of Month	$ 7,770	$ 1,380	$ 2,950	$ 6,600	$12,620

*To be allotted in October and November so that available cash can be kept at the maximum during the months of heavy cash outflows.

Good managers recognize that occasional borrowing is one of the accepted business tools. Your long range plan for borrowing should be based on the fact that each of the various types of money in your business has its specific and appropriate purpose.

Recognizing this fact is important in preventing the misuse of funds. Keep in mind that misuse can cause a shaky financial condition. This point is especially true when operating cash seeps into long term investment in the business. As a result, the business requires a constant renewal of short term borrowings. Such borrowing indicates a capital deficiency in the business and the need for additional permanent capital.

Bear in mind that financial planning is the first step when borrowing. Such planning must be based on facts that come from your records if you are to secure loans and use them profitably.

Copies of this **Aid** and other publications are available from SBA for a small processing fee. Order forms 115A and 115B can be obtained free from SBA, P.O. Box 15434, Fort Worth, TX 76119. **Aids** may be condensed or reproduced. They may not be altered to imply approval by SBA of any private organization, product or service. If material is reused, credit to SBA will be appreciated.

U.S. GPO. 1987-181 712/40061

5

STATE BUSINESS-ASSISTANCE OFFICES

ALABAMA: Development Office, State Capitol, Montgomery, AL 36130, 1-800-248-0033 or (205) 263-0048

ALASKA: Division of Business Development, P.O. Box D, Juneau, AK 99811, (907) 465-2017

ARIZONA: Department of Commerce, 1700 W. Washington St., 4th Fl., Phoenix, AZ 85007, (602) 255-5705

ARKANSAS: Small Business Information Center, One State Capitol Mall, Rm. 4C300, Little Rock, AR 77201, (501) 682-3358

CALIFORNIA: Office of Small Business, 1121 L St., Suite 600, Sacramento, CA 95814, (916) 445-6545

COLORADO: Business Information Center, 1525 Sherman St., Rm. 110, Denver, CO 80203, (303) 866-3933

CONNECTICUT: Small Business Services, 210 Washington St., Hartford, CT 06106, (203) 566-4051

DELAWARE: Development Office, 99 King's Highway, P.O. Box 1401, Dover, DE 19903, (302) 736-4271

DISTRICT OF COLUMBIA: Office of Business and Economic Development, 7th Fl., 1111 E St., NW, Washington, DC 20004, (202) 727-6600

FLORIDA: Bureau of Business Assistance, 107 Gaines St., Tallahassee, FL 32339-2000, 1-800-342-0771 or (904) 488-9357

GEORGIA: Department of Industry and Trade, 230 Peachtree Rd. NW, Atlanta, GA 30303, (404) 656-3584

HAWAII:	Small Business Information Service, 250 S. King St., Rm. 727, Honolulu, HI 96813, (808) 548-7645
IDAHO:	Economic Development Division, Department of Commerce, State Capitol, Rm. 108, Boise, ID 83720, (208) 334-3416
ILLINOIS:	Small Business Assistance Bureau, 620 E. Adams St., Springfield, IL 62701, 1-800-252-2923 or (217) 785-6282
INDIANA:	Division of Business Expansion, Department of Commerce, One North Capital, Suite 700, Indianapolis, IN 46204-2288, 1-800-824-2476 or (317) 232-3527
IOWA:	Bureau of Small Business Development, 200 E. Grand Ave., Des Moines, IA 50309, 1-800-532-1216 or (515) 281-8310
KANSAS:	Division of Existing Industry Development, 400 S.W. Eighth St., 5th Fl., Topeka, KS 66603, (913) 296-5298
KENTUCKY:	Small Business Division, Capitol Plaza, 22nd Fl., Frankfort, KY 40601, 1-800-626-2250 or (502) 564-4252
LOUISIANA:	Development Division, Office of Commerce and Industry, P.O. Box 94185, Baton Rouge, LA 70804-9185, (504) 342-5365
MAINE:	Business Development Division, State Development Office, State House, Augusta, ME 04333, 1-800-872-3838 or (207) 289-2659
MARYLAND:	Office of Business and Industrial Development, 45 Calvert St., Annapolis, MD 21401, 1-800-654-7336 or (301) 974-2946
MASSACHUSETTS:	Small Business Assistance Division, 100 Cambridge St., 13th Fl., Boston, MA 02202, (617) 727-4005

MICHIGAN:	Business Ombudsman, Department of Commerce, P.O. Box 30107, Lansing, MI 48909, 1-800-232-2727 or (517) 373-6241
MINNESOTA:	Small Business Assistance Office, 900 American Center, 150 E. Kellogg Blvd., St. Paul, MN 55101, 1-800-652-9747 or (612) 296-3871
MISSISSIPPI:	Small Business Bureau, 3825 Ridgewood Rd., Jackson, MS 39211-6453, (601) 982-6231
MISSOURI:	Small Business Development Office, P.O. Box 118, Jefferson City, MO 65102, (314) 751-4981/8411
MONTANA:	Business Assistance Center, 1424 Ninth Ave., Helena, MT 59620, 1-800-221-8015 or (406) 444-3923
NEBRASKA:	Small Business Division, P.O. Box 94666, 301 Centennial Mall S., Lincoln, NE 68509, (402) 471-4167
NEVADA:	Office of Community Service, 1100 East William, Suite 116, Carson City, NV 89710, (702) 885-4602
NEW HAMPSHIRE:	Office of Industrial Development, 105 Loudon Rd., Prescott Park, Bldg. 2, Concord, NH 03301, (603) 271-2591
NEW JERSEY:	Office of Small Business Assistance, 1 W. State St. (CN-835), Trenton, NJ 08625, (609) 984-4442
NEW MEXICO:	Economic Development Division, 1100 St. Francis Dr., Santa Fe, NM 87503, 1-800-545-2040 or (505) 827-0300
NEW YORK:	Division for Small Business, 230 Park Ave., Rm. 834, New York, NY 10169, (212) 309-0400

NORTH CAROLINA:	Small Business Development Division, Dobbs Bldg., Rm. 2019, 430 N. Salisbury St., Raleigh, NC 27611, (919) 733-7980
NORTH DAKOTA:	Small Business Coordinator, Economic Development Commission, Liberty Memorial Bldg., Bismarck, ND 58505, 1-800-472-2100 or (701) 224-2810
OHIO:	Small and Developing Business Division, P.O. Box 1001, Columbus, OH 43266-0101, 1-800-282-1085 or (614) 466-1876
OKLAHOMA:	Oklahoma Department of Commerce, 6601 Broadway Ext., Oklahoma, OK 73116, (405) 521-2401
OREGON:	Economic Development Department, 595 Cottage St. NE, Salem, OR 97310, 1-800-233-3306 or 547-7842; or (503) 373-1200
PENNSYLVANIA:	Small Business Action Center, Department of Commerce, 404 Forum Bldg., Harrisburg, PA 17120, (717) 783-5700
PUERTO RICO:	Commonwealth, Department of Commerce, Box S, 4275 Old San Juan Station, San Juan, PR 00905, (809) 758-4747
RHODE ISLAND:	Small Business Development Division, 7 Jackson Walkway, Providence, RI 02903, (401) 277-2601
SOUTH CAROLINA:	Business Development M Assistance Division, P.O. Box 927, Columbia, SC 29202, 1-800-922-6684 or (803) 737-0400
SOUTH DAKOTA:	Governor's Office of Economic Development, Capital Lake Plaza, Pierre, SD 57501, 1-800-952-3625 or (605) 773-5032
TENNESSEE:	Small Business Office, 320 Sixth Ave. N., 7th Fl., Rachel Jackson Bldg., Nashville, TN 37219, 1-800-922-6684 or (803) 737-0400

TEXAS:	Small Business Division, P.O. Box 12728 Capitol Station, 410 E. Fifth St., Austin, TX 78711, (512) 472-5059
UTAH:	Small Business Development Center, 660 S. Second St., Rm. 418, Salt Lake City, UT 84111, (801) 581-7905
VERMONT:	Agency of Development and Community Affairs, The Pavillion, Montpelier, VT 05602, 1-800-622-4553 or (802) 828-3221
VIRGINIA:	Small Business and Financial Services, 1000 Washington Bldg., Richmond, VA 23219, (804) 786-3791
WASHINGTON:	Small Business Development Center, 441 Todd Hall, Washington State University, Pullman, WA 99164, (509) 335-1576
WEST VIRGINIA:	Small Business Development Center Division, Governor's Office, Capital Complex, Charleston, WVA 25305, (304) 348-2960
WISCONSIN:	Small Business Ombudsman, Department of Development, 123 W. Washington Ave., P.O. Box 7970, Madison, WI 53707, 1-800-435-7287 or (608) 266-0562
WYOMING:	Economic Development and Stabilization Board, Herschler Bldg., 3rd Fl. E., Cheyenne, WY 82002, (307) 777-7287

APPROVED CERTIFIED DEVELOPMENT COMPANIES (as of mid-1989)

City, State, Zip	Address	Co. Name, Telephone
ABILENE, TX 79604	1025 East North 10th Street P.O. Box 3195	Big Country Development Corporation (915) 672-8544
AGANA, GU 96910 (Guam)	Suite 204 Calvo Insurance Bldg. 115 Chalan Santo Papa	Small Business Development Corporation (Int. Code 671) 472-8083
AIKEN, SC 29801	P.O. Box 850 Highway 302 North	Lower Savannah Regional Development Corporation (803) 649-7985
AKRON, OH 44308	8th Floor, One Cascade Plaza	MSP 503 Development Corporation (216) 376-5550
ALBANY, NY 12207	City Hall 4th Floor	Albany Local Development Corporation (518) 434-5133
ALBANY, NY 12207	41 State Street	Empire State Certified Development Corporation (518) 463-2268
ALBUQUERQUE, NM 87110	6001 Marbel NE, Suite 6	Enchantment Land Certified Development Company (505) 268-1316
ALEXANDRIA, LA 71315-2248	5212 Rue Verdun Street P.O. Box 12248	Kisatchie-Delta Reg. Planning and Development District, Inc. (318) 487-5454
ALLENTOWN, PA 18105	801 Hamilton Street, Suite 200	Allentown Economic Development Corporation (215) 435-8890
ALTOONA, PA 16601	1212 Twelfth Avenue	Altoona Enterprises, Inc. (814) 944-6113
AMARILLO, TX 79102-1120	2736 West Tenth Avenue	Texas Panhandle Regional Development Corporation (806) 372-3381
ANCHORAGE, AK 99501	619 Warehouse Avenue, Suite 256	Railbelt Community Development Corporation (907) 277-5161
ARCATA, CA 95521	630 Ninth Street P.O. Box 4168	Arcata Economic Development Corporation (707) 822-4616
ARVIN, CA 93203	200 Campus Drive P.O. Box 546	Arvin Development Corporation (805) 854-5561
ASHEVILLE, NC 28802-1011	P.O. Box 1010	Asheville-Buncombe Development Corporation (704) 258-0317
ATHENS, GA 30610	305 Research Drive	Certified Development Company of Northeast Georgia Inc. (404) 542-7064
ATLANTA, GA 30303-1591	230 Peachtree Street, N.W., Suite 1810	Atlanta Local Development Company (404) 658-7066

ATLANTA, GA 30303	Fulton County Certified Development Corporation (404) 525-6205	10 Park Place South, Suite 305
ATLANTA, GA 30339	The Business Growth Corporation of Georgia (404) 434-0273	4000 Cumberland Parkway, Suite 1200A
AUBURN, ME 04210	Androscoggin Valley Council of Governments (207) 783-9186	70 Court Street
AUGUSTA, GA 30904	CSRA Local Development Corporation (404) 828-2356	2123 Wrightsboro Road, P.O. Box 2800
AUGUSTA, ME 04330	Maine Development Foundation (207) 622-6345	One Memorial Circle, Box #4
AUSTIN, TX 78750-1834	Texas Certified Development Company, Inc. (512) 258-8312	13740 Research Blvd.
BAKERSFIELD, CA 93301	Mid State Development Corporation (805) 322-9968	515 Truxtun Avenue
BALTIMORE, MD 21201	BEDCO Development Corporation (301) 837-9305	Suite 2400 Charles Center, 36 South Charles Street
BALTIMORE, MD 21202	The Mid-Atlantic Certified Development Company (301) 539-2449	Maryland National Bank Building, 10 Light Street, 32nd Floor
BANGOR, ME 04401	Eastern Maine Development District (207) 942-6389	10 Franklin Street
BARNESBILLE, GA 30204	McIntosh Trail Area Development Corporation (404) 358-3647	P.O. Box Drawer A
BARTOW, FL 33830	Central Florida Areawide Development Company, Inc. (813) 533-4146	490 East Davidson Street
BARTOW, FL 33830	First Imperial Polk Economic Development Corporation	P.O. Box 1909
BATESVILLE, AR 72501	White River Planning and Development District, Inc. (501) 793-5233	Highway 25 North, P.O. Box 2396
BEAUMONT, TX 77704	Southeast Texas Economic Development Foundation (713) 838-6581	450 Bowie, P.O. Box 3150
BELOIT, KS 67420	Four Rivers Development, Inc. (913) 738-2210	119 North Hersey Street
BENNETTSVILLE, SC 29512	Marlboro County Small Business Development Company, Inc. (803) 479-4046	214 East Market Street, P.O. Box 653
BIRMINGHAM, AL 35203	Birmingham City Wide Local Development Company (205) 254-2799	720 North 20th Street
BOISE, ID 83704	Treasure Valley Certified Development Corporation (208) 375-4651	7243 Potomac

City, State, Zip	Address	Co. Name, Telephone
BOONE, NC 28607	P.O. Box 1820-Furman Road Executive Arts Bldg., Suite 11	Regional D Certified Development Corporation, Inc. (704) 264-5606
BOONVILLE, IN 47601	301 West Main Street	Warrick County Local Development Corporation (812) 897-1506
BOSTON, MA 02111	38 Chauncey Street	Boston Local Development Corporation (617) 725-3304
BOSTON, MA 02109	One Liberty Square	Massachusetts Certified Development Corporation (617) 350-8877
BOWLING GREEN, KY 42101	P.O. Box 154	Barren River Development Council (502) 721-2381
BRATTLEBORO, VT 05301	5 Grove Street P.O. Box 1177	Brattleboro Development Credit Corporation (802) 257-7731
BRENHAM, TX 77833	314 S. Austin	Brenham Industrial Foundation, Inc. (409) 836-3695
BRIDGEPORT, CT 06604	180 Fairfield Avenue	Bridgeport Economic Development Corporation (203) 355-3800
BRISTOL, CT 06010	57 North Main Street	Bristol Industrial Development Corp (203) 589-4111
BROCKTON, MA 02401	One Legion Parkway	Brockton Regional Economic Development Corporation (617) 586-0503
BROWNSVILLE, TX 78520	P.O. Box 911	Brownsville Local Development Company, Inc. (512) 541-8691
BRUNSWICK, GA 31521	P.O. Box 1917 127 F Street	Coastal Area District Development Authority, Inc. (912) 264-7315
BUFFALO, NY 14202	920 City Hall	Buffalo Enterprise Development Corporation (716) 855-5017
BURLINGTON, VT 05402	7 Burlington Square	P.O. Box 786 (802) 862-5726
BURNS FLAT, OK 73624	P.O. Box 569	SWODA Development Corporation (405) 562-4886
BUZZARDS BAY, MA 02523	165A Route 3A Box 304	Cape Cod Economic Development Corporation (617) 888-6209
CAMDEN, NJ 08102	101 North Seventh Street, Suite 201	Camden Local Development Company (609) 963-8230
CAMDENTON, MO 65020	Late of the Ozarks Council of Local Govt. P.O. Box 786	Central Ozarks Development, Inc. (314) 346-5692
CAMILLA, GA 31730	30 E. Broad Street P.O. Box 346	Sowega Economic Development Corporation (912) 336-5617
CANTON, OH 44702	800 Savannah Avenue, N.E.	Stark Development Board Finance Corporation (216) 453-5900

CARIBOU, ME 04736
Main Street
P.O. Box 779
Northern Regional Planning Commission (207) 498-8736

CARLE PLACE, NY 11514
265 Glen Clove Road
Long Island Development Corporation (516) 741-5690

CASPER, WY 82601
145 S. Durbin Street, Suite 201
Small Business Development Corporation for Wyoming, Inc. (307) 234-5352

CATLETTSBURG, KY 41129
3000 Louisa Street
Economic Development Corporation of East Kentucky (606) 739-5191

CHARLESTON, SC 29403
Bus. & Technology Center
701 East Bay Street, Suite 1-548
Berkeley Charleston Dorchester Regional Development Corp. (803) 723-7267

CHARLESTON, SC 29401
180 Metting Street, Suite 310
Charleston Citywide Local Development Corporation (803) 577-7190

CHARLESTON, WV 25305
State Capitol Complex Building 6, Room 525
West Virginia Certified Development Corporation (304) 348-3650

CHARLOTTE, NC 28235
P.O. Box 35008
Centralina Development Corporation, Inc. (704) 372-2416

CHARLOTTE, NC 28202
City Hall-600 East Trade Street
Charlotte Certified Development Corporation (704) 336-2114

CHARLOTTESVILLE, VA 22901
413 East Market Street, Suite 102
Virginia Economic Development Corporation (804) 972-1729

CHATTANOOGA, TN 37402
216 West 8th Street, Suite 300
Southeast Local Development Corporation (615) 266-5781

CHICAGO, IL 60606
222 W. Adams Street, Suite 1398
CANDO City-Wide Development Corporation (312) 845-9696

CHICAGO, IL 60639
4054 West North Avenue
Greater North-Pulaski Local Development Corporation (312) 384-7074

CHICAGO, IL 60624
1111 South Homan Avenue, Suite 204
Lawndale Local Development (312) 265-8500

CHICO, CA 95927
1001 Willow Street
P.O. Box 6250
Butte County Overall Economic Development Corporation (916) 893-8732

CINCINNATI, OH 45203
415 West Court Street
Cincinnati Local Development Company (513) 352-4985

CINCINNATI, OH 45242-2830
10921 Reed Hartman Highway, Suite 108
Hamilton County Development Company, Inc. (513) 632-8292

CITRUS HEIGHTS, CA 95610
7509 Madison Avenue, Suite 111
Economic Development Foundation of Sacramento, Inc. (916) 962-3669

CLEVELAND, OH 44115
690 Huntington Building
Cleveland Area Development Finance Corporation (216) 241-1166

City, State, Zip	Address	Co. Name, Telephone
CLEVELAND, OH 44114	601 Lakeside, Room 210	Cleveland Citywide Development Corporation (216) 664-2406
COLLEGE STATION, TX 77840	1300 Jersey Street	College Station Certified Development Corporation (409) 696-8989
COLLINSBILLE, IL 62234	203 West Main Street	The Small Business Finance Alliance (618) 344-4080
COLORADO SPRINGS, CO 80904	1112 West Colorado Avenue	Pikes Peak Regional Development Corporation (303) 578-6962
COLUMBIA, MO 65201	1015 East Broadway, Suite 210 P.O. Box 566	Enterprise Development Corporation (314) 875-8117
COLUMBIA, TN 38402	P.O. Box 1346 815 South Main Street	South Central Tennessee Business Development Corporation (615) 381-2041
COLUMBUS, GA 31993	P.O. Box 1340	Columbus Local Development Corporation (404) 327-0820
COLUMBUS, GA 31902	P.O. Box 1908	Lower Chattahoochee Development Corporation, Inc. (404) 322-5571
COLUMBUS, OH 43215	140 Marconi Blvd. Marconi Bldg., 8th Floor	Columbus Countywide Development Corporation (614) 222-6171
COLUMBUS, OH 43214	77 South High Street, 28th Floor	Ohio Statewide Development Corporation (614) 466-5043
CONCORD, NH 03301	P.O. Box 664	Concord Regional Development Corporation (603) 228-1872
CONWAY, SC 29526	Horry-Georgetown Tech. College Highway 501 P.O. Box 1288	Intercounty Development, Inc. (803) 347-4604
COOKEVILLE, TN 38501	1225 Burgess Falls Road	Cumberland Area Investment Corporation (615) 432-4115
COON RAPIDS, MN 55433	P.O. Box 33346	Coon Rapids Development Company (612) 786-7334
CORVALLIS, OR 97333	155 S. W. Madison, #5	Cascades West Financial Services, Inc. (503) 672-6728
CUMBERLAND, MD 212502	1 Commerce Drive	Cumberland-Allegany County Industrial Foundation, Inc. (301) 777-5968
DALLAS, TX 75201	Room 6-D N., City Hall 1500 Marilla	Dallas Small Business Corporation (214) 670-3068
DALTON, GA 30720	503 West Waugh Street	North Georgia Certified Development Company (404) 226-1110
DANBURY, CT 06810	57 North Street, Suite 407	Housatonic Industrial Development Corporation (203) 743-0306

DAYTON, OH 45402	Miami Valley Tower 40 W. 4th Street, Suite 1400	Citywide Small Business Development Corporation (513) 226-0457
DAYTON, OH 45402	1700 Miami Valley Tower 40 West 4th Street	Montgomery County Business Development Corporation (513) 225-6328
DENISON, IA 51442	109 North 14th Street	Crawford County Industrial Development Corporation (712) 263-5621
DENVER, CO 80204	1111 Osage Street, Suite 110	Community Economic Development Company of Colorado (303) 893-8989
DENVER, CO 80204	303 W. Colfax Avenue, Suite 1025	Denver Urban Economic Development Corporation (303) 575-5540
DES MOINES, IA 50309	901 Insurance Exchange Building The Armory Building	Iowa Business Growth Company (515) 282-2164
DES MOINES, IA 50307	East 1st & Des Moines Street	The Corporation for Economic Dev. in Des Moines (515) 283-4161
DETROIT, MI 48226	First National Building, Suite 600	Detroit Economic Growth Corporation Development Co. (313) 963-2940
DETROIT, MI 48226	600 Randolph 3rd Floor Wayne County Building	Metropolitan Growth & Development Corporation (313) 224-0735
DODGE CITY, KS 67801	100 Military Plaza, Suite 214, P.O. Box 1116	Great Plains Development, Inc. (316) 227-6406
DONORA, PA 15033	P.O. Box 491	Middle Monongahela Industrial Development Association, Inc. (412) 379-5600
DOVER, DE 19903	99 Kings Highway P.O. Box 1401	Delaware Development Corporation (302) 736-4408
DUBUQUE, IA 52001	P.O. Box 1140 Fisher Building, Suite 22B	E.C.I.A. Business Growth, Inc. (319) 556-4166
DUNCAN, OK 73533	802 Main P.O. Box 1647	Association of South Central Government Econ. Dev. Corp. (405) 252-0595
DURANT, OK 74701	10 Waldron Drive	Rural Enterprises, Inc. (405) 924-5094
EAST BOSTON, MA 02128	72 Marginal Street, 5th Floor	East Boston Local Development Corporation (617) 569-7174
EAST CHICAGO, IN 46312	4525 Indianapolis Blvd.	Downtown Improvement Corporation (219) 392-8203

City, State, Zip	Address	Co. Name, Telephone
EAST LANSING, MI 48823	P.O. Box 6672	Red Cedar Certified Development Corporation (517) 351-6566
EASTMAN, GA 31023	501 Oak Street	Heart of Georgia Area Development Corporation (912) 529-6173
EAU CLAIRE, WI 54701-3707	505 Dewey Street South, Suite 101	Eau Claire County Economic Development Corporation (715) 834-0070
EL CENTRO, CA 92244	1275 Main Street P.O. Box 2343	Commercial Industrial Development Company, Inc. (619) 352-6241
EL PASO, TX 79901	303 N. Oregon	El Paso Certified Development Corporation (915) 543-4000
EL PASO, TX 79999	Two Civic Center Plaza	Upper Rio Grande Development Company (915) 541-4068
ELISABETH, KY 42701	702 College Street Road	Lincoln Trail Development Association, Inc. (502) 769-2393
ELIZABETH, NJ 07208	399 Westfield Avenue	Union County Economic Development Corporation (201) 527-1166
ELIZABETH, NY 07201	1045 East Jersey Street	Elizabeth Development Company of New Jersey (201) 289-0262
ELLAVILLE, GA 31806	P.O. Box 6	Middle Flint Area Development Corporation (912) 937-2561
EMPORIA, KS 66801	Cremer Hall-ESU Campus, Room 208	NEOSHO Basin Development Company, Inc. (316) 343-1200
ENID, OK 73703	1216 West Willow, Suite A	Northern Oklahoma Small Business Development Corp. (405) 237-4810
ESCANABA, MI 49829	2415 24th Avenue South	Central Upper Peninsula Business Dev. Center, Inc. (906) 786-9234
EUREKA, CA 95501	1213 Fifth Street	Six Rivers Local Development Corporation (707) 445-9561
EVANSTON, WY 82930-0721	1101 Main Street P.O. Box 721	Greater Evanston Dev. Co., dba Western Wyoming Cert. Dev. Co. (307) 789-4402
EVANSVILLE, IN 47708	316 Civic Center Complex	Metro Small Business Assistance Corporation (812) 426-5857
EXTON, PA 19341	750 Pottstown Pike	Chester County Small Business Assistance Corporation (215) 363-2569
FAIRMONT, WV 26555	200 Fairmont Avenue P.O. Box 208	Fairmont Industrial and Credit Corporation (304) 363-0447
FARGO, ND 58108	321 N. 4th Street P.O. Box 2443	Fargo-Cass Economic Development Corporation (701) 237-6132
FARIBAULT, MN 55021	City Hall 208-1st Avenue, N.W.	Faribault Industrial Corporation (507) 334-9186

220

FAYETTEVILLE, NC 28305	2504 Raeford Road, Suite B	Old Fayetteville Association, Inc. (919) 323-1313
FITCHBURG, MA 01420	344 Main Street P.O. Box 7330	North Central Massachusetts Development Corporation (617) 343-7345
FLINT, MI 48502	1101 Beach Street	Forward Development Corporation (313) 257-3010
FLORENCE, KY 41402	7505 Sussex Drive, Suite 8	Northern Kentucky Area Development District, Inc. (606) 283-1885
FLORENCE, SC 29502	P.O. Box 5719 U.S. Highway 52	Pee Dee Regional Development Corporation (803) 699-3139
FORT WAYNE, IN 46802	Department of Economic Develop. 840 City-County Building	Community Development Corp. of Fort Wayne (219) 427-1127
FORT SMITH, AR 72902	P.O. Box 2067	Western Arkansas Planning and Development District, Inc. (501) 785-2651
FORT WORTH, TX 76105	2014 East Rosedale, Suite 204	Fort Worth Economic Development Corporation (817) 535-2167
FRANKFORT, KY 40601	2400 Capital Plaza Tower	Commonwealth Small Business Development Corporation (502) 564-4320
FRANKLIN, PA 16323	Biery Building, Suite 406	Uniform Region Nine Certified Development Company (814) 437-3024
FREDERICKSBURG, VA 22401	904 Princess Anne Street P.O. Box 863	Rappahannock Economic Development Corporation (703) 373-2897
FRESNO, CA 93721-2104	2300 Tulare Street, Suite 210	Central California Certified Development Corporation (209) 488-4503
GAINESVILLE, GA 30501	1010 Ridge Road	Georgia Mountains Regional Economic Development Corporation (404) 532-6541
GARLAND, TX 75043	3960 Broadway, Suite 200	Garland Local Development Corporation, Inc. (214) 271-9993
GARY, IN 46402	Gary Chamber of Commerce-S#324 Gainer Bank Bldg.-504 Broadway	Gary City-Wide Development Corporation (219) 883-9691
GAYLORD, MI 49735	P.O. Box 457 123 West Main, Suite 332	Northeast Michigan Development Company (517) 732-3551
GRAND RAPIDS, MI 49503	300 Monroe, N.W.	Grand Rapids Local Development Corporation (616) 456-3199

City, State, Zip	Address	Co. Name, Telephone
GRAND RAPIDS, MI 49503	2 Fountain Place, Suite 240	Region Eight Development Corporation d/b/a REDCO Dev. (616) 458-7287
GRAND RIVER, MI 49417	414 Washington Street	Ottawa County Development Company, Inc.
GREEN BAY, WI 54305	400 South Washington Avenue P.O. Box 969	Area Investment and Development, Inc. (414) 499-6444
GREENVILLE, MS 38702	124 South Broadway Street P.O. Box 1776	South Delta Development Company, Inc. (601) 378-3831
GREENVILLE, NC 27834	201 East Second Street P.O. Box 755	Pitt County Dev. Commission Certified Development Company (919) 758-1989
GREENVILLE, SC 29606	P.O. Box 6668 50 Grand Avenue	Appalachian Development Corporation (803) 242-9733
GULFPORT, MS 39502	P.O. Box 59 #218 Downtown Building	Gulf-Certco, Inc. (601) 864-5657
GULFPORT, MS 39501	1020 32nd Avenue	Southern Mississippi Economic Development Company, Inc. (601) 868-2312
HAMILTON, OH 45011	130 High Street	Certified Development Company of Butler County, Inc. (513) 867-5772
HAMMOND, IN 46324	Office of Economic Development 649 Conkey Street	Hammond Development Corporation (219) 853-6508
HANFORD, CA 93230	1222 West Lacey Boulevard, Suite 101	Crown Development Corporation of Kings County (209) 582-4326
HARRISON, AR 72601	1313 Highway 62-65 P.O. Box 190	Northwest Arkansas Certified Development Company (501) 741-8009
HARTFORD, CT 06106	217 Washington Street	Connecticut Business Development Corporation (203) 241-0670
HARTFORD, CT 06103	c/o HEDCO 15 Lewis Street	Greater Hartford Business Development Center, Inc. (203) 527-1301
HATO REY, PR 00919	Municipal Building 15th Floor Chardon Avenue P.O. Box 1791	Corporacion para el Fomento Economico de la Ciudad Capital (809) 756-5080

HATO REY, PR 00918	Banco Popular Center, Suite 815	North Puerto Rico Local Development Company, Inc. (809) 754-7474
HAYDEN, ID 83835	11100 Airport Drive	Panhandle Area Council, Inc. (208) 772-0584
HELENA, MT 59624	P.O. Box 916 / 555 Fuller Avenue	Montana Community Finance Corporation (406) 442-3820
HENDERSON, NC 27536	238 Orange Street / P.O. Box 709	Region K Certified Development Company, Inc. (919) 492-2538
HERTFORD, NC 27944	512 South Church Street / P.O. Box 646	Albemarle Development Authority, Inc. (919) 426-5755
HICKORY, NC 28201	30 Third Street, N.W.	Region E Development Corporation (704) 322-9191
HILL CITY, KS 67642	317 N. Pomeroy Avenue / P.O. Box 248	Pioneer Country Development, Inc. (913) 674-3488
HILLSBORO, MO 63050	P.O. Box 623	The Economic Development Corp. of Jefferson County, MO (314) 789-4594
HOBBS, NM 88240	Broadmoor Bldg. / P.O. Box 1376	Industrial Development Corporation of Lea County (505) 397-2039
HOLYOKE, MA 01040	42 North East Street	Riverside Development Corporation (413) 533-7102
HOMELAND, AL 35209	90 Bagby Drive, Suite 111	Alabama Community Development Corporation (205) 945-4996
HOMEWOOD, IL 60430	1154 Ridge Road, Suite 100	South Towns Business Growth Corporation (312) 957-6970
HONOLULU, HI 96813-2445	222 S. Vineyard Street, Penthouse 1	HEDCO Local Development Corporation (808) 521-6502
HOPKINSVILLE, KY 42240	609 Hammond Plaza / Ft. Campbell Blvd.	Pennyrile Area Development District, Inc. (502) 886-9484
HOT SPRINGS, AR 71901	ABT Towers, Suite 502 / P.O. 1558	West Central Arkansas Planning and Dev. District Incorporated (501) 624-1036
HOUSTON, TX 77027	3555 Timmons Lane, Suite 500	Houston-Galveston Area Local Development Corporation (713) 627-3200
HUDSON, NY 12534	446 Warren Street	Hudson Development Corporation (518) 828-3373

City, State, Zip	Address	Co. Name, Telephone
INDIANAPOLIS, IN 46205	2506 Willowbrook Parkway, Suite 110	Indiana Statewide Certified Development Corporation (317) 253-6166
INDIANAPOLIS, IN 46204	c/o Indianapolis Growth Project 48 Monument Circle	Mid City Pioneer Corporation (317) 236-6241
ITHACA, MI 48847	215 East Center Street	Greater Gratiot Development, Inc. (517) 875-2083
JACKSON, CA 95642	P.O. Box 596	Amador Economic Development Corporation (209) 223-0351
JACKSON, MI 49201	City Hall, 8th Floor 161 West Michigan	The Jackson Local Development Company (517) 788-4187
JACKSON, MS 39216	P.O. Box 4935	Central Mississippi Development Company, Inc. (601) 981-1625
JACKSON, MS 39205	1201 Walter Sillers Building	Certified Development Company of Mississippi, Inc. (601) 359-6710
JACKSONVILLE, FL 32202	Suite 603, Floor Theatre Bldg. 128 E. Forsyth Street	Jacksonville Local Development Company, Inc. (904) 630-1914
JEFFERSON, OH 44047	25 West Jefferson Street	Ashtabula County 503 Corporation (216) 570-2040
JEFFERSON CITY, MO 65101	1014 Northeast Drive	Rural Missouri, Inc. (314) 635-0136
JERSEY CITY, NJ 07306	870 Bergen Avenue	Jersey City Certified Development Corporation (201) 292-1899
JOHNSON CITY, TN 37604	207 North Boone Street, Suite 800	First Tennessee Economic Development Corporation (615) 928-0224
JOHNSTOWN, PA 15901	551 Main Street East Building, Suite 203	Johnstown Area Regional Industries Cert. Dev. Corp. (814) 535-8675
JONESBORO, AR 72401	1801 Stadium Blvd. P.O. Box 1403	East Arkansas Planning & Development District (501) 932-3957
KALAMAZOO, MI 49007	241 West South Street	Kalamazoo Small Business Development Corporation (616) 385-8050
KANSAS CITY, KS 66101	8th and State Ave., Suite 395 Newbrotherhood Bldg.	Avenue Area Incorporated (913) 371-0065
KANSAS CITY, KS 66101	701 North 7th Street, 7th Floor	Citywide Development Corp. of Kansas City, Kansas, Inc. (913) 321-4406
KANSAS CITY, MO 64105	920 Main Street, Suite 214	EDC Loan Corporation (816) 221-0636
KANSAS CITY, MO 64153	10920 Ambassador Drive, Room 531	Platte County Industrial Development Commission (816) 891-9480

224

KENNEWICK, WA 99336
901 N. Colorado Street
Southeastern Washington Development Association (509) 735-6222

KENOSHA, WI 53140
5455 Sheridan Road, Suite 101
Kenosha Area Development Corporation (414) 654-7134

KILGORE, TX 75662
3800 Stone Road
East Texas Regional Development Company, Inc. (214) 984-3989

KIRKSVILLE, MO 63501
Adair County Courthouse
P.O. Box 965
Northeast Missouri Certified Development Company (816) 665-0202

KNOXVILLE, TN 37919
5616 Kingston Pike
P.O. Box 19806
Areawide Development Corporation (615) 588-7972

LA HABRA, CA 90633-0337
Civic Center
P.O. Box 337
La Habra Local Development Company (213) 905-9741

LAFAYETTE, CA 94549
251 Lafayette Circle, Suite 220
Bay Area Employment Development Company (415) 283-3760

LAFAYETTE, LA 70502
705 W. University Avenue
P.O. Box 4017-C
Lafayette Centre Certified Development Company, Inc. (318) 261-8408

LAFAYETTE, LA 70503
150 Ridge Road
P.O. Box 31978
Louisiana First Certified Development Corporation (318) 837-3410

LAGRANGE, GA 30240
900 Dallis Street
P.O. Box 636
Troup County Local Development Corporation (404) 886-1172

LAKE CHARLES, LA 70601
New City Hall
326 Pujo Street 4th Floor
Imperial Calcasieu Regional Certified Development, Inc. (318) 433-1771

LANCASTER, CA 93535
104 East Avenue K-4
Antelope Valley Local Development Corporation (805) 945-2741

LANDOVER, MD 20785
9200 Basil Court, Suite 200
Prince Georges County Financial Services Corporation (301) 386-5600

LANSDALE, PA 19446
311 North Broad Street
P.O. Box 407
Keystone Small Business Assistance Corporation (215) 368-4880

LANSING, MI 48910
913 W. Holmes Road, Suite 201
Capital Region Business Corporation (517) 393-0344

LANSING, MI 48909
P.O. Box 30234
Michigan Certified Development Corporation (517) 373-6378

LAPEER, MI 48446
449 McCormick Drive
Lapeer Development Corporation (313) 667-0080

LAREDO, TX 78044-2187
P.O. Box 2187
S.T.E.D. Corporation (512) 722-3995

LAS VEGAS, NV 89101
716 South Sixth Street
New Ventures Capital Development Company (702) 384-3293

City, State, Zip	Address	Co. Name, Telephone
LAS VEGAS, NV 89106	2770 South Maryland Parkway #216	Southern Nevada Certified Development Corporation (702) 732-3998
LAWRENCE, KS 66044	901 Kentucky, #206 P.O. Box 1732	Wakarusa Valley Dev., Inc. (913) 841-7120
LEAVENWORTH, KS 66048	518 Shawnee P.O. Box 151	Leavenworth Area Economic Development Corporation (913) 682-6579
LEE'S SUMMIT, MO 64063	600 Miller Street P.O. Box 710	Lee's Summit Economic Development Council (816) 525-6617
LENEXA, KS 66215	11900 W. 87th St. Parkway S-115 P.O. Box 14244	Lenexa Development Company, Inc. (913) 888-3624
LEWISBURG, PA 17837	R.D. #1	SEDA-COG Local Development Corporation (717) 524-4491
LEWISTON, ID 83501	1626 B 6th Avenue North	Clearwater Economic Development Association (208) 746-0015
LEWISTON, ME 04240	95 Park Street	Lewiston Development Corporation (207) 783-3505
LEXINGTON, KY 40507	200 East Main Street	Urban County Community Development Corporation (606) 258-3131
LINCOLN, NB 68510	139 South 52nd Street	The Business Development Corp. of Nebraska (402) 483-0382
LOCKPORT, NY 14094	One Locks Plaza	Greater Lockport Development Corporation (716) 439-6688
LOMPOC, CA 93438	100 Civic Center Plaza	Central Coast Development Corporation (805) 736-1445
LONG BEACH, CA 90802	333 West Ocean Boulevard, 3rd Floor	Long Beach Local Development Corporation (213) 590-6847
LONOKE, AR 72086	112 N.E. Front Street P.O. Box 187	Central Arkansas Certified Development Corporation (501) 374-6976
LORAIN, OH 44052	200 W. Erie Avenue	Lorain 503 Development Corporation
LOS ANGELES, CA 90017	550 S. Vermont Avenue, 3rd Floor	Economic Development Corporation of Los Angeles County (213) 387-0322
LOS ANGELES, CA 90012	200 North Spring Street, Suite 2008	Los Angeles LDC, Inc. (213) 590-6847
LOUISVILLE, KY 40202	515 West Market Street, Suite 650	Jefferson County Local Development Corporation (502) 625-3051
LOUISVILLE, KY 40202	515 West Market Street, Suite 650	Louisville Economic Development Corporation (502) 625-3051
LOWELL, MA 01852	100 Merrimack Street	Lowell Development and Financial Corporation (617) 459-9899

LUBBOCK, TX 79452-3730
P.O. Box 3730
1328 58th Street
Caprock Local Development Company (806) 762-8721

LUMBERTON, NC 28358
711 North Cedar Street
Advancement, Inc. (919) 738-4851

LYNCHBURG, VA 24501
P.O. Box 2526
Central Virginia Economic Development Corporation (804) 845-3493

LYNN, MA 01901
598 Essex Street
Lynn Capital Investment Corporation (617) 592-2361

MACON, GA 31201
600 Grand Building
Mulberry Street
Development Corporation of Middle Georgia (912) 751-6160

MADISON, WI 53703
217 South Hamilton Street
Wisconsin Business Development Finance Corporation (608) 258-8830

MAGNOLIA, AR 71753
600 Bessie Street
P.O. Box 767
Southwest Arkansas Regional Development Corporation (501) 234-4039

MAIMI, FL 33131-2207
300 Biscayne Blvd. Way, Suite 614
Miami Citywide Development Inc. (305) 358-1025

MANHATTAN, KS 66502
104 South Fourth
Big Lakes Certified Development Company (913) 776-0417

MANKATO, MN 56001
410 S. Fifth Street
P.O. Box 3367
Region Nine Development Corporation (507) 387-5646

MAYFIELD, KY 42066
P.O. Box 588
Highway 45 North
Purchase Area Development District (502) 247-7175

MAYSVILLE, KY 41056
327 West Second Street
Buffalo Trace Area Development District, Inc. (606) 564-6894

MCALLEN, TX 78504
4900 N. 23rd Street
The Lower Rio Grande Valley Certified Development Corporation (512) 682-1109

MCPHERSON, KS 67460
P.O. Box 1032
McPherson County Small Business Development Association (316) 241-0431

MEDIA, PA 19063
602 E. Baltimore Pike
Delaware County Economic Development Center, Inc. (215) 565-7575

MEMPHIS, TN 38103
125 N. Mid America Mall, Room 419
Camelot Building
West Tennessee Investment Corporation (901) 528-3307

MENTOR, OH 44060
Lakeland Community College
Lake County Small Business Assistance Corporation (216) 951-2769

MENTOR, OH 44060
8500 Civic Center Blvd.
Mentor Economic Assistance Corporation (216) 255-1100

227

City, State, Zip	Address	Co. Name, Telephone
MERIDEN, CT 06450	43 1/2 Colony Street	Meriden Economic Development Corporation (203) 237-5573
MIAMI, FL 33130	300 S.W.-12th Avenue, Suite A, 2nd Floor	Miami-Date Business Development Corporation (305) 858-9958
MILLEDGEVILLE, GA 31061	Hertiage Road P.O. Box 707	Oconee Area Development Corporation (912) 453-4328
MILWAUKEE, WI 53201	809 North Broadway P.O. Box 324	Metropolitan Milwaukee Enterprise Corporation (414) 223-5812
MINNEAPOLIS, MN 55401	331 2nd Avenue, South, Room 700	Minneapolis Economic Development Company (612) 342-1378
MODESTO, CA 95354	621 14th Street, Suite B	Stanislaus County Economic Development Corporation (209) 521-9333
MOHAWK, NY 13407	26 West Main Street P.O. Box 69	Mohawk Valley Certified Development Corporation (315) 866-4671
MONROE, LA 71201	141 DeSiard Street, Suite 511	Northeast Louisiana Industries, Inc. (318) 387-0787
MONTGOMERY, AL 36130	135 South Union Street, Suite 256	Southern Development Council (205) 264-5441
MONTPELIER, VT 05602	7½ Bailey Avenue	Central Vermont Economic Development Corporation (802) 229-0555
MONTPELIER, VT 05602	East 68- East State Street	Vermont 503 Corporation (802) 828-2385
MT. HOLLY, NJ 08060	49 Rancocas Road	Burlington County 503 Development Corporation
MUSKEGON, MI 49440	349 West Webster Avenue	Greater Muskegon Industrial Fund, Inc. (616) 722-2671
MUSKOGEE, OK 74401-6043	600 Emporia, Suite A	Verd-Ark-Ca Development Corporation (918) 683-4634
NACAGDOCHES, TX 75961	118 East Hospital Street	Deep East Texas Regional Certified Development Corporation (409) 569-0323
NASHVILLE, TN 37201-1502	211 Union Street, #233 Stalman Building—7th Floor	Mid-Cumberland Area Development Corporation (305) 858-9958
NEW BERN, NC 28560	P.O. Box 1717	Neuse River Development Authority, Inc. (919) 638-3185
NEW BRUNSWICK, NJ 08901	303 George Street, Suite 304	Middlesex County Certified Local Development Company (201) 745-4005
NEW HAVEN, CT 06510-3101	770 Chapel Street #B31	New Haven Community Investment Corporation, LDC (203) 787-6023

NEW YORK, NY 10038
c/o Financial Services Corp.
17 John Street 12th Floor

Metropolitan Business Assistance, LTD (212) 566-1358

NEWPORT, RI 02840
c/o Chamber of Commerce
10 America's Cup Avenue

Newport County Certified Development Company, Inc.
(401) 847-8484

NEWS ORLEANS, LA 70130
301 Camp Street, Suite 210

New Orleans Citywide Development Corporation (504) 524-6172

NIAGARA FALLS, NY 14302
745 Main Street

N.F.C. Development Corporation (716) 285-3146

NORFOLK, VA 23510
201 Granby Mall Building, Suite 1000

Urban Business Development Corporation (804) 623-2691

NORTH KANSAS CITY, MO 64117
2900 Rockcreek Parkway, Suite 510

Clay County Development Corporation (816) 472-5775

NORTHBROOK, IL 60062
900 Skokie Blvd., Suite 104

Greater Metropolitan Chicago Development (312) 251-2756

OAKLAND, CA 94612
Dufwin Towers, Suite 111
519 17th Street

Oakland Certified Development Corporation (415) 763-4297

OGDEN, UT 84401
2540 Washington Blvd., 6th Floor

The Historic 25th Street Development Company (801) 399-8241

OKLAHOMA CITY, OK 73102
116 Dean A. McGee Avenue

Metro Area Development Corporation (405) 232-5181

ORLANDO, FL 32801
455 South Orange Avenue

Orlando Neighborhood Improvement Corporation, Inc.
(407) 849-2522

OSHKOSH, WI 54902
P.O. Box 280
120 Jackson Street

Oshkosh Commercial Development Corporation (414) 236-5260

OSWEGO, NY 13126
East 2nd and Schuyler Streets
P.O. Box 4067

Operation Oswego County, Inc. (315) 343-1545

OVERLAND PARK, KS 66204
7200 W. 75th Street, Suite 100

Johnson County Certified Development Company (913) 831-3365

OWENSBORO, KY 42301
3860 U.S. Highway 60, West

Green River 503 Certified Development Corporation (502) 926-4433

OWINGSVILLE, KY 40360
P.O. Box 107

Gateway Certified Development Company, Inc. (606) 674-6355

PARKERSBURG, WV 26101
P.O. Box 247
925 Market Street

Mid-Ohio Valley Development Corporation (304) 485-3801

PASADENA, CA 91101
586 North Lake Avenue

Pasadena Development Corporation (818) 792-5764

PEABODY, MA 01960
20 Peabody Square

Greater Peabody Economic Development Corporation
(617) 531-0454

PEARL RIVER, NY 10965
1 Blue Hill Plaza, Suite 818

Greater Rocklan Local Development Corporation (914) 735-7040

City, State, Zip	Address	Co. Name, Telephone
PENDLETON, OR 97801	17 S.W. Frazer, Suite 20 P.O. Box 1041	Greater Eastern Oregon Development Corporation (503) 276-6745
PEORIA, IL 61602	331 Fulton Street, Suite 407	Peoria Economic Development Association (309) 674-5800
PETERSBURG, VA 23805	P.O. Box 1808	Crater Development Company (804) 861-1668
PETERSBURG, WV 26847	P.O. Box 887 Grant Industrial Park	Potomac Valley Area Development Corporation (304) 257-1221
PHILADELPHIA, PA 19109	123 South Broad Street Fidelity Bldg., 22nd Floor	PIDC Local Development Corporation (215) 735-5050
PHILADELPHIA, PA 19107	One East Penn. Sq. Bldg	Philadelphia Industrial Loan Fund, Inc. (215) 568-2630
PHILADELPHIA, PA 19102	230 South Broad Street	Quaker State Certified Development Company, Inc. (215) 735-3843
PHILADELPHIA, PA 19106	714 Market Street Sovereing Building, Suite 433	Urban Local Development Corporation (215) 561-6600
PHOENIX, AZ 85004	1 North, 1st Street, 7th Floor, Suite D	Phoenix Local Dev. Corp. Phoenix, Arizona (602) 262-6004
PHOENIX, AZ 85007	1700 West Washington, 4th Floor	Arizona Enterprise Development Corporation (602) 255-1782
PIERRE, SD 57501	221 South Central	The South Dakota Development Corporation (605) 773-5032
PINE BLUFF, AR 71611	P.O. Box 6806	Southeast Arkansas Economic Development District, Inc. (501) 536-1990
PITTSBURG, CA 94565	501 Railroad Avenue	Los Medanos Fund, A Local Development Company (415) 439-1056
PITTSBURG, KS 66762	1501 S. Joplin	Mid-America, Inc. (316) 231-8267
PITTSBURGH, PA 15219	437 Grant Street Frick Building, Suite 1220	Pittsburgh Countywide Corporation, Inc. (412) 471-1030
PITTSBURGH, PA 15212	800 Vinial Street, Suite B-310	Southwestern Pennsylvania Economic Development District (412) 323-2800
PITTSFIELD, MA 01201	City Hall, Room 205	Pittsfield Economic Revitalization Corporation (413) 499-9371
PITTSTON, PA 18640	1151 Oak Street	Pocono Northeast Enterprise Development Corporation (717) 655-5587
PLYMOUTH, MA 02361	P.O. Box 321	Plymouth Industrial Development Corporation (617) 746-1050

Location	Address	Organization
POCATELLO, ID 83204	427 North Main, Suite A P.O. Box 626	Eastern Idaho Development Corporation (208) 234-7541
PONTIAC, MI 48053	1200 North Telegraph Road	Oakland County Local Development Company (313) 858-0732
PONTOTOC, MS 38863	P.O. Drawer B	Three Rivers Local Development Company, Inc. (601) 489-2435
PORT JERVIS, NY 12771	14–18 Hammond Street P.O. Box 3105	Port Jervis Development Corporation (914) 856-6911
PORTLAND, ME 04101	233 Oxford Street	Southern Maine Business Financial Corporation (207) 774-9891
PORTLAND, OR 97212	3802 N. E. Union Avenue #203	River East Progress, Inc. (503) 284-7440
PORTSMOUTH, NH 03801	126 Daniel Street P.O. Box 1491	Granite State Economic Development Corporation (603) 436-0009
PORTSMOUTH, OH 45662	729 Sixth Street P.O. Drawer 1606	Scioto Economic Development Corporation, Inc. (614) 354-7779
PORTSMOUTH, VA 23704	1701 High Street, Suite 100	Portsmouth Certified Development Corporation (804) 393-8989
PROVIDENCE, RI 02903	St. RI, Dept. Econ. Dev. Seven Jackson Walkway	Ocean State Business Development Authority (401) 277-2601
PROVO, UT 84603	152 West Center Street P.O. Box 1849	Central Utah Certified Development Company (801) 374-1025
PUEBLO, CO 81002	720 North Main, Suite 444	SCEDD Development Company (719) 545-8680
QUINCY, MA 02169	36 Miller Stile Road	South Shore Economic Development Corporation (617) 479-1111
RACINE, WI 53406	5802 Washington Avenue, Suite 201	Racine County Business Development Corporation (414) 636-3118
RADFORD, VA 24143	1612 Wadsworth Street	New River Valley Development Corporation (703) 639-9314
RALEIGH, NC 27605	820 Clay Street	Capital Economic Development Corporation (919) 832-4524
RANCHO CUCAMONG, CA 91730	9650 Business Center Drive	West Valley Certified Development Company (714) 989-1485
REDDING, CA 96001	737 Auditorium Drive, Suite D	Economic Development Corporation of Shasta County (916) 225-5300
REDMOND, OR 97756	1135 W. Highland P.O. Box 575	Oregon Certified Business Development Corporation (503) 548-8163
RENO, NV 89501	350 South Center, Suite 310	Nevada State Development Corporation (702) 323-3625

City, State, Zip	Address	Co. Name, Telephone
REXBURG, ID 83440	12 North Center Street P.O. Box 330	East-Central Idaho Development Company (208) 356-4524
RICHMOND, VA 23241	201 E. Franklin Street P.O. Box 12324	James River Certified Development Corporation (804) 783-9309
RICHOMOND, VA 23219	600 East Broad Street, Suite 960	Richmond Renaissance Development Corporation (804) 644-0404
RIDGWAY, PA 15853	122 Center Street	North Central Business Development, Inc. (814) 772-6901
RIVERSIDE, CA 92501	3499 Tenth Street P.O. Box 413	Riverside County Economic Development Corporation (714) 788-9811
ROANOKE, VA 24011	145 W. Campbell Avenue, Suite 500	Western Virginia Development Company (703) 343-4416
ROCHESTER, NY 14604	55 St. Paul Street	Monroe County Industrial Development Corporation (716) 454-2220
ROCHESTER, NY 14614	30 Church Street	Rochester Economic Development Corporation (716) 428-6808
ROCK HILL, SC 29730	100 Dave Lyne Blvd. P.O. Box 450	Catawba Regional Development Corporation (803) 324-3161
ROCK ISLAND, IL 61201	1504 Third Avenue	Bi-State Business Finance Corporation (309) 793-1181
ROCKFORD, IL 61103	515 N. Court Street	Rockford Local Development Corporation (815) 987-8127
ROCKVILLE, MD 20850-1436	1014 Neal Drive	Economic and Business Dev. Corp of Montgomery County (301) 984-0999
ROCKY MOUNT, NC 27802	1309 S. Wesleyan Blvd. P.O. Drawer 2748	Roanoke-Tar Rivers Regional Certified Development Inc. (919) 446-5775
ROSEBURG, OR 97470	744 S. E. Rose Street	C.C.D. Business Development Corporation (503) 672-6728
SACRAMENTO, CA 95814	c/o Office of Local Development 1121 L Street, Suite 600	California Statewide Certified Development Corporation (213) 232-2345
SACRAMENTO, CA 95805	917 7th Street P.O. Box 1017	Greater Sacramento Certified Development Corporation (916) 446-8019
SAGINAW, MI 48606	500 Federal Avenue P.O. Box 930	East Central Michigan Development Corporation (571) 752-0100
SALAMANCA, NY 14779	445 Broad Street	Southern-Tier Enterprise Development Organization, Inc. (716) 945-5538

SALEM, IL 62881
Marion County Public Service Bldg.
South Central IL Regional Planning and Dev. Comm. (618) 548-4234

SALEM, OR 97310
595 Cottage Street, N.E.
Oregon Economic Development Corporation (503) 373-7364

SALINAS, CA 93902
3 Howard Street
P.O. Box 634
The Economic Development Corporation of Monterey County, Inc. (408) 424-0154

SALT LAKE CITY, UT 84117
4885 South 900 East, Suite 304
Greater Salt Lake Bus. District DBA Deseret Cert. Dev. Company (801) 266-0443

SAN ANTONIO, TX 78283-0505
P.O. Box 830505
San Antonio Local Development Corporation (512) 224-0518

SAN DIEGO, CA 92101
1100 22nd Street
P.O. Box 8120
San Diego County Certified Development Corporation (619) 234-8811

SAN FRANCISCO, CA 94103
717 Market Street, Suite 204
Bay Area Business Development Company (415) 541-0694

SAN FRANCISCO, CA 94110
987 Valencia Street
San Francisco Business Local Development Corporation (415) 282-8444

SAN FRANCISCO, CA 94102
100 Larkin Street
San Francisco Industrial Development Fund (415) 558-5383

SAN JUAN, PR 00902
P.O. Box 331
La Marketing Development Corporation (809) 783-1646

SANTA ANA, CA 92702
P.O. Box 1988, Department M-25
Santa Ana City Economic Development Corporation (714) 647-6971

SANTA FE, NM 87502
P.O. Box 5115
Development Authority of New Mexico, Inc. (505) 827-8934

SANTURCE, PR 00912
Del Parque St. #352, Suite 202
Advanced Local Development Corporation (809) 721-6797

SAVANNAH, GA 31402
Gamble Bldg., 6 East Bay St.
P.O. Box 1027
Savannah Certified Development Corporation (912) 235-4156

SCRANTON, PA 18501
P.O. Box 431
MetroAction, Inc. (717) 342-7713

SEATTLE, WA 98104
2015 Smith Tower
Evergreen Community Development Association (206) 622-3731

SHREVEPORT, LA 71133
P.O. Box 37005
Ark-La-Tex Investment & Development Corporation (318) 226-7557

SIOUX CITY, IA 51101
400 Orpheum Electric Building
Siouxland Economic Development Corporation (712) 279-6430

SLAYTON, MN 56712
2524 Broadway Avenue
P.O. Box 265
Prairieland Economic Development Corporation (507) 836-8549

SOMERVILLE, MA 02143
City Hall
93 Highland Avenue
Somerville Local Development Corporation (617) 666-5980

City, State, Zip	Address	Co. Name, Telephone
SONORA, CA 95270	55 Stockton Street, Suite C	Gold Country Certified Development Company, Inc. (209) 532-6404
SOUTH BEND, IN 46601	1200 County-City Building	Bus. Dev. Corp. of South Bend, Mishawaka, St. Joseph Cnty, IN (219) 284-9278
	City of South Bend, Dept. of Dev.	
SOUTH HILL, VA 23970	123 S. Mecklenburg Ave.	Lake Country Development Corporation (804) 447-7101
	P.O. Box 150	
SPARTANBURG, SC 29304	145 Broad Street	City of Spartanburg Development Corporation (803) 596-2108
	P.O. Box 1749	
SPEARFISH, SD 57783	P.O. Box 677	Northern Hills Community Development, Inc. (605) 642-7106
	722 Main Street	
SPOKANE, WA 99201	WW. 808 Spokane Fall Blvd.	Greater Spokane Business Development Association (509) 456-4380
SPRINGBORO, OH 45066	280 W. Central Avenue	Certified Development Corp. of Warren County, Inc. (513) 932-3126
SPRINGFIELD, IL 62701	122 S. Fourth Street	Illinois Small Business Growth Corporation (217) 744-0336
SPRINGFIELD, IL 62701	231 S. Sixth	Springfield Certified Development Company (217) 525-2138
SPRINGFIELD, MA 01115	Bay Bank Tower, Suite 1800	Western Massachusetts Small Business Assistance, Inc. (413) 734-3124
	1500 Main Street	
SPRINGFIELD, OH 45503	300 East Auburn Avenue	Clark County Development Corporation (513) 322-8685
ST. ALBANS, VT 05478	2 Federal Street	Franklin County Industrial Development Corporation (802) 524-2194
ST. CHARLES, MO 63301	207 N. 5th Street	Crossroads Economic Dev. Corp. of St. Charles County, Inc. (314) 946-4377
	P.O. Box 1454	
ST. JOHNSBURY, VT 05819	44 Main Street	Northeast Kingdom Development Corporation, Inc. (802) 633-2362
ST. JOHNSBURY, VT 05819	20 Main Street	Northern Community Investment Corporation (802) 748-5101
ST. JOSEPH, MO 64501	1302 Faraon Street	Mo-Kan Development, Inc. (816) 233-8485
ST. LOUIS, MO 63105	121 South Meramec, Suite 412	The St. Louis County Local Development Company (314) 721-0900
ST. LOUIS, MO 63103	1300 Convention Plaza, 3rd Floor	The St. Louis Local Development Company (314) 231-3500
ST. PAUL, MN 55101	150 E. Kellogg Boulevard, Room 900	Opportunities Minnesota Inc. (612) 296-0582
ST. PAUL, MN 55102	25 West Fourth Street	Saint Paul Enterprise Development Corporation (612) 292-6155

234

Location	Address	Organization
ST. PETERSBURG, FL 33701	143–1ST Avenue North, Suite 205	St. Petersburg Certified Development Company, Inc. (813) 823-4311
STERLING, IL 61081	P.O. Box 585	Certified Community Development Corporation (815) 626-2052
	210½ Third Street	
SUMTER, SC 29150	115 N. Harvin Street	Santee-Lynches Regional Development Corporation (803) 775-9215
	P.O. Box 1837	
SYRACUSE, NY 13202	100 East Onondaga Street	Onondaga Industrial Development Second Corporation (315) 470-1343
SYRACUSE, NY 13202	217 Montgomery Street	Syracuse Economic Development Corporation (315) 473-5501
TALLAHASSEE, FL 32399-2000	Duncan Fletcher Building	Florida First Capital Finance Corporation, Inc. (904) 487-0466
	101 East Gaines Street, Room 410	
TAMPA, FL 33602	315 East Kennedy Boulevard	Tampa-Bay Economic Development Corporation (813) 223-8381
TARBORO, NC 27886	112 West Church Street	Taboro Financial Assistance Corporation (919) 823-7194
	P.O. Box 220	
TAUNTON, MA 02780	88 Broadway	South Eastern Economic Development Corporation (617) 822-1020
TEXARKANA, TX 75501	911 Loop 151 Bldg. A	Art-Tex Regional Development Company, Inc. (214) 832-8636
TOLEDO, OH 43605	222 Main Street	East Toledo Local Development Corporation (419) 698-2310
TOLEDO, OH 43624	316 N. Michigan, Suite 700	Small Business Assistance Corporation (419) 255-6077
TOPEKA, KS 66612	820 Quincy, Room 501	Topeka/Shawnee County Development Corporation, Inc. (913) 234-0076
TRACY, CA 95376	803 Central Avenue	Tracy/San Joaquin County Certified Development Corp. (209) 468-3500
	P.O. Box 891	
TRAVERSE CITY, MI 49685	3668 U.S. Highway #31 South	The Greater Northwest Regional Development Corporation (616) 946-3704
	P.O. Box 605	
TRENTON, MO 64683	815 Main Street	Green Hills Rural Development, Inc. (314) 359-5086
TRENTON, NJ 08608	Capital Place One	Corporation for Business Assistance in New Jersey (609) 292-0187
	200 South Warren Street	
TRENTON, NJ 08608	319 East State Street	Trenton Business Assistance Corporation (609) 989-3507
	City Hall Annex	

City, State, Zip	Address	Co. Name, Telephone
TRENTON, TX 75490	106 N. Hamilton Street, Room 101-A	North Texas Certified Development Corporation (214) 989-2720
TRINITY, TX 75862	P.O. Box 549	Trinity Development Corporation (713) 594-3856
TUCSON, AZ 85726-7210	310 W. Alameda P.O. Box 27210	Tucson Local Development Corporation (602) 791-4444
TULSA, OK 74120	130 N. Greenwood	Tulsa Economic Development Corporation (918) 585-8332
TUPELO, MS 38801	c/o Bank of Mississippi One MS Plaza P.O. Box 789	United Local Development Corporation (601) 842-7140
TURTLE LAKE, WI 54889	Route 2, Box 8	Western Wisconsin Development Corporation (415) 986-4310
TWIN FALLS, ID 83303-1844	1300 Kimberly Road P.O. Box 1844	Region IV Development Corporation (208) 734-6587
VALDOSTA, GA 31601	327 W. Savannah Avenue P.O. Box 1223	South Georgia Area Development Corporation (912) 333-5277
VANCOUVER, WA 98661	100 Columbia Way	Columbia River Development Association (206) 694-5006
VIENNA, VA 22180	8300 Boone Boulevard, Suite 450	Virginia Asset Financing Corporation (703) 790-0600
VISALIA, CA 93278	2380 West Whitendale Avenue P.O. Box 5033	Tulare County Economic Development Corporation (209) 627-0766
WACO, TX 76705	c/o Central Texas Econ. P.O. Box 4408	Central Texas Certified Development Company (817) 799-0259
WALTHAM, MA 02154	125 Technology Drive	Bay Colony Development Corporation (617) 891-3594
WARREN, OH 44481	106 E. Market Street–#814	Warren Redevelopment and Planning Corporation (216) 841-2566
WARREN, RI 02885	654 Metacom Avenue P.O. Box 250	Bristol County Chamber Local Development Corporation (401) 245-0751
WASHINGTON, DC 20004	1350 E Street, N.W., Room 201	Washington, D.C. Local Development Corporation (202) 727-6605
WASHINGTON, NC 27889	P.O. Box 1787	Mid-East Certified Development Corporation, Inc. (919) 946-1038
WATERLOO, IA 50701	209 West Fifth Street, Suite N	Black Hawk County Economic Development Committee, Inc. (319) 235-0311

236

WATERTOWN, SD 57201
124 First Avenue, N.W.
P.O. Box 1207
First District Development Company (605) 886-7225

WAUKEGAN, IL 60085
18 North County Street
Lake County Economic Development Corporation (312) 360-6350

WAYCROSS, GA 31501
3243 Harris Road
Southeast Georgia Development Corporation (912) 285-6097

WAYNESVILLE, NC 28786
100 Industrial Park Drive
Smokey Mountain Development Corporation (704) 488-6511

WHEELING, WV 26003
12 and Chapline Streets
P.O. Box 1029
OVIBDC CDC, Inc. (304) 232-2772

WICHITA, KS 67203
River Park Place, Suite 580
727 North Waco
South Central Kansas Economic Development, Inc. (316) 262-5246

WICHITA, KS 67202
350 West Douglas
Wichita Area Development, Inc. (316) 265-7771

WICHITA FALLS, TX 76309
106 N. Hamilton Street, Room 101-A
North Texas Regional Development Corporation (817) 322-9392

WILMINGTON, DE 19801
One Commerce Center, Suite 500
New Castle County Economic Development Corporation (302) 656-5050

WILMINGTON, DE 19801
605 A Market Street Mall
Wilmington Local Development Corporation (302) 571-9087

WILMINGTON, NC 28402
508 Market Street
P.O. Box 1698
Wilmington Industrial Development, Inc. (919) 763-8414

WINSTON-SALEM, NC 27101
280 South Liberty Street
Northwest Piedmont Development Corporation, Inc. (919) 722-9348

WISCASSET, ME 04578
P.O. Box 268 Middle Street
Coastal Enterprises, Inc. (207) 882-7552

WORCESTER, MA 01608
350 Mechanics Tower
100 Front Street
Worcester Business Development Corporation (617) 753-2924

XENIA, OH 45385
50 South Detroit Street
Xenia-Greene County Small Business Dev. Company, Inc. (513) 372-0444

YEMASSEE, SC 29924
P.O. Box 98
I-95 at Point South
Lowcountry Regional Development Corporation (803) 726-5536

YORK, PA 17401
1 Market Way – East
Small Enterprise Development Company (717) 846-8879

YOUNGSTOWN, OH 44505
3200 Belmont Avenue
Mohoning Valley Economic Development Corporation (216) 759-3668

BIBLIOGRAPHY

The following is a list of books on fund-raising and financing for small- to moderate-sized businesses that appears in a reference guide for certified public accountants. The 29 works listed are for the serious investigator of capital-raising methods and techniques. Presumably, if you peruse the following books, you will know as much about this subject as your CPA.

AICPA. *Assisting Small Business Clients in Obtaining Funds*. Small Business Consulting Practice Aid 1. New York: American Institute of Certified Public Accountants, 1982.

Brealy, Richard, and Stewart Myers. *Principles of Corporate Finance*. New York: McGraw-Hill, 1981.

Brigham, Eugene T. *Fundamentals of Financial Management*, 4th ed. New York: Dryden Press, 1986.

Coker, Donald. *Complete Guide to Income Property Financing and Loan Packaging*. Englewood Cliffs, N.J.: Prentice-Hall, 1983.

Colman, Robert. *Modern Business Financing: A Guide to Innovative Strategies and Techniques*. Englewood Cliffs, N.J.: Prentice-Hall, 1985.

Davis, E.W., and K.A. Yeomans. *Company Finance and the Capital Market*. New York: Cambridge University Press, 1977.

Eilon, Samuel. *The Art of Reckoning*. New York: Academic Press, 1984.

Financing the Small Business in the 1980's. CPE Self-Study. New York: American Institute of Certified Public Accountants, 1987.

Friedman, Benjamin M. *Financing Corporate Capital Formation.* (National Bureau of Economic Research—Project Report). Chicago: University of Chicago Press, 1986.

Goldstein, Arnold S. *Strategies and Techniques for Saving Financially Distressed Small Businesses.* New York: Pilot Books, 1976.

Harrington, Diana R., and Brent D. Wilson. *Corporate Financial Analysis,* 2d ed. Plano, Tex.: Business Publications Inc., 1986.

Hayes, Stephen R., and J.C. Howell. *How to Finance Your Small Business with Government Money: SBA and Other Loans,* 2d ed. New York: John Wiley & Sons, Inc., 1982.

Lane, Marc J., and Frederick A. Nicholson. *Corporations: Preorganization Planning.* 101-4th Tax Management Portfolio. Washington, D.C.: Bureau of National Affairs, 1986.

Logue, Dennis E. *Handbook of Modern Finance.* Boston: Warren, Gorham & Lamont, 1984.

McCullough, Burton V. *Letters of Credit.* New York: Matthew Bender, 1987. Looseleaf service.

McKee, Thomas. *Analytical Techniques for Audit and Review Purposes.* CPE Course Handbook. New York: American Institute of Certified Public Accountants, 1986.

National Association of State Development Agencies. *Directory of Incentives for Business Investment and Development in the United States.* 2d ed. Washington, D.C.: Urban Institute Press, 1986.

Norton, Joseph J., ed. *Loan Documentation Guide.* New York: Matthew Bender, 1988. Looseleaf service.

Owen, Robert R., Dan R. Garner, and Dennis S. Bunder. *The Arthur Young Guide to Financial Growth: Ten Alternatives for Raising Capital.* New York: John Wiley & Sons, Inc., 1986.

Pratt, Stanley E., ed. *Guide to Venture Capital Sources.* Wellesley Hills, Mass.: Venture Economics, Inc., 1987.

Price Waterhouse Editorial Staff. *Financing Your Business.* New York: Price Waterhouse, 1985.

Rubin, R.L., and P. Goldberg. *The Small Business Guide to Borrowing Money.* New York: McGraw-Hill, 1980.

Ruda, Howard. *Asset-Based Financing: A Transactional Guide.* 4 vols. New York: Matthew Bender, 1986.

Silver, David A. *Up Front Financing: The Entrepreneur's Guide.* (Small Business Management Series). New York: John Wiley & Sons, Inc., 1982.

____*Venture Capital: The Complete Guide for Investors.* (Small Business Management Series). New York: John Wiley & Sons, Inc., 1985.

____*Who's Who in Venture Capital,* 2d ed. (Small Business Management Series). New York: John Wiley & Sons, Inc., 1986.

Siper, Robert M., ed. *ESOPs in the 1980s.* New York: American Management Association Membership Publications Division, 1988.

Small Business Reporter—Financing Small Business. San Francisco: Bank of America, 1983.

Smollen, Leonard, Mark Rollinson, and Stanley M. Rubel. *Source Guide for Borrowing Capital.* Wellesley Hills, Mass.: Capital Publishing Sources, 1980.

INDEX